PAPAL SIN

PAPAL SIN

Structures of Deceit

GARRY WILLS

IMAGE BOOKS

DOUBLEDAY

NEW YORK • LONDON • TORONTO • SYDNEY • AUCKLAND

An Image Book

PUBLISHED BY DOUBLEDAY

a division of Random House, Inc.

1540 Broadway, New York, New York 10036

IMAGE, DOUBLEDAY, and the portrayal of a deer drinking from a stream are
trademarks of Doubleday, a division of Random House, Inc.

Papal Sin was originally published in hardcover by Doubleday in 2000.

Book design by Julie Duquet

The Library of Congress has cataloged the hardcover edition as follows:

Wills, Garry, 1934–

Papal sin: structures of deceit / Garry Wills.—1st ed.

p.   cm.

Includes bibliographical references and index.

1. Catholic Church—Controversial literature.

2. Papacy.   I. Title

BX1765.2.W54 2000

262'.13—dc21

99-054851

ISBN 0-385-49411-4

First Image Books Edition: October 2001

3   5   7   9   10   8   6   4   2

To Joseph P. Fisher, S.J.
the sanest guide

Contents

   16. The Age of Truth   233

   17. Acton's Reckless Truth   246

   18. Newman's Cautious Truth   261

IV   THE SPLENDOR OF TRUTH   275

   19. Augustine vs. Jerome   277

   20. Augustine vs. Consentius   293

   21. The Truth That Frees   303

      Key to Brief Citations   313

      Acknowledgments   315

      Index   317

Introduction

Catholics have fallen out of the healthy old habit of reminding each other how sinful Popes can be. Painters of Last Judgments—Andrea Orcagna (c. 1308–1368), for instance—used to include a figure wearing the papal crown in the fires of hell, presenting the Pope as a terminal sinner damned forever. This was not only a topos (commonplace), but a preacher's topos—a lesson of the faith, not an attack on it. Authoritative as a Pope may be by his office, he is not impeccable as a man—he can sin, as can all humans.

Of course, there is nothing either new or important about saying that all human leaders are imperfect. If the sermons meant not much more than this—and usually they did not—then they were orthodox but not very searching on the nature of papal sin. But there have been times when the papacy's role in the world created a sustained bias toward a specific kind of sin, when structures of rule or teaching fostered or protected sinful ways, signifying something more than the failings of any individual Pope. The Catholic poet Dante thought that was true of the medieval papacy, whose overriding sin was greed, venality, the desire for wealth—what medieval moralists called avarice. In the first part of *The Divine Comedy*, Dante sees two groups in hell—the misers and the avaricious—running toward each other along opposite sides of a circle. After they run into each other with a crash, they turn about and run back along the circle, only to crash again on the other side of it, and they continue this back-and-forthing through eternity. Prominent in the scene are shaven heads of clergymen:

> *Here Popes and prelates butt their tonsured pates,*
> *Mastered by avarice that nothing sates.*
> —INFERNO 7.46–48

The structural bias toward papal sin in the Renaissance was, according to the Catholic historian Lord Acton, a political desire for earthly power.

Most people are familiar with Acton's famous axiom, "Power tends to corrupt, and absolute power corrupts absolutely" (Acton 2.383). Fewer people remember that he was speaking of papal absolutism—more specifically, he was condemning a fellow historian's book on Renaissance Popes for letting them literally get away with murder.

Happily, those kinds of corruption no longer corrode the papacy. Though there have been financial scandals in the modern papacy (especially that having to do with its involvement in Michele Sindona's Banco Ambrosiano), the spectacle of individual Popes amassing huge fortunes for themselves and their families is no longer the shame that caused Dante's disgust. Similarly, Popes no longer have secular kingdoms for which they are willing to murder and torture and conquer, in ways that Acton illumined with the fierce light of his scholarship. Nor do sexual scandals reach as high up or as deep down as when papal bastards ran the church's bureaucracy. In the tenth century a dissolute teenager could be elected Pope (John XII) because of his family connections and die a decade later in the bed of a married woman.[1]

Indeed, the state of the church is generally so much improved from the past that it might seem to have achieved impeccability after all. The level of scripture scholarship, of liturgical participation, of social concern, of personal holiness, is very high by every comparative measure we can call on. Is it a thing of the past even to think of ecclesiastical sin? One would hesitate to claim that in any case; and there are indications that some things are still not perfect. Even at a surface glance, one finds odd discordant signs. There is, for instance, a kind of double consciousness in the church revealed by this fact: News reports about Catholicism seem to return again and again to matters like birth control, abortion, clerical celibacy, or whether women can be priests—yet in twenty years of regular attendance at Mass in one church, followed by twenty years in another, I have never heard a sermon that touched on any one of those things. What can that mean? That the press is out of touch with what really matters to Catholics in their faith? There may be something to that.

On the other hand, those subjects are not beyond Catholic awareness or concern—especially the marital status of priests as that affects the shrinking numbers of them in the Catholic community. And obviously young couples, and especially young women, are affected by attitudes toward birth control and abortion. I am sure, as well, that priests who are sought out for counseling in those sensitive matters are willing to discuss them in private. But they do not—at least at the campus churches I have attended—mention them from the pulpit. I have asked others at my current church if this impression accords with their memories, and it does. Can this apply to us only because campus churches are "liberal"? Perhaps that is one factor at work. But even so, one would think that some of the young people most affected by such issues, or people with intellectual careers, might be especially attuned to what non-Catholics and the secular press are saying about them. Then why this silence about what the media tell us are burning issues in our Catholic life?

One answer could be that the gospels do not have anything to say about birth control or abortion, married priests or women priests, and that the great truths of the faith—the Trinity, the Incarnation, the Mystical Body of Christ—are more central to our belief than are these controversial items of the day. This answer might be a liberal way to "one-up" people mired in newspaper sensationalism. But, to tell the truth, I do not hear much about those mystical doctrines of the faith in our ordinary course of Sunday sermons. A priest was almost apologetic when he had to refer to the Trinity, "a rather abstruse matter," just because it was Trinity Sunday. I wondered what he thought we were there to hear about if the central doctrines of the faith were irrelevant.

Conservative Catholics claim that the laity are too resistant to "the church's teaching" on controversial subjects to want them discussed in their presence, and that priests are too cowardly to bring up anything distasteful to their audience. Certainly the silence in the pulpit does not come from any failure of the Roman Curia, the Vatican's papal bureaucracy, to demand that its teachings be passed on. If the laity is not listening, it is not because the hierarchy is not loud or insistent enough in its emphases—its demands are, after all, what is being reported in the press. Pope John Paul II, and influential figures around him like Cardinal Ratzinger, have ratcheted up the degrees of obligation on favorite points of doctrine, calling them "definitive" and "irreversible." Yet there is still a gap, a widening lacuna, between the teaching organs in Rome and the laity in the pew. The transmission through priests is faulty or disconnected. Rome has tried to remedy this by severer discipline in seminaries and Catholic universities, insisting that "church teaching" be *taught*. The effort has so far not succeeded. This surprises some people, who have considered the Catholic church the last authoritative institution in the world. The left-wing historian Eric Hobsbawm thinks that religion itself must be fading from modern life if there is a breakdown of docility in the strictest religion of them all.[2] The right-wing jurist Robert Bork says that "the Roman Catholic Church is the test case" by which the issue of authority in modern America will be decided.[3]

What can explain this disparity between what is sent out by the loud maximizers in Rome and what is received by the quietly minimizing lay people in their churches (where they still do turn up in healthy numbers, despite their deafness to Rome's urgencies)? It is not enough to say that lax Catholics have been cafeteria patrons, picking and choosing what dogmas they will have for their Sunday brunch. It is often the most devout lay people (and clergy) who are most serene in tuning out the passionate signals from abroad. We should look to the lines of transmission from one point to the other—to the priests who do the actual preaching, who hear (in dwindling numbers) confession, who minister at weddings and baptisms and deaths. Why do they seem unwilling or unable to bring the high demands from their superiors into contact with the low receptive condition of their congregations? Is it a simple lack of courage or clarity or loyalty on their part? Once again, some conservatives make this charge. For them this *trahison des clercs* brings back to life the first sense of "clerical betrayal."

Why would impaired transmission occur at a time when there has been such improvement in the church's scriptural scholarship, liturgical participation, and intellectual training? It is not simply because priests are resisting the demand that they be celibate. That explains why so many priests have left their status, not why those who stay remain devoted in most other ways but are, nonetheless, fuzzy or muted about what Rome wants them to proclaim with hard-edged clarity. It is not a happy situation, after all, to be ground between the maximizers on high and those minimizing below. Why would anyone want to adopt such an uncomfortable post if he could avoid it?

The priests find they cannot avoid it. It is forced on them, against their own preference and history of service, by a simple inability to keep a straight face or an honest heart—to be truly concerned for those they serve—if they echo what Rome is saying about women or the priesthood, marriage or natural law. Their own integrity rebels, against the calculus of personal gain or the pressures of careerism. The arguments for much of what passes as current church doctrine are so intellectually contemptible that mere self-respect forbids a man to voice them as his own. The very fact that the intellectual level of the church has been raised makes it harder for a priest to swallow the scriptural fundamentalism reverted to by Rome when it claims that priests must be celibate or that women cannot be priests. The cartoon version of natural law used to argue against contraception, or artificial insemination, or masturbation, would make a sophomore blush. The attempt to whitewash past attitudes toward Jews is so dishonest in its use of historical evidence that a man condemns himself in his own eyes if he tries to claim that he agrees with it.

This is a neglected factor in the many discussions of the way vocations to the priesthood (and to nuns' convents) have fallen off so drastically in recent years. It is usual, and easy, and partly right, to say that the requirement of celibacy in the modern world is enough to deter all but a few from becoming priests under the old rules. But another reason, a more disheartening one, is that young idealistic persons, the kind who want to be priests, are just the people for whom matters of honesty with themselves are bound to be most challenging. How can one aspire to a high calling and yet accept low standards for his own truthfulness about what he really believes? How can one be in service to others, yet peddle to them "religious truths" whose truthfulness rings so obviously hollow? I have seen this problem grow over the years, in the cases of men I have known or whose situation I have become familiar with.

When sexual scandal has arisen in the modern church—not as often as in the more lurid past, but with the inevitability of human failing— priests have shown more than the ordinary institutional bias to protect their own. Part of this comes from the bad faith that had them pretending, for the consumption of their superiors, to believe things they did not about celibacy, either for gays or for straight men. Part of it comes from the knowledge that there are many gay priests, by disposition or activity, who have been quietly accepted all along, by friends who do not think what they are doing is so evil (and neither do some in their lay congregations), so long as it is a matter of consenting adults and not of children—that it is not, at any rate, as evil as the odd arguments of Rome would have them openly maintain. So they bend the rules quietly (even those who would prefer to see them maintained)—why, after all, punish one man who gets caught when there are so many others who have not been? Priests' stable heterosexual relations are also known and kept quiet, because some other priests are not convinced that the arguments for celibacy are convincing, even when they remain celibate themselves.

Little dishonesties, built into a situation, lend multiple biases to reactions when scandal arises. Men can find themselves the prisoners of prior compromises they have made. It is in part a revolt against such dishonesty that makes priests unwilling to compound hypocrisy by teaching what they do not believe. A terrible burden is placed on those who try to maintain intellectual integrity in this situation.

But *shouldn't* priests, of all people, believe? Is that not their duty? If they do not want to teach what Rome says is the content of the faith, why do they pretend to be priests at all? In fact, why do not all the Catholics who disagree with the Pope just get out? I receive letters constantly from people who tell me that that is my duty. Who am I—or who is anyone except the Pope—to decide what a Catholic may or may not accept as binding doctrine? That is a serious question, not just the growling of authoritarians who feel they have some of the Pope's excommunicating power themselves. But the question is based on an assumption that is not only challengeable but extremely unhealthy. It assumes that the whole test of Catholicism, the essence of the faith, is submission to the Pope. During long periods of the church's history, that was not the rule—Saint Augustine, for one, would have flunked such a test. And today it is a test that would decimate the ranks of current churchgoers. It is not a position that has a solid body of theology behind it, no matter how common it is as a popular notion (*vulgaris opinio*).

But unfortunately it is an opinion that is acted on, and continually inculcated (though more implicitly than explicitly), by some members of the Roman Curia. Only that can explain the way incoherent views are promoted with fervor by those around the Pope. These are not men who lack intelligence themselves, though it sometimes seems that they believe all others do. How can they sponsor philosophically weird and scripturally simpleminded arguments? It is because they do not come at questions on their own merits, but from above as it were, judging each thing by its likelihood of confirming or calling in question the papacy's record for truthfulness. Thus even as bright and devout a man as Pope Paul VI could endorse a truly perverse teaching on contraception—one rejected by his own picked panel of loyal and intelligent Catholics, priestly and lay, expert and commonsensical—because advisers convinced him that it would shake people's faith in the church for the papacy to reverse its course (see Chapters 5 and 6). In what we shall find is a recurring pattern, truth was subordinated to ecclesiastical tactics. To maintain an impression that Popes cannot err, Popes deceive—as if distorting the truth in the present were not a worse thing than mistaking it in the past. Paradoxically, the teaching part of the church is continually tugged off from the truth, or made to shy away from its consequences, precisely because it claims a special access to the truth. The papal record has to be whitewashed, even when that effort inhibits sincere attempts at good works—as when the effort to express sorrow over the Holocaust was blocked, at every point, by a nervous reassertion of the church's essentially innocent behavior toward the Jews (see Chapter 1). This latter claim must rely on such massive historical misreadings, misinterpretations, and misrepresentations as to become a new act of injustice toward the very people who were being approached with sympathy.

There is nothing here as clear-cut and direct as simple lying. That is why I speak of the "structures of deceit" that recruit people almost insensibly to quiet cosmetic labors buttressing the church by "improving" its substructure. These continual readjustments of the foundation are bound to weaken it, while destroying any standards for honest workmanship in those who think they are saving their church by fiddling it into intellectual irrelevance. The irony is that the very attempt to prove that the church has never changed leads to innovating arguments, to modern adjustments or additions, that just show how ill they accord with the monument they are trying to shore up—as when the gender of the apostles is adduced to support a male monopoly on the priesthood, after the ancient and real reason for that monopoly, a belief in female inferiority, has become unusable (see Chapter 7). When ancient props for certain moral stands are removed, or crumble of themselves, the thing they upheld is not allowed to fall with them. New Jerry-built contrivances are shoved under them to keep them in place—as when the misinterpreted scripture text (Gen 38:9) that had borne the weight of condemnation for contraception proved friable, and some amateur psychology was crammed into its place, a rickety makeshift that tries to pose as an eternal truth.

The Popes themselves do not do most of this innovating. They do not have to. Others are too busy contriving papal deceptions in their name. Yet they usually countenance, if they do not actually encourage, this pattern of untruthfulness. They even let others coax them into disingenuous stands for their own good, as when Paul VI let others bring him to the point of mouthing absurdities about contraception "for the good of the church." There are many people who take on themselves the duty of maintaining in good repair the structures of deceit. By making exaggerated claims of certitude for questionable views these people do what John Henry Newman said the papaloters were accomplishing in the nineteenth century, creating "in educated Catholics a habit of scepticism or secret infidelity as regards all dogmatic truth."[4]

The papaloters' indirect disservice to the truth may seem small potatoes next to the Vatican's lurid sins of the past, the kind that got one painted onto church walls in poses of eternal torment. But it is a deception deeper inside the citadel of spiritual values than mere personal greed or a ruler's ambition. It plays with the truth while using the name of Jesus, who said he *is* the truth (Jn 14:6). It cheapens the gospel. It makes truth look to falsehoods for support. It is the form of deception that Saint Augustine considered most sinful (see Chapters 17 and 18).

It is also a form of deception for which the modern world can muster little tolerance. Truth is a modern virtue in the sense that it took on new urgency in the last century (see Chapter 16). That period saw the birth of history as a scientific discipline, the professionalization of inquiry, the secularization of truth-seeking institutions like the university. It imposed new methodological rigor on just the kinds of bodies—schools, professional groups, keepers of archives and records—that Catholic authorities belong to and direct. To profess a dedication to such standards and yet to deploy evasions and distortions and cover-ups is to be self-condemned, even in the world's eyes, to say nothing of higher calls to truthfulness.

It can be objected that the deceivers in question have first deceived themselves, that they are sincere in their adherence to falsehoods, so they cannot be faulted for acting on genuinely held views. Yet the Roman hierarchy's own most favored theologian, Thomas Aquinas, held that there is such a thing as "cultivated ignorance," *ignorantia affectata*, an ignorance so useful that one protects it, keeps it from the light, in order to continue using it (ST 1–2, q 6, 8r). He called this kind of ignorance not exculpatory but inculpatory. It is a willed ignorance, though an unconfessed one. Certainly in a time that demands intellectual honesty with special emphasis, to remain oblivious of the most basic questions concerning dishonesty is to disqualify oneself for serious exchanges with one's peers—a disqualification hard to ignore, no matter how urgently one tries to blank it out. One cannot escape the point that holding to Catholic truths must now be defended against those who would mingle those truths with obvious and shambling falsehoods, historical or scriptural or philosophical.

My book is a tribute, in part, to the honesty that has led so many priests to keep silent under the burden of deceptiveness called for by their superiors—and it is a plea that the weight be removed. I am not attacking either the papacy or its defenders. My own heroes, it will become clear, are the many truth tellers in Catholic ranks, preeminently Saint Augustine, Cardinal Newman, Lord Acton, and Pope John XXIII. The truth, we are told, will make us free. It is time to free Catholics, lay as well as clerical, from the pressures of deceit that are our quiet modern form of papal sin. Paler, subtler, less dramatic than the sins castigated by Orcagna or Dante, these are the quieter corruptions of intellectual betrayal.

[1] J. N. D. Kelly, *The Oxford Dictionary of Popes* (Oxford University Press, 1986), pp. 126–27.

[2] Eric Hobsbawm, *The Age of Extremes* (Vintage Books, 1996), p. 336: Though Catholics made up "the basic stock of the faithful" in the nineteenth century, "the Church's moral and material authority over the faithful disappeared" in the last part of the twentieth century, while churches "with a less compelling hold over members" collapsed even more spectacularly.

[3] Robert H. Bork, *Slouching Towards Gomorrah: Modern Liberalism and American Decline* (ReganBooks, 1996), p. 292.

[4] John Henry Newman to Ambrose De Lisle, July 24, 1870, in Charles Stephen Dessain et al., *The Letters and Diaries of John Henry Newman* (Oxford University Press, 1973), Vol. 25, p. 165.

I.

HISTORICAL DISHONESTIES

I t is a temptation to our weakness and to our consciences to defend the Pope as we would defend ourselves—with the same care and zeal, with the same uneasy secret consciousness that there are weak points in the case which can best be concealed by diverting attention from them. What the defense gains in energy it loses in sincerity; the cause of the Church, which is the cause of truth, is mixed up and confused with human elements, and is injured by a degrading alliance. In this way even piety may lead to immorality, and devotion to the Pope may lead away from God.

— L O R D   A C T O N   (3.79)

1.

Remembering the Holocaust

We Remember

The debilitating effect of intellectual dishonesty can be touching. Even when papal authority sincerely wants to perform a virtuous act, when it spends years screwing up its nerve to do it, when it actually thinks it has done it, when it releases a notice of its having done it, when it expects to be congratulated on doing it—it has not done it. Not because it did not want to do it, or did not believe it did it. It was simply unable to do it, because that would have involved coming clean about the record of the papal institution. And that is all but unthinkable.

A good example is the long-awaited document on the Holocaust, *We Remember,* issued by a papally appointed commission on March 16, 1998, and recommended in an accompanying letter by John Paul II. This document had been in preparation for over a decade. It was supposed to go beyond the Second Vatican Council's assurance, in 1965, that Jews cannot, after all, be blamed for the death of Jesus (an assurance that *We Remember* refers to). Though expressions of sympathy for Jewish suffering are voiced in the new statement, it devotes more energy to exonerating the church—and excoriating the Nazis for not following church teaching—than to sympathizing with the Holocaust's victims. The effect is of a sad person toiling up a hill all racked with emotion and ready to beat his breast, only to have him plump down on his knees, sigh heavily—and point at some other fellow who caused all the trouble.

The key distinction labored at through the text is between anti-Semitism, as a pseudo-scientific theory of race always condemned by the church, and anti-Judaism, which some Christians through weakness suc-

cumbed to at times but not "the church as such." The former is a matter
of erroneous teaching—which the church is never guilty of. The latter is
a matter of "sentiment" and weakness, sometimes using misinterpreted
scriptural texts as a cover for prejudices of a basically nonreligious sort:

> In a climate of eventful social change, Jews were often accused of
> exercising an influence disproportionate to their numbers. Thus
> there began to spread in varying degrees throughout most of Eu-
> rope an anti-Judaism that was essentially more sociological and po-
> litical than religious.[1]

Since the "sentiment" was not really religious, that lets the church off the
hook. It never caused "anti-Judaism," though individual members of the
church succumbed to it on their own. Thus the document can direct its
animus against scientific racism (the real anti-Semitism) and present it as
the common enemy of Christian and Jew:

> At the level of theological reflection we cannot ignore the fact that
> not a few in the Nazi party not only showed aversion to the idea of
> divine Providence at work in human affairs, but gave proof of a def-
> inite hatred directed at God himself. Logically, such an attitude also
> led to a rejection of Christianity, and a desire to see the church de-
> stroyed or at least subject to the interest of the Nazi state. It was this
> extreme ideology which became the basis of the measures taken,
> first to drive the Jews from their homes and then to exterminate
> them. The Shoah was the work of a thoroughly modern neo-pagan
> regime. Its anti-Semitism had its roots outside of Christianity and,
> in pursuing its aim, it did not hesitate to oppose the church and per-
> secute its members also (16).

Did Christians have anything to do with the persecuting? Well, only in
the sense that some did not oppose it quite as strenuously as they ought
to have done:

> Did Christians give every possible assistance to those being perse-
> cuted, and in particular to the persecuted Jews? Many did, but oth-

ers did not. Those who did help to save Jewish lives as much as was in their power, even to the point of placing their own lives in danger, must not be forgotten. During and after the war, Jewish communities and Jewish leaders /expressed their thanks for all that had been done for them, including what Pope Pius XII did personally or through his representatives to save hundreds of thousands of Jewish lives. Many Catholic bishops, priests, religious and laity have been honored for this reason by the State of Israel. Nevertheless, as Pope John Paul II has recognized, alongside such courageous men and women, the spiritual resistance and concrete action of other Christians was not that which might have been expected from Christ's followers. We cannot know how many Christians in countries occupied or ruled by the Nazi powers or their allies were horrified at the disappearance of their Jewish neighbors and yet were not strong enough to raise their voices in protest. For Christians, this heavy burden of conscience of their brothers and sisters during the Second World War must be a call to penitence (17–18).

So this document—which the Pope commends for calling "memory to play its necessary part in the process of shaping a future" (7)—establishes three entirely separate categories:

1. Those who caused the Holocaust—irreligious Nazis with a godless scientism about race, who were anti-Christian as well as anti-Jewish.
2. Those who opposed the Holocaust—Pope Pius XII and bishops and other authorities encouraging their followers to act in accord with the church's teaching.
3. Those who did not oppose the Holocaust *enough*—Christians too fearful to follow their brave leaders. It is only in the name of this last category that the document expresses "penitence."

What is left out of this picture? To begin with, the bishops and priests who were supportive of the Nazis are expunged from the memory that Pope John Paul says is supposed to guide us into the future.

The [papal] nuncio to Berlin throughout the war, Archbishop Cesare Orsenigo, was a Nazi sympathizer, and far from the only friend of the Nazis in the hierarchy. The rector of the German College in Rome, Archbishop Alois Hudal, who was useful in dealing with the Nazis during their occupation of Rome, was another, and many members of Hitler's government, like Ernst von Weizsacker, the ambassador to the Vatican and an old acquaintance of the Pope [Pius XII], professed to be good Catholics. When Weizsacker was credited to the Vatican in 1943, the papal limousine that took him to his audience flew the papal flag and the swastika side by side, "in peaceful harmony," as Weizsacker noted proudly.[2]

There may (or may not) have been extenuating circumstances for some of these collaborators. But to pretend—nay, to assert—that they did not exist is to remove *We Remember* from any serious consideration as an honest confrontation with a complicated history. Its "memory," far from being useful to the cause of true understanding that would prevent another Holocaust, is useful only to the fictions that the Vatican wants to maintain about itself. It can take such a fanciful approach to the historical record because it is imposing on that record a theoretical template that has three parts—"the church," and "science," and the relations between church and science.

First, we are told that "the church" as such cannot have been involved in the Holocaust since it has never taught any theoretical difference in the races. I attended a Jesuit seminary whose oldest building was erected, in the nineteenth century, by slaves owned by the Jesuit order—men who were the property of the whole order since individual Jesuits had all taken a vow of poverty. That building is concrete evidence for a practical treatment of the races as unequal, no matter what theoretical propositions were being formulated at the time. But the main problem here is not historical but theological. What is the church? The Vatican authorities continue to use the term in ways that the Second Vatican Council rejected. According to the Council, the church is the people of God, the body of believers baptized into the life and death of Christ.[3] The church, no more than the Pope, can be impeccable. If the concrete reality of the historical church has been involved in the guilt of slavery, inquisitions, and conquest, we cannot say that this does not count because it was not the *real* church that was sinning—that it was just lay churchmen, or nonhierarchical elements, or people who could not claim the teaching authority (magisterium) of the church, as if the magisterium were itself the whole people of God.

The Vatican reverts, in *We Remember*—and in many places—to the older usage that equates the church with its highest organs of doctrinal statement. That is what is meant when we hear that Catholics no longer follow "the church," or are defying "the church." How can they defy themselves? Was the church guilty of the Holocaust? No, says the Vatican, since the magisterium never advocated it or defended it in a formal teaching. If Catholics singly or in groups were implicated in the crime, this was something the magisterium could not be convicted of.

Let us apply that kind of thinking to a current situation. The teaching church says that abortion and contraception are mortal sins and crimes against human persons. Is the church guilty of those crimes (assuming, for the sake of argument, that they are such)? No, says the Vatican, because the Pope has condemned them. On the other hand, polls confirm that a majority of Catholics (88 percent in 1993) accept contraceptive methods in theory, and those in a position to act on that acceptance do so.[4] Catholics are also no different from the rest of the population in the number of abortions they undergo. The church, then, is "committing" abortion and contraception, though its leaders say that they must not. In the same way, Catholics were active in the Nazi state, even though their leaders (some of them, some of the time) told them not to be.

Second, the blaming of science is something with a long history in Vatican documents. We do not have to go back to Galileo to see that ecclesiastical authorities have been suspicious of science, of human knowledge when that seems to run counter to scripture or tradition. Authorities with a large body of changeless truth to maintain tend to look with apprehension on anything so vertiginously changeable as the experimental sciences. Apprehension deepened to entrenched acrimony under Pius IX (a hero to Pope John Paul), an acrimony that lingers in some curial enclaves. Whenever evil views can be attributed to science, that effectively removes them from the sacred domain the church authorities are protecting. That is why *We Remember* is careful to pick up National Socialism with tongs, as it were, and drop it into the sterile confines of a laboratory:

> At the same time, theories began to appear which denied the unity of the human race, affirming an original diversity of races. In the twentieth century, National Socialism in Germany used these ideas as a pseudo-scientific basis for a distinction between so-called Nordic-Aryan races and supposedly inferior races (14).

We are supposed to conclude that any form of thought so distant in ethos from a Catholic mentality could not mix with it easily or at all. But prejudice regularly mingles contradictory items, so long as they can be made to pull in the desired direction. The anti-Semite draws readily on science, faith, legend, history, or law—on any snippet of fact or theory that hatred can fuse into a rationale for action.

This is a picture very far from the neat little schema of three disparate types offered by *We Remember*. That document tries to draw a clear line of demarcation between secular anti-Semitism and "sociological" anti-Judaism. But empirical studies show that the two reinforce rather than fight each other. The most thorough proof of this was made, so far as America is concerned, when the Anti-Defamation League (ADL) of B'nai B'rith commissioned a major series of studies from the Survey Research Center of the University of California at Berkeley. The survey was commissioned while the Vatican Council was sitting, and carried out after it was dissolved. Pollsters first set up categories of orthodox belief among Christians—categories in which Catholics, as expected, scored higher than Protestants. Then they tested those who scored high in these categories with the range of secular anti-Semitic views. They found that "the respondents' anti-Semitism varies in direct relation to their positions on this measure [of orthodoxy] . . . *the more the religious beliefs are subscribed to, the greater the anti-Semitism*" (emphasis added). Orthodox beliefs are in fact "a powerful predictor of secular anti-Semitism."[5] The degree of secular anti-Semitism is often linked to specifically theological positions—e.g., that the Jews are a cursed race, guilty of rejecting their own Messiah, responsible for killing Christ. That view is still powerful, despite the assurance in *We Remember* that the church has denied its legitimacy. The ADL study found, even after that official denial, that 11 percent of Catholics in America still agreed with this statement: "The reason Jews have so much trouble is because God is punishing them for rejecting Jesus." An amazing 41 percent said that they were not certain about the curse, but they considered it a possibility. History is not easily altered by a single decree, especially one that comes out of the blue, as Vatican II's did.

Vatican II (1962–65)

We Remember quotes a 1997 speech by Pope John Paul II: "In the Christian world—I do not say on the part of the Church as such—erroneous and unjust interpretations of the New Testament regarding the Jewish people and their alleged culpability have circulated for too long" (13). The Pope can clean the skirts of "the church as such" only in the highly technical sense (and by the theologically narrow definition of "the church") that the supreme magisterium never *infallibly* said that the Jews are deicides, cursed for their killing of Christ (though it never authoritatively denied it, either, until 1965). Besides, this Pope likes to emphasize that encyclicals, though they may not be infallible, are authoritative, are "the church's teaching," and Pius XI said in a 1937 encyclical that "Jesus received his human nature from a people who crucified him"—not some Jews, but the Jewish *people*.[6] And the same Pope suppressed a Catholic organization, the Friends of Israel, that tried to discontinue the charge of deicide.[7] Furthermore, Catholic preachers over the centuries have continually made the deicide charge, and seminaries taught it, and biblical commentaries explained it, and persecutions were based on it. In finally rejecting this claim, the Second Vatican Council said nothing about the church's past record. It did not express penitence for official encouragement of such a view, or for pogroms and other actions taken on the basis of it. The price of getting the statement through the Council's sessions was that it *not* admit that the church had ever said or done anything wrong.

Some Council fathers even said that the charge of deicide should not be brought up, since they had never heard of it.[8] They had to be shock-

ingly ignorant of history, including recent history. Others thought that it
was unwise to mention anything so unpleasant, that the best course was
to forget the whole matter. Monsignor John M. Oesterreicher, who
helped draft the statement and worked it past the objections of many
bishops, recounts one exchange:

> There came up to me one day a certain bishop, who is widely
> known outside America and is by no means attached to the "bad old
> days." He said, "Look here, this won't do. One cannot simply de-
> clare, in public, that the Jews are not deicides." I answered, "Why
> not?" Upon which the bishop explained his objection like this:
> "Why not? Simply because it is insulting even to put the word into
> one's mouth. What would you say if someone suddenly announced,
> in public, 'Oesterreicher is no thief'? How would you like that?"
> "Your Excellency, that depends on the situation. If this 'defence'
> came like lightning out of a clear sky, I should of course be thun-
> derstruck. But if, for years, I had been the victim of a slander, then
> I should feel that I had been set free by such a public vindication. I
> should in fact be pleased about it." The bishop was evidently im-
> pressed by this argument, as he asked me to prepare a memorandum
> for him on the matter. But I am not sure that I convinced him in
> the depths of his heart.[9]

There was no excuse for the Council fathers to be (or to play) ignorant
about the church's record on the charge of a Jewish curse. The theologian
the hierarchy has considered most authoritative, Thomas Aquinas, said
that the Jewish mob did not know what it was doing when it said "His
blood be our responsibility, and our children's" (Mt 27:25), but the leaders of the Jews knew the scriptures well enough to recognize the Messiah and deliberately reject him, which means they were not only
"crucifiers of Christ as a man but as God" (ST 3, q 47, 5 ad 3). They were
deicides.

There is no need to go through the whole dreary round of obloquy
heaped on the Jews by early Fathers of the church—especially by John
Chrysostom, with his rant about Christ killers (*Christoktonoi*).[10] The medieval tales of the cursed race were not rejected by reformers like Luther

or Calvin, who prove that anti-Semitism is a *Christian* sin, not just a Catholic one.[11] That it is a modern sin, not just an ancient one, is made clear from Charlotte Klein's survey of what respected theologians have said and written even since the Holocaust. One of the leading liberal theologians at Vatican II, Karl Rahner, could publish, in the very year of the Council's statement, these words about the Jews: "We could almost say that a supernatural demonism is exercising its power in the hatred of this people against the true kingdom of God."[12] More astonishingly, the priest who edited the *Revue biblique* (Pierre Benoit) brought out this accusation three years after the Council's decree: "The religious authority of the Jewish people took on itself the actual responsibility for the crucifixion. Israel closed itself off from the light that was offered it, from the expansion of view demanded of it . . . That refusal has continued, down through the ages, to this very day . . . Every Jew suffers from the ruin undergone by his people when it refused Him at the decisive moment of its history."[13]

Of course, there was a countertradition, which was less harsh to Jews, but it ameliorated rather than canceled the main tradition. Augustine, for instance, said that Christ's words "Forgive them, for they know not what they do" meant that those killing him did not realize that he was God, so they could not have committed deicide, just homicide.[14] In a very influential chapter of his *City of God* (18.46), Augustine argued that the diffusion of Jews throughout the world was a providential blessing, since they bore witness to the authenticity of the ancient scriptures on which Christians relied—no one can say the Christians invented or falsified documents kept so carefully by the Jews. This idea of the Jews as unwilling witnesses to the truth was condescending, but at least it discouraged attempts to get rid of Jews. In fact, it was the basis of a series of papal decrees modeled on the bull of Callistus II, *Sicut Judeis* (1120), which guaranteed Jews legal protection.[15]

These are minimal points of light in the dark story of vituperation and accusation, especially when we consider the commonsense and historical arguments against the idea of a divine curse imposed on an entire people. For one thing, "the Jews" did not kill Christ, even if one could make the (uncertain) case that *certain* Jews were more responsible than the Romans who actually executed him. Besides, while religions are persecuting and persecuted by turns—e.g., there were Catholic martyrs in England under Elizabeth I, Protestant ones under Mary Tudor—we do not say that one or other side is cursed forever. As we shall see later (Chapter 18), certain Christians betrayed Peter and Paul to their execution—does that mean that Christians have a curse on them? But there is a deeper theological reason why believers in Christian theology should never have considered one part of mankind the killers of Jesus. Since he died for all sins, the only racial solidarity expressed in his suffering is that of the sinful human race, the joint cause and beneficiary of the redeeming death.

One reason the Catholic church lagged behind some other parts of Christianity in its recognition of such basic facts is that biblical norms established in the sixteenth century by the Council of Trent froze Catholics' scriptural scholarship until the 1950s (when Pius XII opened some avenues to the new learning). Before then, the gospel accounts were taken as conventional history written by eyewitnesses. Most modern scholars have concluded that the gospels took their present form after the destruction of the Jewish Temple by Rome in 70 CE and reflect the current urgencies (*Sitz am Leben*) in which and for which they were composed. After the death of Jesus, Christians were persecuted as Jewish heretics by some Jewish leaders, who killed Stephen and James.[16] The responsibility of Rome for Christ's death was muted during this process, and that of the Jews played up, as "the body of Christ" (his believers united to him) underwent new suffering. The ancient creeds go back to an older tradition that emphasizes Roman primacy in the execution ("suffered under Pontius Pilate"), as does the only secular source on the death of Jesus, Tacitus (*Annals* 15.44).

The theologians who went to Vatican II in the 1960s were acutely conscious of the ways Catholic scholarship had lagged on this vital matter of seeing the New Testament's treatment of the Jews in a theological perspective.[17] They felt a pressing need, in the name of intellectual integrity as well as justice to the Jews, to give their corrected views authoritative expression, a need that looked mysterious to many bishops, who had not kept up with the new scholarship. That is why the statement on the Jews was stalled, over and over, and had a hard time finding a home in the documents prepared by the Council. It would never have survived these difficulties but for the insistence of Pope John XXIII.

While the Council was being planned, Pope John had greeted a delegation of American Jews by saying, *"Son io Giuseppe, il fratello vostro"*—"I am Joseph, your brother"—echoing the words of the biblical Joseph (Gen 45:4), and using Roncalli's personal name, not his papal one (Giovanni).[18] At the same time, he asked Cardinal Bea, of the Secretariat for Promoting Christian Unity, to prepare a Council draft (schema) on the subject of the Jews. This decision would itself be challenged repeatedly, on the grounds that Bea's was an ecumenical group dealing, before then, only with Christian denominations. It was also attacked because Bea's Secretariat was not one of the formal commissions directed to prepare schemata, and Bea was known to be too liberal for the comfort of many in the Curia. John solved the first problem by making the Secretariat a commission, after the Council had begun.[19] As for the cardinal's liberalism, that seems to be the very reason John was determined to keep Bea in charge of this sensitive matter. There were later efforts to take the Jewish schema away from Bea's commission, and to split the decree up into three anodyne additions to other documents, but he was able to fight these off.

A different kind of challenge arose, early on, when the World Jewish Congress, accepting the invitation for other religious bodies to send official observers to the Council, sent Dr. Chaim Wardi. Wardi had performed this kind of service before, acting as official observer at the World Council of Churches in 1961 and at a Pan-Orthodox Conference in the same year. He was a minister of religion in the Israeli government, which did not disqualify him in the eyes of those bodies; but the Council's Central Preparatory Commission took the occasion of his appointment to withdraw the draft decree on the Jews from the Council's schedule, saying the matter had become "politicized." Again Bea had to go to the Pope in order to revive the decree. John sent a message to the Central Commission saying, "We have read Cardinal Bea's memorandum with care and entirely share his opinion that a profound responsibility requires our intervention."[20]

The adventures of the draft decree on the Jews, in its voyage through the four sessions of the Council, were a series of hairbreadth escapes on the order of *The Perils of Pauline.* With the death of the spontaneous Pope John before the second session of the Council, and the installation of the cautious Paul VI, conservative bishops took heart and began to invite the Pope's intervention on their side, to make up for John's earlier interventions for the liberals. In fact, the cardinals of the Curia became so confident of their control of the Pope that they misrepresented an order as coming from him, one that would have set up a special review commission to abbreviate the decree on the Jews and remove it from Cardinal Bea's control. Fourteen cardinals of great reputation sent an urgent message of objection to Paul, who modified the new commission's authority without entirely disowning what had been done in his name.[21] At another time, more rumors that the decree would be suppressed led two cardinals from America and one from Germany to tell the Pope they would have to leave Rome if that were to occur.[22]

Though many other points were debated in the statement on the Jews as it evolved, the deicide issue caused the most heated disagreement. Some thought it bad policy to bring it up, since that would just admit that the accusation had been made in the past. Better to state the positive new view and bury in oblivion the past. The liberals did not want to bury the past, but to draw attention to it, since it was an injustice still to be redressed. The same Council fathers who did not want a reference to deicide also wanted to exclude any mention of past persecutions by the church, or of Christian guilt for them. They won on all three issues. Only the substance of the deicide matter survived, but by a jettisoning of the term. Here is the progress of the drafts as they dealt (or not) with this specific matter:

First Draft (December 2, 1961)

Even though the greater part of the Jewish people remained separated from Christ, it would nevertheless be an injustice to call this people accursed, since they are beloved for the sake of their fathers and the promises made to them. [No mention of deicide, the grounds on which any unspecified people might call the Jews accursed. This was the preliminary draft, done in Rome when it was uncertain how much freedom the Council would have under John].

Second Draft (March 2, 1963)

The chosen people cannot without injustice be termed a deicidal race, as the Lord has expiated through his suffering and death the sins of all men—the cause of his Passion and his dying. [The issue is stated clearly, using the term at issue—and this led to many protests.]

Third Draft (March 6, 1964)

May all, therefore, take care that in catechetical instruction, in preaching the Word of God, and in daily conversation the Jewish people are not represented as rejected, and equally that nothing is said or done that could alienate souls from the Jews. They should also guard against attributing to the Jews of our time what was done during Christ's Passion [The term "deicide" removed, along with the *theological* reason for rejecting it. Even this statement was resisted.][23]

Final Statement

True, authorities of the Jews and those who followed their lead pressed for the death of Christ (cf. Jn 19:6); still, what happened in His passion cannot be blamed upon all the Jews then living, without distinction, or upon the Jews of today. Although the Church is the new people of God, the Jews should not be presented as repudiated or cursed by God, as if such a view followed from the holy Scripture . . . Besides, as the Church has always held and continues to hold, Christ in His boundless love freely underwent his passion and death because of the sins of all men, so that all might attain salvation. [Deicide gone as a term, but the theological argument against it restored.][24]

In an item-by-item vote of the whole Council, the vote against the sentence that opposed blaming Jews for the death of Christ was 188, and that against opposition to calling the Jews cursed was 245. Admittedly, this is a small minority—the votes for the statements were 1,875 and 1,821, respectively.[25] But it is astounding that even the weakened form of the statement, unaccompanied by any recognition of past persecution or any expression of sorrow and repentance, could still be rejected by hundreds of Catholic bishops.

Hopeful Catholics and generous Jews settled for this imperfect document (called *Nostra aetate* from its opening words in Latin), since it did represent progress, given the terrible conditions that preceded the Council, and it could be the basis for building new attitudes. But that would happen only if the statement were to be understood as a first tentative step, leading to a more open effort at justice. Rabbi David Polish spoke for many other Jews when he called the statement "a unilateral pronouncement by one party which presumes to redress on its own terms a wrong which it does not admit."[26] There was still work to be done at remedying past injustices.

The logical place for the next step to be taken was the Vatican study of the Holocaust that resulted in *We Remember*. But that document took the Council statement as having closed the issue of Christian actions in the past rather than opened a discussion of them. It was a step back in the matter of acknowledging guilt and redressing wrongs. It not only ignored the past centuries of persecution, like the Council, but it denied that Christians had any role in inflicting the Holocaust (as opposed to resisting it too feebly). The Council dismissed history. *We Remember* rewrote it. What we see, then, is a sad repetition of the kind of muted and aborted effort at justice that was undertaken at the very time when the Holocaust was about to occur. The conciliar decree (*Nostra aetate*) is a link in the process that goes from the first effort at response to German atrocities, by Pius XI, and the belated effort to deal with the accomplished horror by Pope John Paul II. A consideration of Pius XI's effort sets the stage for the current difficulty in being honest about Jewish-Christian relations.

---

[1]Commission for Religious Relations with the Jews, *We Remember: A Reflection on the Shoah*, Vatican translation (Pauline Books, 1998), p. 14. Numerical references in my text are to pages of this edition.

[2]Charles R. Morris, *American Catholic: The Saints and Sinners Who Built America's Most Powerful Church* (Times Books, 1997), p. 239. John F. Morley, a historian who is also a priest, con-

cluded, on the basis of the extensive diplomatic correspondence between Orsenigo and the Vatican: "Whether aware or not, Orsenigo was indifferent to what happened to the Jews. His superiors in the [Vatican] Secretariat of State, however, were well informed, and yet they manifested no concern for the Jews." Morley, *Vatican Diplomacy and the Jews During the Holocaust, 1939–1943* (KTAV Publishing House, 1980), p. 128.

[3]Dogmatic Constitution on the Church (*Lumen Gentium*), Chapter 2, *The Documents of Vatican II*, edited by Walter M. Abbott, S.J. (Herder and Herder, 1966), pp. 14–24. Father Abbott's note stresses that the use of "the people of God" as the church's definition "met a profound desire of the Council's to put greater emphasis on the human and communal side of the Church, rather than on the institutional and hierarchical aspects, which have sometimes been overstressed in the past for polemical reasons" (p. 24). The only thing to argue with in that sentence, published in 1966, is the words "in the past."

[4]Chester Gillis, *Roman Catholicism in America* (Columbia University Press, 1999), p. 187.

[5]Harold E. Quinley and Charles Y. Glock, *Anti-Semitism in America* (The Free Press, 1979), pp. 97–107.

[6]Pius XI, "With Burning Anxiety" (*Mit brennender Sorge*).

[7]See footnote 8.

[8]John M. Oesterreicher, "Declaration on the Relationship of the Church to Non-Christian Religions: Introduction and Commentary," in Herbert Vorgrimler (editor), *Commentary on the Documents of Vatican II* (Herder and Herder, 1969), p. 65.

[9]Ibid.

[10]For the patristic record, see Rosemary Radford Ruether, "The Adversus Judaeos Tradition in the Church Fathers: The Exegesis of Christian Anti-Judaism," in Jeremy Cohen, *Essential Papers on Judaism and Christianity in Conflict: From Late Antiquity to the Reformation* (New York University Press, 1991), pp. 174–92. John Chrysostom, in the first of his eight orations against the Jews, delivered in Antioch in 386/7, said that a synagogue is worse than a pagan temple, since that is "where Christ-killers gather, where the cross is banished, where God is blasphemed, where Father goes unacknowledged, Son is assaulted, and Holy Ghost's grace cannot prevail—where the demons are the Jews themselves" (PG 48.852).

[11]For Luther's anti-Semitism, see Mark U. Edwards, Jr., "Against the Jews," and for Calvin's, see Salo W. Baron, "John Calvin and the Jews," both in Cohen, op. cit., pp. 345–400. For the anti-Semitic theology of Reform theologians during Hitler's regime, see Robert P. Erickson, *Theologians Under Hitler: Gerhard Kittel, Paul Althaus, and Emmanuel Hirsch* (Yale University Press, 1985).

[12]Charlotte Klein, *Anti-Judaism in Christian Theology*, translated by Edward Quinn (SPCK, 1978), pp. 100–01, quoting Rahner's "Meditation on the Spiritual Exercises of St. Ignatius." A Protestant liberal does not escape Klein's survey either: in a 1933 lecture, Dietrich Bonhoeffer (who would, however, protest the Holocaust) said, "In the Church of Christ we have never lost sight of the idea that the 'chosen people,' which placed the Savior of the world on the cross, must bear the curse of its actions through a long history of suffering." Klein, p. 118.

[13]Pierre Benoit, O.P., *Exégèse et théologie*, Vol. 3 (Editions du Cerf, 1968), p. 420.

[14]Augustine, *Explaining the Psalms* 61.5 (PL 36.791).

[15]Solomon Grayzel, "The Papal Bull *Sicut Judeis*," in Cohen, op. cit., pp. 231–59.

[16]Ac 6.9–7.60, Josephus, *Antiquities of the Jews* 20.200.

[17]For a balanced treatment of Jews and the death of Jesus, see Raymond E. Brown, *The Death of the Messiah* (Doubleday, 1993), Vol. 1, pp. 328–97.

[18]Oesterreicher, op. cit., p. 6.

[19]Giuseppe Alberigo (editor), *History of Vatican II*, Vol. 2 (Orbis, 1997), pp. 44–46, 55.

[20]Oesterreicher, op. cit., pp. 41–44.

[21]Ibid., pp. 83–85.

[22]"Xavier Rynne" (F. X. Murphy), *The Third Session: The Debates and Decrees of Vatican Council II, September 14 to November 21, 1964* (Farrar, Straus & Giroux, 1965), pp. 261–62.

[23]Oesterreicher, op. cit., pp. 40, 47, 61–62.

[24]Vorgrimler, op. cit., pp. 665–67.

[25]Oesterreicher, op. cit., p. 128.

[26]Rabbi Polish quoted by Claud Nelson in the Response printed after *Nostra aetate* in Abbott, op. cit., p. 668.

2.

Toward the Holocaust

Pius XI

One of the saddest attempts to reverse the church's terrible record with Jews occurred when two good men found each other in what seemed a historically destined moment—the darkening summer of 1938, as Hitler's war was about to begin—and tried to do secret good. They were prevented from doing this when they encountered the papal structures of deceit. The two men were a learned and generous Pope, Pius XI, and a progressive American Jesuit, John LaFarge. The aging Pius, then eighty-one, whose record had not been a good one on Jewish matters during his seventeen years as Pope, was sincerely shocked and angered when Fascist professors, at Mussolini's direction, issued a Racial Declaration on July 14, 1938, saying that "Jews do not belong to the Italian race," which was declared "a pure Aryan race." On September 6, in a spontaneous outburst during an audience with pilgrims, Pius actually wept as he remembered the Jewish origins of the church and said, "Anti-Semitism is inadmissible. We are spiritually Semites."[1]

The Pope's prepared statements did not reflect this sensitivity. Even later (November 10 and 11), when Mussolini's government promulgated harsher anti-Semitic laws, the Vatican's official complaint was limited to the aspects of the law that broke the church-state concordat (by taking the marriages of baptized Jews away from church jurisdiction).[2] This had been the strategy of Pius all along, in dealing both with Nazi Germany and with Fascist Italy. Against Germany he had issued an encyclical, "With Burning Anxiety" (1937), that was smuggled into that country for simultaneous reading from Catholic pulpits. It condemned Fascist measures—though, once again, only those that broke the concordat with the Vatican (no mention was made of the sufferings of Jews).[3]

But Pius had a secret. Ever since June he had been preparing a new encyclical, one that would attack anti-Semitism directly. That is where John LaFarge came in. LaFarge, an editor of the Jesuit magazine *America,* was a pioneer in the struggle against southern segregation laws. He had written a book attacking the racism on which such laws were based, *Interracial Justice* (1937). In 1938 he went, as part of his duties at *America,* to a Eucharistic Congress in Budapest, and made a brief visit to Rome before returning home. While he was staying at the Jesuit residence, he received a mysterious message from the Pope, asking him to call at his summer home, Castel Gandolfo. Pius, it turned out, had read his recent book—this Pontiff had spent most of his life before his papacy as the director of two of the world's great archives, the Ambrosian Library in Milan and the Vatican Library in Rome, and he read incessantly, closely, and well, even in his eighties.

Pius wanted LaFarge to draft an encyclical for him, calling for justice in the cause of European Jews on the same grounds that LaFarge had used as an advocate for American blacks. He expressly wanted a new approach, which is why he went outside his regular circle of Roman advisers: "Say simply what you would say if you yourself were Pope."[4] Pius spoke to LaFarge even before informing his superior, the formidable General of the Society of Jesus, Wladimir Ledochowski, who had helped the Pope in forming earlier encyclicals. LaFarge felt flattered but a bit overwhelmed by his assignment. To an assistant of his provincial superior in New York he wrote: "Frankly, I am simply stunned, and all I can say is that the Rock of Peter has fallen on my head."[5] Naturally, he turned for guidance to Father Ledochowski—thus inadvertently defeating Pius's strategy for getting a fresh approach to the problem.

Ledochowski said that LaFarge should be assisted by two other Jesuits—one German, one French—who had experience in drafting encyclicals. They had both worked separately on Pius's social encyclical *Quadragesimo Anno* (1931), and the Frenchman had helped draft the same Pope's anti-Communist encyclical *Divini Redemptoris* (1937). LaFarge therefore went to Paris to work with the men he would come to think of as his "two Guses"—Gustav Gundlach and Gustave Desbuqois. They labored at a text provisionally titled *Humani Generis Unitas* ("The Unity of the Human Race") from July to September, creating drafts in four languages (Latin, French, German, and English).

After they turned in their work—not directly to the Pope but to Father Ledochowski—nothing happened for months. Father Gundlach, frustrated at the silence, began to suspect sabotage on the part of "our Boss" (the Jesuit General). In time they heard that Ledochowski had turned the draft over for corrections to another Jesuit, Enrico Rosa, the editor of *Civiltà Cattolica,* the Society's newspaper run in close collaboration with the Vatican. After that, only rumor said that the draft might have reached an ailing Pius a month or so before his death in February 1939. The Vatican later claimed that Pius XII, Pius XI's successor, knew the draft and used elements of it in some of his own papal statements— but not in any directly condemning anti-Semitism. The whole encyclical project might as well not have occurred, so far as the world at large knew. The Pope had enjoined secrecy on the drafting process, and Father Ledochowski would not let that ban drop, even after Pius XI (like the project itself) was dead. Biographers of Pius XI knew nothing of his effort to address the dreadful fate of the Jews. Even in LaFarge's autobiography, *The Manner Is Ordinary,* which came out in 1954, no mention was made of Pius's effort to come to the aid of the Jews. The world would not learn of this encyclical-that-might-have-been for another third of a century. Men working in the papers of LaFarge and Gundlach in the 1970s turned up traces of the encyclical project and tried to search out more information about it. A French version of the draft mysteriously disappeared from the LaFarge papers, but not before a microfilm was made of it. A German draft was in the Jesuit papers of Gundlach's province, but researchers were denied access to it. The Vatican said it had a copy of the Latin draft (which Pius XII saw), but will not produce it. What has been discovered, from the French draft and from letters in the LaFarge papers, was published in 1997, along with an account of the frustrations preventing further discovery so far, by the men who pursued the evidence most assiduously, Georges Passelecq and Bernard Suchecky. Their book, which appeared in France as *Encyclique cachée de Pie XI,* was translated into English in the same year (*The Hidden Encyclical of Pius XI*).

What happened to abort this carefully prepared and potentially historic encyclical? After news of it spread, many expressed regret that it had not come out in 1939—though others, considering the shortcomings of the draft, and wondering what would have been done to it before official promulgation (by Father Rosa, members of the Curia, and Pius's Secretary of State, Eugenio Pacelli), were just as glad that it did not. Certainly the draft was deficient, even as it left the hands of its three authors. But if anything like its severe condemnation of anti-Semitism had been adopted by the papacy in Pius XI's final months—a condemnation that had so far been lacking in the papal record—that would have made it harder for Pius XII to maintain his ambiguities and silences about the Holocaust as it was occurring. Indeed, preserving that ambiguity for future Pontiffs was an indirect reason for the suppression of the encyclical.

Yet the encyclical project was doomed from its inception—not because those working on it did not want to do something about the fate of the Jews, but because none of them could escape the structures of deceit that were in place all around them as they labored. Everyone but LaFarge had skeletons in the closet, so far as the Jews were concerned— beginning with the Pope himself. In the sixth year of his pontificate (1928), he had suppressed a Catholic organization, the Friends of Israel, that, in order to work for reconciliation with the Jews, tried to reverse past stands taken by the church. The group called for the abandonment of all talk of deicide, of a curse on the Jews, and of ritual murder. The papal decree of suppression said that this program did not recognize "the continual blindness of this people," and the Friends did not give the church credit for the way it had "protected this people against unjust persecutions." The Friends' approach was "contrary to the sense and spirit of the Church, to the thought of the Holy Fathers and the liturgy."[6] We saw in the last chapter what horrible things were said of the Jews by the "holy" Fathers of the church (e.g., John Chrysostom's claim that Jews are devils), but what did the decree mean by "contrary to the [Catholic] liturgy"? This was no doubt a reference to the notorious words "the perfidious Jews" contained in the liturgy of Holy Week—words still said by the church down to the time of John XXIII, who finally removed them.

Catholic commentary on the decree suppressing the Friends of Israel said that it is illegitimate "to conceal the role played by Israel with regard to Christ," to neglect "the Divine Punishments of the destruction of Jerusalem," to downplay "the long centuries of [Jewish] disbelief," and to show disrespect for the writings of the Fathers of the church.[7] We know that LaFarge was familiar with this decree of suppression, because it is actually quoted in the draft of the new encyclical—for a sad reason. The decree argued that its own act was not anti-Semitic, drawing a distinction between religious views and secular anti-Semitism in the same kind of skirt-clearing that we have seen in *We Remember*. But even this pro forma renunciation of anti-Semitism *was the only renunciation of it that the drafters of the new encyclical could find to attribute to a Pope!* Even to quote this renunciation out of context—suggesting that, thus isolated, it expressed a true papal position of long standing—was disingenuous and shows how easily structures of deceit can skew things written to express official attitudes of the teaching church.

Given his action in this decree, Pius XI's record up to 1939 was not likely to show a strong stand against persecution of the Jews—not because he approved of it, exactly, but because he was too much concerned with what he saw as the modern world's persecution of Catholics. Pius inherited the problem of the Vatican state bequeathed him by Pius IX (1846–78). When the unification of modern Italy took away from the church its temporal domains in Italy (1871), the new Italian government guaranteed the Pope independence within his walled palace and basilica grounds (the modern Vatican state) and offered financial reparations for the lands seized from him. Pius IX, calling the new state illegitimate, refused to accept the terms or the recompense. He made himself "a prisoner in the Vatican," and forbade Catholics to have anything to do with the usurping power—they could not even vote in Italian elections, under pain of excommunication.

Pius's successors (Leo XIII, Pius X, and Benedict XV) slowly backed off from some of the extremes of this noncommunication policy with the Italian government. But relations had still not been formally restored when Pius XI came to the papacy. In 1929, however, at a time when Mussolini wanted church approval for his actions, Pius signed the Lateran Treaty, in which the Vatican recognized the legitimacy of the Italian government, and that government paid the Vatican reparations for its lost domains (though less than the amount that was originally offered Pius IX in 1871).[8] At the same time, Pius signed a concordat making the church politically neutral in Italy, though Catholicism was recognized as the state church, with rights over marriage and the education of children.

Pius liked the idea of such concordats. He signed similar ones with Mexico and Germany. Concordats allowed the church a sphere of freedom in what was perceived to be the hostile world of secular states. The church gave up direct political action, replacing it with "Catholic Action" (mainly evangelizing work with the young and devotional organizations). This withdrawal from politics, in order to protect the church's spiritual realm, undercut the leaders of Catholic parties—Don Luigi Sturzo in Italy, Gil Robles in Spain, and the Center Party in Germany—making it easier for fascism to take over the politics of those countries. Pius XI was not deeply concerned about this, since he had the anti-democratic distrust of parliaments that was another bequest from Pius IX (see Chapter 10). Ratti, like the good librarian he was, relied on binding paper agreements with the heads of state, not electoral bargaining with the shifting moods of "the people." When he protested the growth of totalitarianism in European countries, it was always on the basis of their violation of the concordats he had drawn up with them. This meant that he was always speaking out only for Catholic rights specified in the concordats.

Eugenio Pacelli, the future Pius XII, had been a papal nuncio in Germany, and as Secretary of State he drew up the German concordat. He would be especially protective of his handiwork, helping maneuver Pius XI's protests against its violation ("With Burning Anxiety") into that country. His attitude as a diplomat was that the Vatican was on its legally strongest ground—if not the only one allowed it by the concordat—when it criticized specific departures from the governments' own commitments. The result was a busy patrolling of the network of concordat provisions, which would later be referred to as the church's fight against totalitarianism. If Pius XI attacked particular governments in terms that went beyond the concordats, he would be endangering the concordat diplomacy with other powers. When governments sized up this situation, as they were bound to, they realized that what was a cobweb for them could become an iron mesh for the Vatican, which kept placing all its hopes on this one slim and clever weave of deals, satisfactory to the librarian who shuffled his papers like the rare documents that had been under his care for decades, and the legalistic Secretary of State who could spin out their provisions with subtlety.

Such an approach had precluded conflict with the governments on matters like Jewish persecution, especially when the approach was bolstered by two other things—the Vatican's attitude toward Bolshevism in general, and toward the Jews' supposed affinity with Bolshevism. Cardinal Pacelli was the leading proponent of the Vatican's prevalent view that Bolshevism posed the gravest threat to the church in the modern world. Nazis might corrupt the churches, but they let them exist. Bolshevists abolished them outright. Even when Nazism began to look evil, it remained not only the lesser of two evils but a bulwark against the greater one. That made criticisms of Germany, when they had to be made, cautious and negotiatory.

This caution would especially be called for with regard to Jews, since they were felt to be deep in the secret councils of the socialist international (despite their persecution in Russia). For proof of this Vatican obsession, we need look no further than the draft of Pius XI's encyclical itself. *Humani Generis Unitas,* which was supposed to defend Jews, has this passage, lumping Jews together with the misguided souls who are driven "to ally themselves with, or actively to promote revolutionary movements that aim to destroy society to obliterate from the minds of men the knowledge, reverence, and love of God."[9]

How could such a passage make its way into a document that was supposed to be *anti*–anti-Semitic? It is simple. Father Ledochowski made sure of it when he appointed collaborators for LaFarge who were "safe" in his eyes. Desbuquois, after all, had cooperated with Pacelli on the anti-Communist encyclical, *Divini Redemptoris,* and Gundlach had written the entry on a "permissible anti-Semitism" in the *Theology and Church Lexicon* of 1930. There he taught that anti-Semitism is to be condemned only when it is "politico-racial," not when it is "politico-governmental." Jews should not be discriminated against just because they are Jews. But governments must protect themselves against "the 'assimilated' Jews who, being for the most part given to moral nihilism and without any national or religious ties, operate within the camp of world plutocracy [i.e., Jewish bankers] as well as within that of international Bolshevism, thus unleashing the darker traits of the soul of the Jewish people expelled from its fatherland." Gundlach clearly thought that this was not a pejorative attitude, since it treated equally "not only Semitic but also 'Aryan' vermin." And Jews tend to be not only radicals but libertines, forcing Gundlach to praise an anti-Semitism "linked to the rise of moral decadence (the decline of births)."[10]

That a priest who referred to fellow human beings as vermin was recruited to champion human rights in the Pope's name is a telling indicator of the Vatican's attitude toward Jews in the 1930s. Nor did Gundlach suppress his views in the draft he created with his fellow Jesuits. Here are other parts of that "hidden encyclical":

> But however unjust and pitiless, this [current] campaign against the Jews has had at least this advantage, if one can put it so, over racial strife, that it recalls the true nature, the authentic basis of the social separation of the Jews from the rest of humanity . . . [The Savior] was rejected by that people, violently repudiated and condemned as a criminal by the highest tribunal of the Jewish nation, in collusion with the pagan authority . . . The very act by which the Jewish people put to death their Savior and King was, in the strong language of Saint Paul, the salvation of the world. On the other hand, blinded by a vision of national domination and gain, the Israelites lost what they themselves had sought.[11]

So Pius XI was being asked to embrace the cause of the Jews by saying that they should not be persecuted even though they are Christ-killers.

In a further, sadder irony, the encyclical that took its rise from La-Farge's arguments against the segregation of blacks in the American South went on to argue *for* the segregation of Jews:

> As a result of the rejection of the Messiah by His own people, and of His corresponding acceptance by the Gentile world, which had not shared in the special promises delivered to the Jews, we find a historic enmity of the Jewish people to Christianity [blame the vicims], creating a perpetual tension between Jews and Christians . . . [thus the Church's hopes for the Jews] do not blind her to the

spiritual dangers to which contact with Jews can expose souls, or make her unaware of the need to safeguard her children against spiritual contagion . . . The Church has warned likewise against an over-familiarity with the Jewish community that might lead to customs and ways of thinking contrary to the standards of Christian life.[12]

These are the passages that made some people, when the draft of the encyclical came to light in the 1970s, express relief that it was never issued. It fed old prejudices while denouncing new persecutions. Father Johannes Nota, a Dutch Jesuit, wrote: "If one puts these sentences back into the context of the racist legislation adopted in Germany at that period, one can say today: 'God be praised that this draft remained only a draft!' "[13] In fact, embarrassment over these passages may explain why the Vatican and the Jesuits have refused cooperation with the effort to bring this whole story to light, keeping Gundlach's draft, and possibly more compromising notes and letters, inaccessible.

Yet that is hardly the reason the encyclical was aborted in 1938. The key factor in that derailment was Father Ledochowski's request that the editor of *Civiltà Cattolica* correct the draft created in Paris. That journal, and its Ledochowski-appointed editors, had been very far from showing any sympathy for Jews in the 1920s and 1930s (Ledochowski's period in office). A 1920 article talked of Jews as "the filthy element . . . avid for money . . . wanting to proclaim the communist republic tomorrow." It was the synagogue that was "urging on this rabble of parties, leagues and [Freemason] lodges" to create a universal revolution. A 1936 article quoted a French Jesuit to prove that Jews are "uniquely endowed with the qualities of parasites." A 1937 series of articles developed the theme of Jews as "a foreign body that irritates and provokes the reaction of the organism it has contaminated." In 1938, it was said that Hungary could be saved from the influence of Jews, "disastrous for the religious, moral, and social life of the Hungarian people," only if "the government forbids [Jewish] foreigners to enter the country." Finally, Father Rosa himself, to whom the General of the Jesuits turned over the draft of *Humani Generis Unitas* for correction, endorsed these sentiments from an earlier article in *Civiltà Cattolica*:

The equality that anti-Christian sectarians have granted Jews, wherever the government of the people has been usurped, has had the effect of bringing Judaism and freemasonry together in persecuting the Catholic Church and elevating the Jewish race over Christians, as much in hidden power as in manifest opulence.[14]

Read those words again, and remember when they were written—in September 1938, when Jews were being harried and driven and terrorized just outside the Vatican's own walls. In fact, this was just three weeks after the Italians marked all foreign Jews for expulsion (and two weeks after Pius XI had said, "We are spiritually Semites"). In fact, this was just about the time when the draft encyclical was being delivered to Father Ledochowski, who would almost immediately turn it over to the author of these very words.

We can be sure, then, that the encyclical was not diverted by Father Ledochowski because the authors—(Gundlach especially?)—had been too harsh in it toward Jews. It was the liberal words, echoing LaFarge's earlier book, that must have frightened the Jesuits of the Vatican. Ledochowski delayed (if he did not prevent) the delivery of the encyclical to the man who had requested it, though it was delivered by the man from whom he had requested it. The Pope was old and ailing. Delay at this point was critical, because of his health and because of the world's condition, as Hitler and Mussolini reached new levels of mutual accommodation on the handling of Jews. This was not a time to hesitate or delay, unless one meant to sabotage.

And, of course, Ledochowski did. It is not hard to reconstruct his thinking. Here was a Pope old and about to die. He had gone outside channels to commission a draft from an inexperienced American, and though Ledochowski had largely controlled what LaFarge could do, and with whom, the American had nonetheless turned in a draft that made the Pope attack governments for singling out Jews for persecution:

It becomes clear that the struggle of racial purity ends by being uniquely the struggle against the Jews. Save for its systematic cruelty, this struggle is no different in true motives and methods from persecutions everywhere carried out against the Jews since antiquity.[15]

Those were words to set all kinds of alarm bells ringing in the Vatican. We have seen how bishops reacted even a quarter of a century later, at Vatican II, when the subject of past persecutions came up. That was not a subject the authorities wanted to go into—and not, certainly, to connect the Nazi activities of the day with the suppressions "since antiquity." Besides, to single out the treatment of the Jews went against the whole strategy that Rome had been following, which was to speak only of general rights for all people or for specific Catholic rights under various concordats. The concordats themselves called for neutrality on "political" issues, and the point of all prior protests mounted against both Hitler and Mussolini was strict and literal observance of the concordats.

Father Ledochowski took it upon himself to prevent the encyclical's timely delivery to the Pope. Why saddle the next Pope with a dying man's erratic and ill-considered lunge outside the tested policies of the institution? It was clear to all insiders (and Ledochowski was one of the inmost) that the next Pope would be Pacelli—he would be chosen in a one-day conclave on March 2, 1939—and the entire structure of Vatican diplomacy had been his creation over the past decade. It would not be surprising if Ledochowski consulted Pacelli on giving the encyclical another round of corrections from a trusted man like Rosa. The Jesuit General had worked with Pacelli on other encyclicals. Is Pacelli's involvement the reason for the Vatican's unwillingness to reveal anything in its custody about the fate of *Humani Generis Unitas*?

In any event, the cards were stacked against Rome's effort to fight the persecution of the Jews—which would soon become the Holocaust. The Ratti Pope sincerely wanted to tell the truth, and he would probably have been able to but for one thing. He was the Pope, and that can make telling the truth impossible. Even the outsider he brought in, the one man who came to this task with clean hands, was not able to deliver a document unstained by racism, bad theology, anti-Communist hysteria, and segregation. So far as we know from the incomplete record now available, he did not protest what his collaborators put in about Jewish "contamination." How could he question his own superior, or the men who had created the Pope's texts on other occasions—or the words of the Pope himself, calling Jews the ones who killed Christ, in the one document we know with certainty that he read while drafting the encyclical, the decree suppressing the Friends of Israel? Instead of breaking out with his overture to LaFarge, Pius drew the American into the structures of deceit that afflict those trying to tell the truth from the Vatican.

The Vatican's conviction that Jews were in alliance with international socialism, secularism, rationalism, banking, libertinism, and birth control—with the whole of modernity as that had been defined pejoratively in the nineteenth century—was another bequest of Pope Pius IX, who is a presence in the Vatican to this day.

Pius IX

ius IX—Pio Nono to Italians—drew the line of opposition against modernity in the twelfth year of his long (thirty-two-year) reign, in 1858. That is the year he kidnapped a six-year-old Jewish boy in Bologna, took him to Rome, and kept him there. The act caused an outcry against Pius, a formerly popular Pontiff, all over the world, even from some Catholics. But Pius said this was just a sign that friends of the Jews hate Christians. *Civiltà Cattolica* reported a dialogue at the time in which a foreign minister told Pius that the whole modern world was calling for the Jewish boy's return. "What you call the modern world," said Pius, "is simply Freemasonry."[16] A prominent Catholic newspaper made the connection between Jews and revolutionaries even more dramatic: *L'armonia della religione colla civiltà* (*The Harmony of Religion and Culture*) headlined a story on the case, "The Jew of Bologna and the Bombs of Giuseppe Mazzini."[17] Pius himself told a sympathetic Catholic newspaper editor that the "hubbub" over the Jewish boy was caused by "the freethinkers, the disciples of Rousseau and Malthus [the latter an evil man for fostering birth control]."[18]

How did a Pope in the nineteenth century get into the kidnapping business? It happened because a young Christian woman in the papal state of Bologna told friends that she had secretly baptized a sick child, Edgardo Mortara, in the Jewish home where she was a servant. The child was only a year old at the time. The Inquisition in Bologna investigated the matter—very possibly at the instigation of Pius IX himself, according to the definitive three-volume biography of Pius by Giacomo Martina, S.J.[19] When it was decided to believe the woman, despite problems with her story, the police were sent to take the boy (now six) away from his mother and father. Bologna was still part of the Pope's temporal domain, so the police were his officials.

When they took the child, the police did not even give the parents a reason for the seizure—in the early days, the Mortaras had no way to contest the story told about their son, since they did not know what the story was. They had to undertake investigations of their own to find the woman who had secretly testified to the Inquisition. By that time, Edgardo had been sent to Rome, where the Pope received him fondly and said he would be brought up a Christian. When Edgardo's parents came from Bologna to recover him in Rome, they were allowed to visit their son in the Esquiline palace, but not to take him away. *Civiltà Cattolica* reported that Edgardo's mother, at the sight of a Marian medal on her son, ripped it off contemptuously, proving herself an unfit mother.[20]

The Pope maintained that he was defending spiritual values against a secular world indifferent to matters of faith—a Christian boy could not be trusted to be brought up by Jewish parents. *Civiltà Cattolica* predicted that the boy, if returned, would be pressured by his family to renounce the faith (as if there were no pressure being used to foist faith on him at the Esquiline). He might even be tortured, the Jesuit author of the article suggested: "Would it seem right and generous to place this innocent boy on this cross?"[21] By raising the image of a boy being crucified, the paper was tickling the vicious old charge that Jews engaged in ritual murder of Christian boys—and, sure enough, that charge was renewed during the Mortara affair. The newspaper *Il Cattolica* published this report: "While the libertine press was creating such an uproar against the Pope because of the case of the Mortara boy, the most horrendous assassination of a Christian boy was being committed by Jews in Folkchany, a Moldo-Wallachian city." A four-year-old, after disappearing, had been discovered dead from multiple wounds. That was proof, said *Il Cattolica*: "The type of torture was too much like that of Our Lord for them to be fooled about the intention of the murderer or murderers."[22] Other papers picked up this story—but failed to report, later on, that the boy's own uncle was found to have killed him.

Some Catholics were not convinced that the Pope was right to be holding a child against his parents' wishes. Even Thomas Aquinas had said that children should not be baptized without their parents' consent, since they have the immediate authority over them (ST 3 q 68, 10 ad 2). But Pius was impervious to argument. When a Catholic wrote a respectful letter suggesting that Edgardo should be returned, the Pope scribbled on the bottom of the letter, "aberrations of a Catholic . . . doesn't know his catechism."[23] When his own Secretary of State, Cardinal Antonelli, suggested that Pius might be alienating other countries by such a high-handed use of power, the Pope answered that he did not care who was against him: "I have the blessed Virgin on my side." He told the Catholic ambassador from France that the Mortaras had brought their trouble on themselves by illegally employing a Christian as their servant.[24] To other emissaries coming to speak of Mortara, the Pope pointed to the figure of Christ on a crucifix and declared, "I rely on the One there."[25]

The Pope, who genuinely loved children, pampered little Edgardo, who was dazzled, like any little boy, by the coaches and soldiers and vestments and splendor of the palace. Even after he was enrolled in a religious school, he frequently visited his "father" at the Esquiline. He would later recall how the Pope, "like a good father, had fun with me, hiding me under his grand red cloak, asking jokingly, 'Where's the boy?' and then, opening the cloak, showing me to the onlookers."[26] When Edgardo became aware of the criticisms directed at the Pope, Pius told him: "My boy . . . you have cost me dearly and I have suffered a great deal because of you." To others he said, "Both the powerful and the powerless tried to steal this boy from me." He stood firm because "I, too, am his father."[27]

When delegations from Rome's Jewish community came to plead with the Pope, he loosed his famous temper on them, blaming them for "stirring up a storm all over Europe about this Mortara case." One Jewish leader he excoriated as "Crazy! Who are you?" To another he said, "Lower your voice. Do you forget before whom you are speaking?" Since, in his liberal early days as Pope, Pius had freed Rome's Jews from some earlier requirements (like compelled attendance at proselytizing sermons), he now blew up at them:

I suppose these are the thanks I get for all the benefits you have received from me! Take care, for I could have done you harm, I could
have made you go back into your hole. But don't worry, my goodness is so great, and so strong is the pity I have for you, that I pardon you.[28]

The distinguished British-Jewish philanthropist, Sir Moses Monte-
fiore, made a special trip in his own old age to plead with the Pope in
Rome, but he was rebuffed.[29] In England and the United States, the
plight of Edgardo was used by anti-Catholics to discredit the church. The
case was important enough to generate thirty-one major news articles in
the *Baltimore American,* twenty-three in the *Milwaukee Sentinel,* and more
than twenty in the *New York Times.* The *New York Herald* said that interest in the affair had reached "colossal dimensions." Pressure was put on
President James Buchanan to speak out against the capture of the boy. He
was forced to respond that he could not meddle in another country's internal affairs.[30] He was paralyzed by the fact that children were still being
separated from their parents in America's slaveholding Southern states in
1858, two years before the beginning of the Civil War. The international
protests embarrassed the French government, whose troops were occupying Rome in support of the Pope against his own rebellious subjects.
The French did not want to be seen as complicitous in this crime, and
their ambassador discussed with the Italian nationalist leader, Camillo di
Cavour, the idea of ending the crisis by kidnapping the child back.[31]

In 1864, six years after Edgardo's kidnapping, a nine-year-old Jewish
boy, Giuseppe Coen, was baptized without his parents' permission in
Rome, and sequestered from them. The outrage over the Mortara child
was renewed, with such effect that some claim this contributed to the
Pope's loss of his temporal holdings in 1870—a government that could
do this to children, it was argued, is insupportable by civilized allies.
When the French removed their troops from Rome, precipitating Pio
Nono's fall, they had other reasons for their action, but they also felt no
regret at ceasing to prop up the discredited papal regime. It was the
Catholic countries that were most shamefaced about the matter. The
Austrian ambassador wrote: "Italy [the triumphant secular government]

should be erecting arches of triumph in honor of this little Jew [Coen]."[32]
The veritable unanimity among the nations had made Pius complain to
Edgardo in 1867:

> Your case set off a worldwide storm against me and the Apostolic
> See. Governments and peoples, the rulers of the world as well as the
> journalists—who are the truly powerful people of our times—de-
> clared war on me. Monarchs themselves entered the battle against
> me, and with their ambassadors they flooded me with diplomatic
> notes, and all this because of you . . . And in the meantime no one
> showed any concern for me, father of all the faithful.[33]

Pius felt vindicated, not only by the "persecution," which made him one
with his Savior, but by the fact that Edgardo completed his Catholic education, entered a seminary, and became a priest. Pius plunged further
into wild charges against "the modern world"—he issued his disastrous
Syllabus of Errors in the very year Coen was kidnapped, and five years later
called an ecumenical council to declare himself infallible (see Chapter
12). Now it was not secular governments that were accusing him of
despotism but a loyal Catholic like John Henry Newman, who wrote in
1870: "We have come to a climax of tyranny. It is not good for a Pope to
live twenty years [in office]"(N 163).

The atmosphere Pio Nono created was not dissipated in Rome between the time of his reign and Pius XI's. In fact, Pius X instituted a
crackdown on Catholic intellectuals that has been called a form of theological McCarthyism, accusing his own priests of surrender to modern
rationalism. And the Jesuit journal of the Vatican kept up its drumbeat
against Jews as the spokespersons of modernity. In 1886 it ran an article
alleging that "Jews have always persecuted Christians." In 1892 the paper
accused Jews of "a remorseless, pitiless war against the Christian religion,
and especially against Catholicism, and then an unbridled arrogance in
usury, monopolies, and a series of thefts of all sorts, to the damage of the
very people who gave them their civil liberty."[34] Father Rosa was defending the *Civiltà*'s 1890s articles on the Jews at the very time when he
was about to receive the draft encyclical *Humani Generis Unitas* from his
Jesuit superior.

This is the kind of billingsgate that poured out of the Vatican in a continual stream right up to the time when Pius XI tried to back away from the church's record. Such a break is not easily accomplished, not for any institution, and least of all for an institution that claims never to have been wrong, never to have persecuted, never to have inflicted injustice. Given so much to hide, the impulse to keep on hiding becomes imperative, automatic, almost inevitable. The structures of deceit are ever less escapable—the cumulative product of all the past evasions, the disingenuous explainings, outright denials, professions, deferences, pieties, dodges, lapses, and funk. It is thought, no doubt, that to let the truth slip through this intricate outwork, this riddle of baffles and lattices and shutters, would embarrass the church. But to keep on evading the truth is a worse embarrassment, and a crime—an insult to those who have been wronged, and whose wrong will not be recognized. When truth lies blatant on the doorstep, the instinct is to lock oneself in behind the door and never look out. This is nothing less than imprisonment in the dark, done in feigned service to the Light of the World.

[1]Georges Passelecq and Bernard Suchecky, *The Hidden Encyclical of Pius XI*, translated from the French by Steven Rendall, with an Introduction by Garry Wills (Harcourt Brace & Company, 1997), pp. 138–39.

[2]Ibid., pp. 144–51.

[3]Ibid., pp. 101–10. The Jews are mentioned only when the right of Catholics to teach the Old Testament is affirmed—and here occurs the unfortunate passing reference to Jews as "the people" who killed Christ. See Chapter 1, note.

[4]Ibid., p. 36.

[5]Ibid., p. 37.

[6]Ibid., pp. 97–98.

[7]Ibid., pp. 98–99. The quotes are from an article in *Nouvelle revue théologique,* where the Latin text of the decree had been published. The commentary was by the Jesuit father, Jean Levie.

[8]Mussolini so wanted church approval in the middle of the 1930s that he moved almost to the right of the Pope on some issues, outlawing divorce, contraception, and abortion, adding to the legal penalties for anyone convicted of adultery, syphilis, or immodesty. Dennis Mack Smith, *Mussolini* (Alfred A. Knopf, 1982), pp. 159–61.

[9]Passelecq and Suchecky, op. cit., p. 252 (*Humani Generis Unitas*, paragraph 1142).

[10]Ibid., p. 48 (*Lexikon für Theologie und Kirche,* Vol. 1, second edition [Herder, 1930], pp. 504–5).

[11]Passelecq and Suchecky, op. cit., pp. 247–49 (*Humani Generis Unitas,* paragraphs 133–36).

[12]Ibid., pp. 251–53 (paragraphs 141–42).

[13]Ibid., p. 12.

[14]Ibid., pp. 124–35.

[15]Ibid., p. 246 (paragraph 131).
[16]David I. Kertzer, *The Kidnapping of Edgardo Mortara* (Alfred A. Knopf, 1997), p. 157.
[17]Ibid., p. 139.
[18]Ibid., p. 158.
[19]Giacomo Martina, S.J. *Pio IX (1851–1866)*, *Miscellanea historiae ecclesiasticae in Pontificia universitate Gregoriana 51* (1986).
[20]Kertzer, op. cit., p. 112.
[21]Ibid., p. 113.
[22]Ibid., pp. 136–37.
[23]Ibid., p. 85.
[24]Martina, op. cit., p. 32.
[25]Kertzer, op. cit., pp. 81, 157.
[26]Ibid., p. 255
[27]Ibid., p. 161,
[28]Ibid., p. 159.
[29]Ibid., pp. 163–70.
[30]Ibid., p. 127.
[31]Ibid., pp. 119–21.
[32]Ibid., p. 259.
[33]Ibid., p. 260.
[34]Ibid., p. 136.

3.

Usurping the Holocaust

dith Stein, who was born a Jew in 1891 and died a nun at Auschwitz in 1942, lived one of the most intellectually adventurous lives of the twentieth century. She is, by any measure, a giant—profound in thought, dedicated in service, challenging in originality. Then why should anyone be offended that her church has called her holy? Yet many Jews (and quite a few Christians) have been upset at the canonization of Sister Teresa Benedicta de Cruce, to give her the name she went by as a Carmelite nun. All through the process by which John Paul II first beatified Stein (1987) and then made her a saint (1998), there have been strenuous objections to placing her in the Christian calendar of those to be prayed to in heaven. It may seem odd that non-Catholics should care to whom Catholics do their praying. If we are to have freedom of speech, does that not include freedom of prayer? But matters are more complicated than that.

Some object to the fact that she has not been known by her religious but by her ethnic name, as if she were still a Jew when she died. "It is clear that Edith Stein as Sister Teresa Benedict of the Cross—as the one blessed by the Cross—does not fulfill the categorical definitions nor obligations of one who is a Jew. Yet the Church insists that she died as 'a daughter of Israel.' "[1] Others find in the treatment of her a suggestion that the only good Jew is a converted Jew. Still others feel with her niece, who attended Stein's beatification and then went to a synagogue as to a cleansing ceremony and said, "The Christian religion to which Edith Stein converted was in our eyes the religion of our persecutors."[2] But most of the uneasiness comes from a suspicion that Stein is a symbol

being manipulated to give Catholics a claim that the Holocaust victimized Catholics as well as Jews.

Some of these reactions are extreme, some of them ill stated, but when
one surveys the range of them, it is easy to see that what is resented is not
Stein herself but the use being made of her. Consider, for instance, this
question, posed by Judith Herschcopf Banki:

> If Edith Stein had been born a Jew in another time, had converted
> to Christianity, had joined a Roman Catholic order, had been sent
> to the Far East or to Africa, and had been murdered there in an out-
> break of anti-Christian violence, would her beatification have
> stirred the same concern among Jews?[3]

The answer is no, of course, and for reasons that go even deeper than
Banki suggests. We might ask, rephrasing her, would Stein in those circumstances have been proposed for canonization at all, would the rules
of the process have been bent for her, would the history of her ordeal
have been rewritten, would a miracle have been jiggered into place to
make sure she won her halo? For that is what is at issue here, not Stein's
own great merits and deep holiness. Not what she was, but what posthu-
mous service she is being asked to perform, is the issue.

Before we go into these matters, we should step back first, and consider
who she was and what she did. That will make it seem all the more egregious that she is being deployed against her own people. She was the last
of seven surviving children (four died in childbirth) of a devoutly Orthodox mother who heroically raised this large family and ran an orphaned
business after her husband died (when Edith was two). Born on Yom Kippur, Edith was her mother's darling, the most brilliant child in a bevy of
bright ones, a prodigy who had to push out toward the unknown—ini-
tially into teenage atheism, then into training as a professional philosopher. She took her doctorate summa cum laude at Göttingen, where she
was the favored student of the founding father of phenomenalism, Edmund Husserl. She also studied informally with the dissolute Catholic
phenomenologist Max Scheler, on whose book, *The Nature of Sympathy,*
she based her doctoral dissertation, *The Problem of Empathy.* (Another person who did a doctoral dissertation on Scheler, without having her ad-

vantage of studying with him, was Karol Wojtyla.) Her first scholarly work is a clue to her spirituality. We form a self, she argued, we achieve our own interiority, only by the interplay with other interiorities. Ours is a reflexive subjectivity. I explore other persons like me and different from me, and define a self in that process—so that the isolated person is a non-person. Moral progress is a matter of making a self that pays its debts to the other selves that helped it come into being. To break off or diminish that respectful interplay with other minds is morally to die:

> To consider ourselves in inner perception, i.e., to consider our psychic "I" and its attributes, means to see ourselves as we see another and as he sees us . . . This is how empathy and inner perception work hand in hand to give me myself to myself . . . By empathy with differently composed personal structures we become clear on what we are not, what we are, more or less than others. Thus, together with self-knowledge, we also have an important aid to self-evaluation . . . When we empathically run into ranges of value closed to us, we become conscious of our own deficiency or disvalue . . . We learn to see that we experience ourselves as having more or less value in comparison with others.[4]

This moral theory was partly formed and partly tested when she broke off her studies, during World War I, to serve as a nurse in the typhoid section of a military hospital, where she cared for people of many nationalities and entered into the differences in their way of facing suffering.[5] When the professor she felt closest to, Adolf Reinach, died at the front, Stein was impressed by the Christian way his young wife coped with this severing of one self from another. Sensing that the greatest interplay of subjectivities is with God, she considered becoming a Lutheran like the Reinachs. That would shock her mother less than to join the church known for its past persecution of the Jews. Yet despite her genuine love of her past, she was drawn to a spectacular break with it, as if the challenge of the harder act of empathy brought out more of her selfhood. Her hunch was always that to gain a self was to transcend a self. That is why, eventually, it would not be enough to be a Catholic, she must be a Carmelite.

Yet the farther off she launched herself from her starting point, the more important it became to circle back and include in her experience all that went before. Even as a Catholic, she did not stop taking her mother to synagogue and praying with her. She never tried to convert her mother, or any other Jew. She never thought of herself as an ex-Jew. In fact, she said of her conversion, "My return to God made me feel Jewish again"—a claim Jews rightly resent, but one that was integral to her way of seeing empathy as a voyage out into other minds without losing one's earlier sense of self.[6] Her claim was, subjectively at least, less a theological affront than a psychological necessity. She deeply regretted Husserl's loss of his Jewish faith, and was overjoyed when he returned to religion before his death:"As regards my dear Master, I have no worries about him.To me it has always seemed strange [to think] that God could restrict his mercy to the boundaries of the visible Church."[7]

Even as a Carmelite nun she used her birth name when publishing as a philosopher, though she knew publishers would be afraid of its Jewish sound. "In 1936, having completed her magnum opus, *Bounded and Unbounded Being,* she found out that the treatise could not be published under her Jewish name. Stein refused to adopt a name eligible from the guild of Aryan writers."[8] Just before Easter, in 1933, she wrote to Pius XI, begging him to direct an encyclical against the persecution of the Jews— something he tried to do six years later, unsuccessfully. Well before she was killed for being a Jew, she had lost teaching appointments for being a Jew. She was even sent away from one of her order's convents for being a Jew (she posed a threat to the other sisters' safety). In 1933, as the persecution of Jews was intensifying, she began her *Life in a Jewish Family* in the hope that even persecutors might be enabled to empathize with the humane family she describes, so far from the picture created by Nazi propaganda: "Is Judaism represented only by, or even only genuinely by, powerful capitalists, insolent literati, or those restless heads who have led the revolutionary movements of the past decades?" She offers a warm portrait of her mother as the living refutation of such caricatures—and she never brings her own Christianity into the story.

Even a Jewish scholar who cannot admire her conversion does not feel it was a desertion. In some measure, according to Judith Herschcopf Banki, her earlier faith failed her:

We may regret her conversion to what her niece has called "the religion of our persecutors." But given the extraordinary combination of intellectual brilliance and spiritual hunger that came together in her, where could she have turned in the Jewish community of her time? Was there a Talmud Torah or rabbinical academy that would have taken her speculative philosophical interests seriously? How could she have latched onto the rich and demanding legacy of rabbinic thought as a woman, and an argumentative woman at that? Recalling the much-told story that Franz Rosenzweig was called back from the very threshold of conversion to Christianity by a visit to an Orthodox synagogue on the eve of Yom Kippur, Rabbi Nancy Fuchs-Dreimer asks whether Rosenzweig would have remained a Jew if he had been hurried upstairs to sit behind a *mehirz*—the screen separating women in the synagogue—that fateful night. We do not know the answer, but the question should spur us to find a hospitable home in Judaism for women with the gifts of an Edith Stein.[9]

Does this mean that Edith Stein stands less for conversion from Judaism to Christianity than for a convergence of Judaism and Christianity, as Rachel Feldhay Brenner argues in a profound and moving essay? Not really. Though Stein thought constantly of "her people," it was always as a people whose scripture was fulfilled in Jesus. She did not think so much that Jews had to be converted, individually, as that Jesus would include them in the salvation that was promised them despite their lack of belief in him. That is the meaning of her supposed words to her sister when the guard came to take them to their death: "Come, we are going for our people." *For* them, not *with* them. She offered her own sufferings, in unison with Christ's on the cross, as redemptive of her people. She wrote—before she was captured, but with a knowledge that she might well be killed in the persecution—that she offered her life "for the Jewish people, that the Lord may be received by his own and his kingdom come in glory."[10] It is significant that she does not offer her sacrifice to redeem the sins of the persecuting Christians, but to redeem the unbelief of the persecuted. This makes the presentation of Stein as a basis for reconciliation futile. Reconciliation of two faiths is not the same as replacement of one by the other.

Stein's life and writings are inspiring, aside from any claim she might make on her church's part for victimization by the Holocaust. In fact, her first promotion in the process of beatification did not describe her death as a martyrdom. She was promoted as a "confessor" of the faith. In the nomenclature of Catholic sainthood, confessors are those who live exemplary lives of holiness, as opposed to martyrs, who give their lives for their faith. In the early days of the church, martyrs were the first to be acclaimed as saints and have their relics honored. They are still the "privileged" saints. The martyrs may not have lived as exemplary lives as some confessors, but their sins are purged by their blood. Under the church rules now followed, a martyr's case is so much stronger than a confessor's that the former does not need to have two officially ascertained miracles in order to be beatified, while the latter does.[11] (Actually, if the presumption of the martyr's dignity is stronger, the working of miracles should be easier and more common with him or her, by the logic of the system.)

Stein was offered for consideration as a confessor, since it was assumed she did not, as a martyr must, die for her faith. She was not killed for being a Catholic. One of her early champions, himself a convert from Judaism, Monsignor John Oesterreicher (whose great work for the Jewish statement at the Vatican Council we have noticed), said, "Of course, she would never have been killed had she not had Jewish parents."[12] Let us assume, for a moment, that her cause had proceeded on these lines and been vindicated—that she had been first beatified and then canonized as a confessor. Even in that case, if her own sense of suffering for her unbelieving relatives were brought up at all, there would be no reason to say she was a figure of reconciliation, but there would also have been no occasion for Jews' taking any particular offense at this honor given her. No claim would have been made that she died for some reason different from that of her relatives.

That is not what happened. A confessor, as I said, differs from a martyr in the need for two confirmed miracles to be declared a *beata* (blessed)—and for years not even one could be attributed to Stein. As we are about to see, the miracle needed for her canonization would be hard enough to come by. At the beatification stage there wasn't even a plausible miracle to work with. Well, it is not unusual for a person to be proposed for beatification and then to languish in that state for many years—indeed, forever—if the miracle cannot be established. But there was an urgency about Stein's case that did not really depend on her virtues alone.

Canonization has a didactic purpose in the church. Saints are proposed for the lessons they teach, the needs they meet, the priorities church leaders want to emphasize. Martyrs are role models in times of persecution, monks in periods of asceticism. Most confessors have been either virgins, priests, or religious, teaching that those states were superior to married life. When a layman was canonized, it was often because he was (like Thomas More) also a martyr. There has always been special pressure to canonize founders of religious orders, to show their legitimacy and to encourage membership in them. Saints specially devout to Mary (like Bernadette of Lourdes) would promote the Virgin's cult. National sensibilities are sometimes taken into account. For years, the Jesuit priests martyred in Elizabeth I's time were not canonized because that might have offended the English. On the other hand, Paul VI put a hold on martyrs from the Spanish civil war out of his disapproval of the Franco regime that was promoting them.[13] Yet the sensibilities of Jews were not allowed to have any weight in Stein's process.

What *was* the aspect of Stein's life that made officials feel a special urgency for her promotion, despite the openly expressed misgivings of Jews? The Vatican plausibly denies that it was to encourage conversions from Judaism. The urgency was not originally to celebrate her martyrdom, since she was not called a martyr for the first years of her process. Or was she a martyr after all? What seems to have been described at first as just a way to get beyond the problem of dispensation from the need for miracles soon became an issue on which Stein's advocates became enthusiastic—the idea that she died for her faith, not for her parentage. But to establish that, these officials must prove that her killers were animated by *odium fidei,* a persecuting hatred of her religion. The indication of such a motive in the traditional martyr tales was that the victim was asked to renounce the faith or to perform an act that violated it—like sacrificing to pagan idols, or committing sacrileges against the crucifix. None of this applies to Stein. She was not told to renounce Christianity, or tempted toward sacrilege. She was a Christian—but so were all the other nuns in the convent she was taken from, and they were not arrested with her.

Only her sister Rose, another Catholic convert staying at the convent (though she was not a nun), was taken with her. The nuns of her order had recognized what was at stake when they shifted her about—her Jewish origin led to her being treated in a different way even by her fellow Carmelites.[14] There is no indication that her treatment at the death camp was in any way differentiated from that of her fellow ethnic Jews.

The fact that she did not see her own death as a witness for the faith is indicated by the fact that she tried to escape it—she left notes at the train stops to the death camp asking for aid from the Swiss Consulate and offering to pay for it. There was nothing questionable about doing anything so sensible if she was just fleeing anti-Jewish hatred. If, however, it meant refusing to bear witness for the faith, it would be somewhat less admirable—a bit like trying to bribe your way out of the company of Christians about to face the lions in the arena. She clearly did not think it was hatred of the Catholic faith that would be on the minds of her murderers. There is no question what their motives were.

But Stein's promoters were determined to raise such a question. They created a historical lie to promote her cause. Was this done just to get around the requirement for a miracle? If we restrict ourselves to her beatification, that might be argued. But when we look at her canonization, too, and put it in conjunction with other canonizations centering on the Holocaust, it becomes clear that Stein is very useful for maintaining the argument of *We Remember,* that the church was more with the persecuted than with the persecutors during the Holocaust. In order partly to clear the church of guilt for the Holocaust, it would partly usurp the sufferings of the Jews from whom Stein is now being separated in her death. She was being made a sign of division, the last thing she would have wanted.

How did the Vatican make the ludicrous case that Stein died for being a Catholic, not for being a Jew? In a very tricky and roundabout way. Stein was arrested as part of a roundup of Dutch Jews that Holland's Christian leaders were protesting. In a joint statement of Catholic bishops and Protestant ministers against the deportation, the churchmen made the mistake of singling out one group with special emphasis: "In the case of Christians of Jewish descent, we are moved by a further consideration: namely, such measures would sever them from participation in the life of the Church."[15] That provided the Nazis with a bargaining chip. They said they would make an exception of the baptized Jews if the bishops would cease their protests, which was the immediate result. But when the deportations continued, the churchmen decided to speak out again. Most of them backed down when Holland's Reichkommisar forbade their interference, but the bishop of Utrecht sent a pastoral letter to his parishes denouncing the deportations. The Nazis, in return, canceled the exception for the baptized, and Edith Stein was taken from her convent at that point.

Advocates of Stein's cause argue that Nazi response to the bishop's protest amounted to *odium fidei,* and that was the immediate cause of Stein's death. But, first of all, religion was not at issue in the attempted blackmail of the Nazis. They had a group of people they were going to deport *as Jews.* They showed that, in order to buy the bishop's silence they would not treat the converts *as Jews,* but otherwise they would continue to treat them *as Jews.* The punishment was not of just any Catholics, or of Catholics as Catholics. If it had been, other nuns would have been taken from the convent, not just the one with Jewish parents. Rose Stein was the only lay person taken from the convent, where she had been staying with Edith. She, too, was a Catholic convert, but she was not arrested for that reason.

If hatred of the bishop was the issue, the Nazis should have arrested him. But no Catholics other than those of Jewish birth were punished as a result of his letter. No new policy was formulated to focus on Catholics. The old policy toward Jews was carried out without any exemptions. If you had asked any official up the Nazi chain of command if the Steins were being arrested in accord with any other program than the anti-Jewish one, they would not have known what you were talking about. Besides, the immediate response to the bishops' statement was confined to the Dutch deportation. There was no message we know of passed on to Poland, to those receiving the deportees at Auschwitz, saying that the Steins were to be treated not as Jews but as Catholics. There are no reported indicators to say, "*These* we are killing as Jews but *those* as Catholics." If, furthermore, the *odium fidei* existed for Edith, why not for Rose? Why was her martyrdom not good enough to make her a *beata?* She may not have been as saintly as her sister, but the martyr's blood is

supposed to purge all sins, and Rose, too, needed no miracle for beatification if she was a martyr.

So weak is the causal link between the bishops' statement in Holland
and the murderers' work in Poland that even Stein's official Vatican *relator* (champion of beatification) had to make vaguer and larger (and more
ecclesiastically useful) claims about the persecutors as having a general
anti-Catholic animus. Since there was no overt policy to persecute the
Catholic church as such, the German Dominican promoting her cause,
Ambrose Eszer, claims that the very lack of evidence for such a policy
proves how diabolically clever the persecution was:

> The modern tyrant is very sophisticated. He pretends not to be
> against religion or even interested in it, so he doesn't ask his victims
> what their faith is. But in reality he is either without religion or
> makes some ideology into an erzatz religion. We see that with the
> Communists and we saw it with the Nazis. In my *positio* [advocat-
> ing document] on Edith Stein, my main argument was that the
> church cannot accept the arguments of criminals and persecutors of
> herself. We cannot give in the process an advantage to people who
> are liars just because they say they are not against religion.[16]

In a significant lapse, Father Eszer talks of the death camp officials as if
they were arguing against Stein's beatification, and lying by their silence
concerning their real motives. They could not argue against a process
they knew nothing about, or be "given an advantage" in it. Eszer is clearly
conflating the silent executioners with those arguing against Stein's beatification, with one of whom, the Stein biographer James Baaden, he had
an angry public exchange. Baaden, he expressly said then, is the one who
should not be heard in the process (given an advantage), since "the
Catholic Church is sovereign regarding matters of faith and morals and
does not depend on interference from outside."[17] He also had Baaden in
mind when he said this:

> Today, many Jewish writers don't admit that the Catholics did any-
> thing for the Jews. But I know that in the case of Edith Stein she
> was killed because the Catholic Church did something for the Jews.

Our critics say that she must be honored as a Jewish martyr, and that we cannot accept.[18]

It is disturbing that a man so important to the beatifying of Stein should so completely misunderstand the motives of those objecting to it. They did not want to honor Stein as a Jewish martyr. They wanted to say that she was not a Catholic martyr—which is a quite different, and quite obvious, thing. For that Stein's motives are not the issue. Her killers' are. If they were acting on an *odium fidei,* the *fides* was Jewish. Eszer's inability to understand that seems all the worse when we remember that he was defending a person who made empathy, the entry into others' minds, the very basis of her moral system.

Kenneth Woodward, who interviewed Eszer for his fine book on canonization, noticed that Eszer was eager to exonerate not only his church but his fellow Germans—and especially his family—from any guilt for the Holocaust. He says that his father was a Nazi officer who did not like the Nazis but "a Jesuit advised him to go in and try to Christianize the army." He also denies that Catholics—well, real Catholics anyway, convinced Catholics—worked in the death camps: "The extermination camps were all outside of Germany. There were few real Catholics involved in the extermination camps because the SS did not want convinced Catholics. They even excluded them."[19] One wonders what test the SS had to distinguish real from apparent Catholics, convinced from doubting ones, what system they had for sorting out these categories. He also plants the ugly implication that Protestants—even real Protestants, even convinced ones—were the only Christians left to do all the dirty work.

After Stein was beatified in 1987, the next step in the process was canonization, and for that a martyr, under the Vatican's modern rules, does need a miracle. The difficulty with establishing that a miracle has been performed is not simply to show that something occurred that escapes natural explanation, but that it was directly tied to intercession by the candidate for sainthood. In the past, that was often established by contact with a relic of the person, either a primary relic (some body part) or a secondary relic (things worn by or used by the person). But the death camp left no identifiable remains of Stein, not even a note or a prayer book. Lacking such a connection, officials in the past had to rely on the word of the person for whom the miracle was worked, or on behalf of whom it was worked, that they prayed for this to the relevant dead person—and, presumably, not to other saints (or not as hard to them), lest there be a mix-up in the lines of responsibility.

Actually, the connection with Stein was pretty clear in the case that was finally decided to be her miracle. It occurred to a girl who was born on August 8, the eve of the presumed date of Stein's death (there is no official record), and who was named Benedicta, part of Stein's religious name, by parents devoted to Stein. When the girl was two, she swallowed much of a bottle of Tylenol pills, became unconscious, and was rushed to a hospital. There, Dr. Ronald Kleinman began treating her, and also called Dr. Michael Shannon, a pediatrician and toxocologist specializing in Tylenol overdose in children, at the Massachusetts Poison Control division of Boston's Children's Hospital. Shannon, who wrote the chapter on Tylenol in a standard textbook on overdoses, was the most authoritative person consulted in the case. Meanwhile, the girl was moving toward a coma that could have proved fatal despite the best efforts of Dr. Kleinman, acting in conjunction with Dr. Shannon's recommendations. The parents, informed of this, prayed to Edith Stein, and the girl recovered. Was it a miracle? Dr. Kleinman would not pronounce one way or the other: "I'm Jewish. Thinking about miracles is not part of the way I think."[20]

The parents, understandably grateful for what they considered a miracle by their beloved Sister Benedicta, told their story to *Catholic Digest,* which alerted the Vatican to a possible solution to the problem of canonizing Stein. Church officials interviewed Dr. Shannon, the best expert in the matter: "I remember being asked point-blank, 'Do you think this was a miracle?' To which I responded, 'No.' That was it. They left. I got a thank-you note letter in February, 1993, and never heard from them again."[21] Interviewed by James Carroll of *The New Yorker,* Shannon expanded on his view of the case:

> As a toxocologist for the last fourteen years, I have taken care of hundreds of Tylenol-overdose cases every year, and probably, in my career, thousands. I have seen the complications that Benedicta had.

They happen sometimes. But it doesn't change the fact that ninety-nine percent of the time children with Tylenol overdoses fully recover.[22]

Despite the fact that the two doctors most qualified to judge the case refuse to say it is a miracle, it was on the basis of little Benedicta's cure that Stein was canonized. What can explain this? No doubt the same thing that explains the distortion of history to make a bishop's letter the cause of Stein's death—namely, a determination to find in Stein a Catholic victim of the Holocaust, no matter what structures of deceit had to be deployed in order to bring that off.

The canonizers have managed to accomplish what Edith Stein worked hard in her lifetime to avoid, that she should be separated from her people—worse, that she should be the cause of offense to them. We are all the losers for this, since the divisiveness caused by her canonization makes it harder for people to approach her valuable writings with an open mind. Even the sisters of her own order seem to have missed her message of empathy and regard for other minds. With a callousness toward Jewish feeling, they placed a convent in 1978 right beside the Dachau death camp (Karol Cardinal Wojtyla himself dedicated it). In 1985, they went further, placing another convent at the gates of Auschwitz, in a building the Nazis had used for storing their exterminating gas. When Jews protested at this attempt to say that Edith Stein was the real (and Catholic) martyr of Auschwitz, Cardinal Glemp of Poland would not defer to their feelings. Finally, Cardinal Macharski of Krakow, whose diocese includes Auschwitz, agreed to move the convent by 1989. When it was not yet moved by that year, violent demonstrations occurred there.[23] Catholics were still claiming that they had no intention of usurping the Holocaust, but the Stein case does not stand alone. There were other co-opting activities, to be considered in the next chapter.

[1]Zev Garber, "Jewish Perspectives on Edith Stein's Martyrdom," in Harry James Cargas (editor), *The Unnecessary Problem of Edith Stein* (University Press of America, 1994), p. 42.

[2]Suzanne Batzdorff, "Witnessing My Aunt's Beatification," Cargas, op. cit., p. 42.

[3]Judith Herschcopk Banki, "Some Reflections on Edith Stein," Cargas, op. cit., p. 44.

[4]Edith Stein, *On the Problem of Empathy,* translated by Waltraut Stein (ICS Publications, 1989), pp. 88–89, 116.

⁵Edith Stein, *Life in a Jewish Family, 1891–1916,* translated by Josephine Koeppel, O.C.D. (ICS Publications, 1986), pp. 333–41.

⁶Banki, op. cit., p. 46.

⁷Herbstrith, op. cit., p. 78.

⁸Rachel Feldhay Brenner, "Ethical Convergence in Religious Conversion," Cargas, op. cit., p. 78.

⁹Banki, op. cit., p. 48.

¹⁰Herbstrith, op. cit., p. 95.

¹¹Kenneth L. Woodward, *Making Saints* (Simon & Schuster, 1990), pp. 84–85. The general rule now is two miracles needed for beatification of confessors, and two more (different ones) for canonization, but no miracles needed for a martyr's beatification and only one for canonization.

¹²Banki, op. cit., p. 49.

¹³Woodward, op. cit., p. 133.

¹⁴Herbstrith, op. cit., pp. 93–96.

¹⁵Ibid., p. 104.

¹⁶Woodward, op. cit., p. 141.

¹⁷Ibid., p. 143.

¹⁸Ibid., p. 142.

¹⁹Ibid., p. 142.

²⁰James Carroll, "The Saint and the Holocaust," *The New Yorker,* June 7, 1999.

²¹Ibid.

²²Ibid.

²³Jonathan Kwitny, *Man of the Century: The Life and Times of Pope John Paul II* (Henry Holt and Company, 1997), pp. 602–3.

4.

Claims of Victimhood

$\mathcal{T}$hough Edith Stein's is the most famous example of the determination to make Catholics in death camps martyrs for their faith, it was not the earliest. Even before she was beatified, Maximilian Kolbe had been canonized. There were reasons why Pope John Paul II would have a special interest in Stein, who was a fellow philosopher, another Schelerian phenomenologist. But his emotional attachment to Father Kolbe was earlier and deeper. Kolbe was a Polish priest, a Conventual Franciscan who had set up a worldwide organization, Knights of Immaculata, that reflected his own "intense, almost fanatical devotion to the Virgin Mary" (in Kenneth Woodward's words).[1] Some Polish chapters of the group reflected the general anti-Semitism of Polish culture at the time, and had rioted against Jewish-owned businesses.[2] Of Kolbe himself, the Catholic magazine *Commonweal* wrote:

> Although Maximilian Kolbe was by no means the violent anti-Semite his accusers suggest, there is no denying the anti-Semitic character of some of his beliefs and remarks. Plainly and simply, Kolbe was a believer in the *Protocols of the Elders of Zion* and in the existence of a Communist-Freemason-Zionist conspiracy to subvert and destroy Christianity.[3]

Karol Wojtyla was never an anti-Semite in any sense; but he shared Kolbe's ardent devotion to the Immaculate Conception, and personally admired the undoubted heroism of Kolbe's death. Arrested early for his group's resistance to Nazi control of youth groups, Kolbe sacrificed his life for a fellow prisoner he did not even know. As punishment for an escape from the camp, ten men were chosen at random to be starved to death. When one of those chosen begged to be spared, since he had a family, Kolbe stepped forward, said he was a priest, and went in the man's stead to a drawn-out and sordid form of death. The starving men drank their own urine. After sixteen days without food or water, six were dead and the others, including Kolbe, barely surviving. They were finished off by lethal injection.[4]

Father Kolbe's selfless act, well documented, made him the leading candidate for canonization among all the Catholics who died at Auschwitz. Unlike Edith Stein, who tried to escape going into the camp, he chose his death when he could have avoided it. (The man for whom he substituted himself lived to testify at his beatification process.) Kolbe's prison cell was identifiable, and pilgrimages were made to it, encouraged by Wojtyla. When Wojtyla was bishop of Krakow, within whose confines Auschwitz lies, he celebrated Mass every All Souls Day at the death camp, and his sermons highlighted Kolbe's noble end. When Kolbe was beatified in 1971 by Pope Paul VI, Wojtyla conducted 1,500 Poles to the ceremony and gave the most moving speech connected with the event.[5] Kolbe easily met the two-miracles standard of beatification as a confessor—the problem Edith Stein had did not arise for him.

Since the requisite new miracles were also testified to for his canonization, there was no need to invent a case that he was a martyr in order to get him past that hurdle. But Wojtyla and others, including members of his Knights of the Immaculata, were determined that he be celebrated as a martyr. They petitioned Pope Paul in large numbers. He gave Kolbe a kind of courtesy title, "martyr of charity" instead of martyr for the faith, but beatified him under the formal designation of confessor.

When Wojtyla became John Paul, he was certain to canonize Kolbe, but he wanted to make him a martyr for the faith. This would not only quiet any doubts about Kolbe's anti-Semitic ties in the past (a martyr's blood cleanses all past sins) but would advance the Pope's thesis that Catholics were the victims of the Holocaust, not the victimizers. The problem, however, was that—in all the investigations for the beatification and the canonization being prepared—no one had been able to construct a convincing argument that Kolbe died for his faith. He was arrested on political charges. If the guards had wanted to kill him as a priest, they would have chosen him instead of the family man. When he substituted himself, it was a noble act, but one a nonpriest or non-Catholic could have performed. Sydney Carton, after all, was not a priest. The Jesuit who drew up the *positio* advocating Kolbe's canonization, Kurt Peter Gumpel, said there was no way to present Kolbe's imprisonment as aimed at his religion. After investigating the circumstances of his arrest in detail, Gumpel described them to Woodward:

> It was part of a big operation, a large sweep. The Nazis were preparing to invade Russia, and as part of that operation they had to make sure, from a logistical point of view, that the lines of supply were safe for the transport of ammunition, foodstuffs, fuel, spare parts for tanks, and the like. So to assure the safety of all this, they arrested all the intellectuals who could possibly cause them trouble: atheists, Communists, Catholics. So Kolbe was not arrested for reasons of his faith.

Nor was anything made of Kolbe's faith when he was condemned to death:

> Now there has been a most searching investigation of the survivors who saw and heard what happened. We asked them whether they heard or saw in the commander's face or in the face of any of the guards any satisfaction that they were glad for a chance to kill a priest. There was none of this. The commander simply said to Kolbe, well, if you want to, go ahead.[6]

Kolbe, in other words, did not get a *relator* like Edith Stein's Father Eszer, one willing to cook the historical evidence.

Nonetheless, the Pope wanted his favorite Polish victim to be declared a martyr. Giving up on the formal bodies involved so far, he appointed a special twenty-five-member commission to meet at Cardinal Ratzinger's Congregation of the Doctrine of the Faith and reconsider the case for Kolbe's martyrdom. Polish and German bishops on the commission argued strenuously for the Pope's desire, which they shared, but Father

Gumpel testified to the findings of the various investigating groups, and a majority on the commission had to conclude that the decisions of their predecessors had been the right ones. Despite pressure to comply with anything the Pope so energetically desired, they informed him that Kolbe did not qualify as a martyr. But this is not a Pope used to taking no from others. When he canonized Kolbe in 1982, he declared: "And so, *in virtue of my apostolic authority* I have decreed that Maximilian Kolbe, who, after his beatification was venerated as a confessor, shall henceforward be venerated also as a martyr [emphasis added]."[7] Not for the last time, the Pope showed that, where Catholics in Nazi death camps are concerned, he will follow special rules of his own making.

Three years after Kolbe's canonization, a Carmelite priest, Titus Brandsma, was beatified as a martyr. Brandsma died at Dachau, after being arrested for his activities as the leader of the Catholic press in Holland, where he had asserted the right of the papers he supervised not to print Nazi propaganda or to accept Nazi advertisements. He also refused to expel Jewish children from the Carmelites' school. His *relator* decided he was acting on Catholic principles, therefore he died for his faith. But as Kenneth Woodward points out, freedom of education and of the press are not specifically Catholic doctrines—the church does not even have an unbroken record of upholding them. A journalist of conscience would have taken Brandsma's stand without being a Catholic.[8] But the desire to have Catholic victims of the Holocaust was making the church authorities regularly break their own rules.

In 1999, the Pope was able to canonize as a martyr a Polish nun taken by the Gestapo in 1939 and shot in the Piasnica Forest after she had been forced to dig her own grave. It was claimed that she suffered for the faith because she hid liturgical vessels from a Nazi search party—though it seems the soldiers were after the gold and silver rather than any religious item as such.[9] The attempt to claim the Holocaust for the church goes forward on many fronts, so we should not be surprised at the audacity of the historical distortion that could say Edith Stein died as a Catholic rather than a Jew.

The claim of Catholic victimization goes so far, even, as to claim that Pope Pius XII is a victim, because Jews are not properly grateful for all the quiet work he did to save them. This produces books like Michael

O'Carroll's *Pius XII, Greatness Dishonored*. Pope Paul VI, when dedicating a monument to Pius XII in Saint Peter's, felt he had to defend him from "unjust and ungrateful clamors of blame and accusation" about his silence during the Holocaust.[10] The Jesuit Kurt Peter Gumpel, whom we met as the *relator* in the beatification process of Maximilian Kolbe, is also a *relator* in the process to make Pius XII a saint, and he has gone public (a rare thing for *relatores*) to deplore "unjustifiable attacks against this great and saintly man."[11] The Vatican could not issue its supposed apology to the Jews, *We Remember*, without praising "what Pope Pius XII did personally or through his representatives to save hundreds of thousands of Jewish lives," and appending to that remark a long, argumentative footnote (the only one not a mere citation in the whole document) on "the wisdom of Pope Pius XII's diplomacy."[12] Commiseration with victims who lost their lives has to pause while the document takes time to defend this victim—a thing that might more properly have been undertaken elsewhere, since Pius, though perhaps a defensible figure, is hardly an ecumenical one.

Paul VI, not content with calling Pius defensible, describes his "heights of heroism," and argues:

> In as far as circumstances allowed him, circumstances which he assessed with intense and conscientious reflection, he used his voice and his activity to proclaim the rights of justice, to defend the weak, to give help to the suffering, to prevent greater evils and to smooth the path of peace. One cannot attribute it to cowardice, lack of interest, or the selfishness of the Pope if innumerable and immeasurable evils befell humanity.[13]

I do not mean to renew here the arguments over Pius XII's wartime diplomacy. For the purposes of this book, I am willing to stipulate that he did much privately to help Jews, that he was hemmed in by fear of provoking tyrants to worse repression, that he felt the church could play a peacekeeping role if it stayed neutral. Those are all matters being thrashed out and still *sub judice*. This book's concern is with honesty in the church authorities' account of themselves, and on that score it should be noted that others are continuing what Pius himself initiated, the rewriting of his historical performance. Pius never explained his silence on the Holocaust, since he claimed there was no silence to be accounted for, that he spoke up on the tragedy not once but on several occasions. On August 3, 1946, for instance, he noted that "We condemned on various occasions in the past the persecution that a fanatical anti-Semitism inflicted on the Hebrew people."[14]

That is a deliberate falsehood. He never publicly mentioned the Holocaust. His silence on the subject was a matter of grave concern to many people. In 1942, after the British ambassador to the Vatican, Francis Osborne, passed on a letter to the Pope pleading with him to speak out, he confided to the writer of the letter his disappointment that nothing, he felt, would come of it: "It is very sad. The fact is that the moral authority of the Holy See, which Pius XI and his predecessors had built up into a world power, is now sadly reduced."[15] Later that year, when the Pope appealed to the Allies not to bomb Rome, Osborne reflected: "I am revolted by Hitler's massacre of the Jewish race on the one hand and, on the other, the Vatican's apparently exclusive preoccupation . . . with the possibilities of the bombardments of Rome."[16] When an American representative, Myron Taylor, arrived at the Vatican, he repeated Osborne's calls for the Pope to break his silence. A memo of the Pope's Secretary of State, Cardinal Tardini, records one such appeal: "Mr. Taylor talked of the opportunity and the necessity of a word from the Pope against such huge atrocities by the Germans. He said that from all sides people are calling for such a word."[17]

Pius's defenders note that these extracts from the record precede the Pope's Christmas address of December 4, 1942, the one speech that is cited to prove that he did speak out against the Holocaust. That address, which maintained the Pope's posture of neutrality, blamed the war on neither side exclusively but on a general "lust for power and profit." He called for humanity in general to repent and return to the laws of God:

> Humanity owes this vow to those innumerable exiles whom the hurricane of war has torn away from their native soil and dispersed in a foreign land, who might make their own the prophet's lament: "Our inheritance is turned to aliens, our houses to strangers." Humanity owes this vow to those hundreds of thousands who, without

any fault of their own, sometimes only by reason of their nationality or race, are marked down for death or gradual extinction.[18]

Displaced persons and racial animosities of many sorts were what earned the conflict he was describing the title of a *world* war. In an address that presented itself as neutral, that refused to name Jews or Nazis or Germans specifically, this hardly qualifies as what the Pope would later call his "various" condemnations of "a fanatical anti-Semitism." The Pope himself admitted that he did not single out the Nazis when he responded to the French ambassador at the Vatican, who had asked him why he did not name the Nazis, by saying that he would have had to name the Communists too if he were going to be specific. His own words prove he was *not* specific about the Nazi atrocities. Yet it is out of these two sentences that he would later construct a claim to have attacked anti-Semitism, specifically, on various occasions. The mere fact that he made that false later claim may indicate that he wished he had spoken out, or at least that he wanted people to think he had—just as the French ambassador's question proves that people did not believe that he had clearly condemned the Nazis.

Pius's admirers have taken his cue and made him not only guiltless about the Holocaust, but a hero of the Holocaust, one who courageously spoke up when others were silent—one, in fact, who is victimized if anyone expresses doubt about that claim. And insofar as he did maintain any silence, they say, it was only for the highest and most selfless motives. Let me repeat that I am stipulating that Pius may have been sincerely following what he thought was the best course for everyone caught up in a tragic situation—even if he was mistaken in the course he took, it could have been an honest mistake, since prudence had to face problems where all responses involved risk. But the issue of honesty arises when arguments are made defending Pius with false readings of history. Some, for instance, have taken up a defense of Pius's silence based on a story told by Sister Pasqualina, the devoted assistant and confidante of Pius, who said that the Pope had written a document denouncing the Nazis, but that he burned it before her eyes when he heard that the Bishop of Utrecht's letter denouncing the deportation of Jews from Holland had led to the savage retaliation of deporting forty thousand Jews.[19] This is the

episode looked at in the last chapter, which involved the arrest of Edith
Stein. But the bishop's letter in that incident did not cause the deportation of Jews—that was going on unchecked, which is why the letter was
written, after all. Nor did forty thousand Jews suffer as a result of the letter. It was only *baptized* Jews who were restored to the deportation—
ninety-two of them—and they would have been deported with the
others, in the first place, but for the temporary exception made of them
in hopes that church leaders would accept this bribe for their silence
about what was happening, in far greater numbers, to *un*baptized Jews. In
other words, Pius could not have been basing his silence on what was
happening to Jews—if Sister Pasqualina's story is to be believed at all—
but on the fate of Catholics. Pius XI and his successor always did speak
out (no one has ever questioned this) on behalf of Catholics who had
been Jews before changing faiths, since their lot was a matter of express
provision in concordats. Use of the Holland episode to determine Pius's
attitude toward Jews in general is illegitimate.

If Pius is beatified, as many now wish, it will be the occasion of a controversy even greater than that which surrounded the beatification and
canonization of Edith Stein. Hers did not involve criticism of Stein herself, but of the use made of her to indicate that Catholics were more the
victims than the victimizers in the period of Nazi persecution. That
would be even more true of an elevation of Pius XII. Whatever his own
virtue or merits, he is now caught up in the long series of distortions by
which the Vatican tries to deny its own sorry history with regard to the
Jews. Pius's denial of his own silence, perpetrated by those who must make
false claims in order to defend the words of a saint, would make him the
source of a new round of deceit structured into past dishonesties.[20]

---

[1] Kenneth L. Woodward, *Making Saints* (Simon & Schuster, 1990), p. 144.

[2] Jonathan Kwitny, *Man of the Century: The Life and Times of Pope John Paul II* (Henry Holt
and Company, 1997), p. 237.

[3] Harry James Cargas, *The Unnecessary Problem of Edith Stein* (University Press of America,
1994), pp. i–ii.

[4] Woodward, op. cit., p. 144.

[5] Kwitny, op. cit., pp. 237, 240.

[6] Woodward, op. cit., p. 146.

[7] Ibid., p. 147.

[8] Ibid., p. 134.

⁹Diane Struzzi, "Nuns Savor Step to Sainthood for One of Their Own," *Chicago Tribune,* August 16, 1999.

¹⁰Paul VI, *Heights of Heroism in the Life of Pope Pius XII,* Vatican translation (St. Paul Editions, 1964), p. 5.

¹¹Kurt Peter Gumpel, S.J., "Pius XII As He Really Was," *The Tablet,* February 12, 1999, p. 106.

¹²Vatican Commission for Religious Relations With the Jews, *We Remember: A Reflection on the Shoah,* Vatican translation (Pauline Books, 1998), pp. 17–18.

¹³Paul VI, op. cit., p. 7.

¹⁴Pius XII, "Address to the Supreme Council of the Arab People of Palestine" (AAS 38, p. 323) cited in John Cornwell, *Hitler's Pope* (Viking, 1999), p. 197.

¹⁵Ibid., p. 284.

¹⁶Ibid., pp. 290–91.

¹⁷Ibid., p. 289.

¹⁸Ibid., p. 292.

¹⁹Ibid., p. 287. It is highly unlikely that Pius would destroy a document that was part of the official Vatican record, which would have involved the assistance of others in drafting and copying it (yet no one but Sister Pasqualina gives evidence of knowing about it), and which would reflect his attitude if he had to vindicate that afterward. There would be no reason to take Sister Pasqualina's story seriously if she had not offered it in considered testimony to the beatification investigation of Pius, and if so many of the stories about his sanctity were not derived, directly or indirectly, from her accounts at various times.

²⁰Guenter Lewy offers one plausible explanation for the silence of Pius XII. A threat of excommunication for all those collaborating with Hitler would have been massively disobeyed in the patriotic fervor of Germany's mood—which makes nonsense of *We Remember*'s claim that Catholics were not complicitous with the Nazi regime. See Lewy, *The Catholic Church and Nazi Germany* (McGraw-Hill, 1964), pp. 90–91, 303–4.

II.

DOCTRINAL DISHONESTIES

We [bishops] do not want any license to fool you.

—SAINT AUGUSTINE

5.

The Tragedy of Paul VI: Prelude

ope Paul VI, with his sad sunken eyes in their smudgy Italian sockets, was a good and noble man, a man of wide-ranging intellect and rich emotional friendships. His pontificate (1963–78) had many moments of greatness—his intervention in the Vatican Council to strengthen the decree on ecumenism, his plea for peace at the United Nations, his joint declaration with Patriarch Athenagoras renouncing the enmities between Eastern and Western Christianity, his renunciation of the papal crown and the chair carried on men's shoulders. The scene that moves me most is the last one—his casket of plain wood, with no ornament but the gospels lying open on it. He deserved our respect, as a man of God trying to do what was best for the world as well as for his church.

Yet he dealt the most crippling, puzzling blow to organized Catholicism in our time. Perhaps, in the long run, he will be remembered for the good he did—especially for continuing Pope John's Council, against great opposition, through the remaining contentious sessions needed to complete its work. But he stands out in our current (shorter) memory for having issued the most disastrous papal document of this century, the encyclical letter *Humanae Vitae* (1968). It was the equivalent, for sheer wreckage achieved, of the nineteenth century's most disastrous papal document, Pius IX's *Syllabus of Errors*, with its accompanying encyclical *Quanta Cura* (1864). That such totally different men should fall into the same kind of blunder is stunning proof that the papal constraint on truth imposes a continuing pattern. In terms of personality and institutional strategies, these men present a study in opposites—Paul studious, diplo-

matic, cautious (sometimes to the point of paralysis), Pius poorly educated, tactless, volatile (sometimes to the point of frenzy).

Nor could the two documents differ more, at least to a superficial
glance, than theirs do. The *Syllabus* was grand in its crazy way—it took
on science, secularism, materialism, relativism, democracy, freedom of
speech, and the competency of all modern governments. It dumbfounded the world (see Chapter 10). Paul's birth control encyclical was,
by contrast, petty and parochial. From the viewpoint of an undumb-
founded world, it seemed caught up in the comic agonies of Catholic
couples trying to cope with the "rhythm method" for limiting their families. Yet the missives were really about the same thing. They mark two
stages in a continuing battle against the modern world—Pius rolling out
the big guns and training them on everything in sight, Paul shooting his
own wounded after the battle was over. *Humanae Vitae* is not really about
sex. It is about authority. Paul decided the issue on that ground alone. He
meant to check the notion that church teaching could change. Instead,
he promoted that idea. Five years after the letter, 42 percent of the priests
in America thought that issuing it was an abuse of the Pope's authority
and 18 percent thought it was an inappropriate use of that authority, leaving less than a third of his own closest legions to give it feckless support.
Lay persons were even more indignant. In 1963, 70 percent of them
thought that the Pope derived his authority to teach from Christ by way
of Peter. In 1974, that number had shrunk to 42 percent, a drastic depar-
ture from historic attitudes in the American church.[1]

How did Paul VI make such a miscalculation? He was trapped by his
and his predecessors' former statements. On the issue of the church's
moral authority in the modern world, all the papal eggs had foolishly
been put in one basket, the result of another papal encyclical, Pius XI's
Casti Connubii, issued in 1930. That document is the connecting link between the *Syllabus* and *Humanae Vitae*. It put the church magisterium, the
endangered authority that had been pitted against modernity, at stake on
a single issue: birth control. This was a major reorientation of Catholics'
moral energy. It offered a new teaching under the mask of ancient truth.
Then a drumbeat of assertions from the next Pope, Pius XII, made the
condemnation of birth control resonate ceaselessly from classrooms, pam-

phlets, confessionals, with a kind of hysterical insistence. Contraception was a mortal sin. Its unrepenting practitioners were going to hell.

The whole of modern Catholic culture thus became characterized by large families, the proof that some people, even in the "godless" world, were still true to natural law and the will of God. If the Vatican was sure on any one thing in the moral sphere, it was this. On this it had asked for tremendous sacrifices in the lives of everyday believers. If the Pope was wrong on it, he might have no claim left to supervise the most intimate lives of his followers. Or so the defenders of *Casti Connubii* would themselves insist. When the teaching on contraception was finally called into question in the 1960s, Rome's defenders did not go back to earlier teachings, which had been confused and erratic. The modern authority claimed for encyclicals themselves, and for the Pope in his relatively new garb of infallibility, made *Casti Connubii* the bedrock of embattled Catholic teaching. This was the rock that would be tied around Paul VI's neck as he prepared to issue his own subversive encyclical on birth control. Its formulation gives the essential background for understanding Paul VI's great disaster.

Casti Connubii (1930)

Although it is true that some kind of criticism of contraception can be found in Christian history from the third century on, it is misleading to call this a constant teaching. To read the best (and massive) book on the subject—*Contraception* (1966) by the conservative legal historian John T. Noonan, Jr.—is to wander through a galaxy of vivid battles fought, on a dizzying variety of fronts, against shifting combinations of adversaries, in alliance with shifting platoons of allies. The most consistent early attacks on contraception treated the potions used for it as magic and witchcraft.[2] But there were many other rationales for condemning contraception. Early on, church Fathers shared with Stoics the certainty that all sex acts not directly aimed at procreation were immoral. That was Saint Augustine's view, and Piux XI would cite Augustine in *Casti Connubii*. But Augustinian Stoicism made no allowance for things later accepted even by Pius—intercourse in old age, for instance, or when a partner was sterile. On still other fronts—in conflict with various heresies that opposed sex, marriage, women, or procreation (heresies from Gnosticism to Manicheism to Catharism)—church instructors made tactical concessions to extremes of asceticism while trying to retain basic values of respect for life or the family.

So, when we look to the patristic era and its legacy, we find a variety of campaigns against contraception limited to particular contexts. And the great issue in those battles was usually not contraception in itself but some larger struggle—over the goodness or the evil of the body, or the apocalyptic expectations of history, or the sacrifice of marriage to virginity. The whole attitude toward sex in late antiquity—pagan and Jewish as well as Christian—was marred by misogynism, fear of the body, and the lure of false spiritualisms. It is not the place to look for sanity on these matters. It was a time when the bestiality of sex was proved by a belief that the serpent had sodomized Adam and Eve in Eden.[3] Strange notions of what was "natural" in sex would persist for a long time in Christianity. Even in the thirteenth century, Thomas Aquinas would still be saying that natural law makes it a sin for sex to take place in any position but with the man on top, or that contraception is a worse sin than incest.[4] The Middle Ages added their own weird views on what is normal, including the doctrine of *amplexus reservatus*—the teaching that *coitus interruptus* can be engaged in so long as no seed is spilled.[5]

One particularly disturbing aspect of modern papal claims is the assertion that contraception violates natural law. If it is a matter of moral right or wrong perceptible to natural reason, the ancient pagans should have been bound to see its immorality. Yet the classical Greeks and Romans, who originated Western moral theory (including the theory of natural law), had no inkling of the evil of contraception—and not because there were no contraceptive devices available to them. As Noonan concludes: "The absence of reference to the subject in Roman classical literature is perhaps best understood as due to a general calm acceptance of contraceptive practices."[6] Even more disturbing for Catholics, who believe in the inspiration of Jewish scripture, is the fact that Jews had no prohibition of contraception in their extensive and detailed laws (though Pius tried to wrest one from a false interpretation of the Onan story in Genesis). Even today, some conservative Protestants inform their political allies in the Catholic church that they agree with them in opposing abortion but they find no moral basis for opposing contraception.[7] As a final blow to natural law claims, some of the theologians who helped craft *Humanae Vitae* for Paul VI agreed with the ban on contraception but not with the natural law justification for that ban.[8]

The history of the theology on contraception, then, had this anomaly as it entered the modern world: It claimed to be basing its views on a philosophy of natural law derived from classical antiquity (which had no ban on contraception) but was taking its supposedly empirical views on sex from late antiquity and the Middle Ages (which were full of superstitions). These problems called for sorting out by the nineteenth century, when science, the industrial revolution, the study of demography, and scientific psychology changed family patterns. Concern over demographic imbalances—combined with urban living, improved technologies, and higher living standards—led to a limiting of births. (Condom technology made progress after Charles Goodyear vulcanized rubber in 1839 and Thomas Hancock improved this process in 1843.)

Instead of taking this opportunity to reassess the mixed heritage of views on contraception (and on sex itself), the papacy during Pius IX's long reign (1846–78) saw the whole of modernity as an assault on religion. It put up a stout resistance to science as a Faustian desire to remake nature. Darwin was as unacceptable as Galileo had been—but without the church's power to silence Darwin. Psychology's contribution to sexual enlightenment was dismissed as disguised hedonism. The attempt to adjust procreation to industrial patterns was a way of giving free rein to sexual indulgence—we saw in the last chapter how Jews were branded as libertines because of their low birth rate. Early in the twentieth century a Belgian Jesuit, Arthur Vermeersch, organized the Catholic counterattack on contraception. When an international birth control conference met in 1905 at Liège, Vermeersch denounced it and inspired Belgian bishops to instruct priests that they must fight this modern evil to the death. When the Anglican church, meeting at their Lambeth Conference of 1930, allowed the practice of contraception, the aging Vermeersch, still on the battlements, said that Anglicans could no longer claim to be Christians at all, and he wrote for Pius XI that year's encyclical *Casti Connubii*.[9]

Though that encyclical claimed to be expounding natural law, it brought in revelation as well. John Noonan has shown that the story of Onan, who "spilled his seed on the ground" at Genesis 38:9, had been used occasionally through the centuries to condemn contraception, though it was never a principal source of teaching on this issue. For one thing, even if one views Onan's as a contraceptive act, it condemned only the specific practice described—*coitus interruptus*. A subsidiary use was sometimes made of the passage to condemn masturbation. But Vermeersch-Pius now made it a biblical injunction against every form of contraception, from douches to chemicals to condoms, and European theologians' preferred term for contraception became "onanism":

> Small wonder, therefore, if Holy Writ bears witness that the Divine Majesty regards with greatest detestation this horrible crime and at times has punished it with death. As St. Augustine notes, "Intercourse even with one's legitimate wife is unlawful and wicked where the conception of the offspring is prevented. Onan, the son of Juda, did this and the Lord killed him for it."[10]

There is a major problem with this passage. Modern scholars universally agree that what is condemned in the Onan passage is not contraception considered in itself (there is no direct condemnation of that in all the detailed provisions of Jewish law), but the deprivation of a brother's line of its proper heir (Deut 25:5–6).[11] Thus, in this most authoritative condemnation of "onanism," the thing the Pope is supposed to have greatest authority over, the "deposit" of revealed truths, is erroneously cited (and would be omitted from *Humanae Vitae* and all recent papal documents on contraception).

Yet the reasoning Pius used in issuing his statement was less important, for later church authorities, than the fact that he *had* issued it, making it formal and binding, and summoning the church to use all its resources against this peril. Pius gave priests a mandate to patrol individual consciences that was unparalleled in past instructions on contraception:

> We admonish, therefore, priests who hear confessions, and others who have the care of souls, in virtue of Our supreme authority and

in Our solicitude for the salvation of souls, not to allow the faithful entrusted to them to err regarding this most grave law of God, much more that they keep themselves immune from such false opinions, in no way conniving in them. If any confessor or pastor of souls, which may God forbid, lead the faithful entrusted to him into these errors or should at least confirm them by approval or by guilty silence, let him be mindful of the fact that he must render a strict account to God, the Supreme Judge, of the betrayal of his sacred trust, and let him take to himself the words of Christ: "They are blind and leaders of the blind, and if the blind lead the blind, both fall into the pit."[12]

The drilling of Catholics on this one aspect of their lives had now begun in earnest. And since the prohibition was based on natural law as well as the Bible, even non-Catholics were supposed to be held to its dictates. That meant making or keeping the sale of contraceptives illegal. In America, bishops tried to prevent Margaret Sanger from speaking in favor of birth control. When an Irish policeman arrested her at a New York rally, he said it was at the bidding of Archbishop Patrick Hayes.[13] Sanger tried to get President Franklin Roosevelt to back her attempts to legalize the sale of contraceptives, but she found her way blocked by Monsignor John A. Ryan, a man known as "the Right Reverend New Dealer" for his alliance with Roosevelt (the President needed him to counter the appeal to Catholics of the anti-Semitic priest, Charles Coughlin).[14]

The more this discipline was enforced, the more impossible it became to consider reversing the grounds on which it had been imposed. How could the church, after over a century of insistence on this particular discipline, confess that it had got things wrong? As a priest would say when experts were brought to Rome to consider the matter during the Second Vatican Council, "What then with the millions we have sent to hell if these norms were not valid?"[15] Another priest, who would have a great deal to do with the encyclical *Humanae Vitae*, said that if the church reversed itself now, it would prove that the Holy Spirit had been with the Anglicans at Lambeth, not with the Pope in Rome.[16] That was an admission Rome could not make.

Given the papal uneasiness about science, it is surprising that the first changes to *Casti Connubii* came from improved technical knowledge. Studies by Kyusaku Ogino in Japan and by Hermann Knaus in Austria were popularized in the years immediately following 1930, the year of Pius's encyclical. These doctors more accurately pinpointed the monthly infertile days in women's ovulation cycle, making it seem possible to limit births if intercourse took place only on those days. Could exploitation of this information give Catholics a permissible new way to limit family size? Some theologians said yes, since church authorities had (despite Augustine) allowed couples to have intercourse even though they were infertile. It seemed, then, that Catholics could take advantage of a naturally infertile interval in the month, and have intercourse only then—a conclusion to which Pius XII gave authoritative support in a 1951 address to Catholic midwives. The "rhythm method" was declared a natural, not an artificial, form of birth control.

This decision changed the teaching on contraception. Before, it was the contraceptive *intent* that was objected to. Now, people could space their sex acts with the intent to avoid conception, so long as they did not interfere with "the integrity of the act"—which put a sacrosanct mechanics of sex above the motives of the actors, reversing the normal priorities of moral reasoning. The mechanics of killing a person, for instance, had not been considered the primary factor in judging the morality of killing. Catholic moralists had approved the infliction of death, no matter what means were used, if the motive was one of permissible self-defense, or the authorized execution of a criminal, or engagement in a just war. But the sex act, it now appeared, was good if performed "naturally," *apart from the contraceptive intent* of the couple involved. Augustine, for one, would have been astonished at this. His Manichean opponents had an early theory of infertile days and relied on it to avoid procreation (which they considered immoral). Augustine directed his first and harshest attacks on contraception against this early form of "rhythm." As John Noonan remarks:

> The method of contraception practiced by these Manichees whom Augustine knew is the use of the sterile period as determined by Greek medicine . . . In the history of the thought of theologians on

contraception, it is, no doubt, piquant that the first pronouncement on contraception by the most influential theologian teaching on such matters would be such a vigorous attack on the one method of avoiding procreation accepted by twentieth-century Catholic theologians as morally lawful.[17]

An emphasis on the integrity of the act, on the way nature intends it to be performed, had the further unhappy result of recalling earlier limitations of the sex act to the one right way, including Thomas Aquinas's teaching that incest, if it preserved the fertilizing integrity of the act, was less sinful than contraception.

This stress on observance of the proper mechanics stored up trouble for the Pope when the next scientific breakthrough occurred—the anovulant pill, which was being tested at the very time Pius XII approved of rhythm (though it would not be approved for use in America until 1960). These pills did not interfere with the sex act itself—though they did suppress ovulation, ahead of time, by artificial means (chemistry). Catholic theologians' first responses to this development were generally negative, and they were confirmed by Pius XII in 1958 when he condemned the pill in an address to Catholic hematologists. But Pius in his old age had become oracular, pronouncing on all kinds of news before all the facts were in, and—as a sign of a new mood in the church—some theologians and Catholic doctors continued to explore questions raised by the pill.

In 1963—when the Second Vatican Council was already in session, prompting hopes for changes in church instruction—John Rock, a Catholic doctor at the Harvard medical school who had helped develop the pill, published a book, *The Time Has Come*, arguing that nature itself suppresses ovulation to prevent conception, not only in the infertile monthly period but during pregnancy and lactation. Nature, however, is sometimes faulty, as different women's departures from the norm demonstrated. Why not let the pill confirm or stabilize what nature was doing anyway? After all, doctors give people chemicals, or mechanical implants, to stabilize irregular heartbeats or other physical syndromes.

Nervous prelates in Rome felt that the pill was just an excuse to jettison the Vatican's position on birth control, which was resented and

under siege. The euphoria over new freedoms was part of the social gid-
diness that characterized the 1960s, in the church as in the secular world.
It was a time of the sexual revolution, feminism, and new attitudes toward authority. In this atmosphere, the papal pronouncements about natural law were brought under closer scrutiny by natural reason, and they
grew flimsier with every look. There was great fear in the Curia of the
Vatican that this mood would invade the Council Pope John was assem-
bling (as, in fact, it did). The whole matter of birth control was considered especially endangered, and it would be fought over strenuously in
two Roman arenas, one open and one secret. The former battle, carried
on in the sessions of the Vatican Council, reached a kind of stalemate in
the conciliar decree on the church in the modern world, *Gaudium et
Spes*. The other battle, waged in secret by the Pope's own special commission, led to that commission's stunning defeat by the Pope's own encyclical *Humanae Vitae*.

Gaudium et Spes (1965)

ope John XXIII upset conservatives in the church with his two
social encyclicals, *Mater et Magistra* (1961) and *Pacem in Terris*
(1963)—the latter issued during the first session of the Council itself.
Those letters' openness toward the world, their call for cooperation with
it, were considered naïve by the Pope's own staff (Curia), as was his calling of the Council. The various congregations of the Vatican set themselves the task of containing the Council, primarily by preparing the draft
documents (schemata) to be considered, and putting up a slate of candidates for chairing the Council's own commissions. The paper work was
meant to bury discussion in a confusion of detail that only the resident
curial experts could guide the assembled bishops through—there were
seventy schemata waiting for each participant as he arrived in Rome in
1962, 2,000 pages of folio size, all written in the curial Latin that most
bishops had forgotten since their seminary days.[18] The schemata restated
the positions held by the officials. They offered nothing new to the
world. They were abristle with anathemata and condemnations, though

Pope John had let it be known that he wanted a pastoral approach, not a doctrinal one.

On sexual matters, the Curia felt a special urgency to set parameters that would contain the bishops and their attendant theological advisers (periti). The schema on sex morality was written by a conservative favorite of the Curia, the Franciscan Ermenegildo Lio, and its four chapters contained twenty-one condemnations.[19] Its very title showed where the emphasis lay: "On Marriage, Chastity, and Virginity."[20] When Bishop McGrath submitted a written objection to the schema, Father Lio, the expert on marriage in the Holy Office (formerly the Inquisition), responded with an accusing letter. The bishops, it was clear, were there to listen to the experts, not to take matters into their own hands.[21]

But they did take matters into their own hands. Presented with a slate of officers drawn up by the Curia, and told to vote on it before the bishops had time to become acquainted with alternate candidates, Cardinal Lienart of Lille spoke up in the Council's first working session, breaking the rules to ask that the vote be postponed until the bishops could draw up their own slates.[22] It was the first unmistakable sign that the Curia was losing control. It would fight an obstructive action henceforth with the help of a well-placed but shrinking minority of the bishops present. The schema prepared on chastity was changed to one on married love—which Father Lio fought inch by inch, with the support of his Holy Office superior, Cardinal Ottaviani. This draft would be totally rewritten five times (not counting the numerous tamperings with each draft by way of emendation). Ottaviani called in for help the American ethicist, John Ford, who with his Jesuit colleague had written the manual on ethics used in seminaries and schools to enforce the precepts of *Casti Connubii* and the rhythm method. Ford, it would turn out, had Pope Paul's ear, but the majority kept winning on the Council floor as the decree on marriage became more oriented toward its treatment as a sacrament of love, not a mere mechanism for procreation.

Since it had proved impossible to get modern scientific information into the drafting process on marriage, where celibate theologians thought laymen had no contribution to make, Cardinal Leo Joseph Suenens of Belgium had persuaded Pope John to set up a special commission to weigh the empirical evidence on birth control. Four of the six men ap-

pointed to this pontifical commission were laymen, and all were married—two medical doctors, a demographer, and an economist. Of the
two priests, one was a diplomat and the other a sociologist. The Pope was
looking in a new direction for light on this subject. The commission met
between the first two sessions and was hesitant to suggest fundamental
change. But it did call for further study—which meant a call for its own
continued existence. When Pope John died during the second session,
this commission, whose existence was still a secret (even to most of the
Council fathers), was inherited by Pope Paul. Though he might have dissolved it, he actually expanded it, making its membership more representative. For the first time, women were asked to contribute their
insights on a question affecting their lives so intimately.

After leaks about the commission's existence occurred, the Pope admitted, between the second and third sessions of the Council, that a separate study on birth control was being conducted, but that "in the
meantime" the old strictures applied.[23] This information was used by the
majority in the Council to keep the Lio faction from sneaking back into
the schema on marriage a sweeping reaffirmation of *Casti Connubii*'s
condemnations. This was a matter "reserved," they said. Such jockeying
led to the penultimate vote on the marriage schema, the one that preceded a final editing. Though the editing body was not supposed to
change the substance of what had been agreed on by the whole body of
the Council, a last-minute intervention by the Pope seemed to cancel all
the preceding work of the Council fathers. On November 24, 1965, Cardinal Ottaviani, presiding over the Mixed Commission to edit the document, ordered that a letter from the Pope's Secretary of State be read. A
"higher authority," according to the letter, was demanding the insertion
of four *modi* (emendments) to the document, including a specific condemnation of "contraceptive devices" and a reassertion of the authority
of *Casti Connubii* by name.

Striking while the iron was hot, Ottaviani said that these directives
were not matter for discussion but for "holy obedience," so the theological advisers could be dismissed. Cardinal Browne said *Christus ipse locu-
tus est* ("This is Christ himself speaking"), while Fathers Ford and Lio
looked triumphant—though Ford would later blush when a grammati-
cal error was pointed out in the letter's Latin, marking him as its author.[24]

The majority then challenged Ottaviani's claim that no discussion was allowed. Was the Council no longer operative? Was the Pope dissolving it in order to issue his own statement? If they were to have any part at all in the statement, how could they not be allowed to discuss it? The imperious cardinal had to bend, somewhat. The majority fathers then whittled away at the *modi* without rejecting them outright. The express ban on "contraceptive devices" became, finally, one on "illicit practices against human generation." Wiggle room was left for the pontifical commission to suggest changes in how one judges whether any practice is illicit. *Casti Connubii* was mentioned, but only in a footnote, and in conjunction with a reference to the pontifical commission considering the subject as still open to investigation.

The resulting section of *Gaudium et Spes* (Chapter 2, paragraphs 47–52) is carefully ambiguous on certain points—enough so for Popes Paul VI and John Paul II to claim, later, that the Council reaffirmed *Casti Connubii* and for Bernard Häring and others to claim that it moved some way off from that encyclical.[25] What cannot be doubted is that the Council's liberty was severely compromised when the Pope altered the free expression of two thirds of the assembled bishops of the church. Despite claims that the Holy Spirit was speaking through the whole assembly of the church's assembled bishops, the Council itself existed within a structure of deceit. And still the matter of birth control had not been settled. Though its groundwork had been laid, *Humanae Vitae*, the disastrous encyclical, had still to be written.

---

[1]National Opinion Research Center polls reported in Andrew Greeley, *The American Catholic: A Social Portrait* (Basic Books, 1977), pp. 134, 156. Other indicators of acceptance of guidance from the clergy dropped as well, including donations to the parishes. In 1963, Irish Catholics educated in parochial schools said they would be very pleased to have a son enter the priesthood. By 1974, that number had sunk to 45 percent (Greeley, p. 162).

[2]John T. Noonan, Jr., *Contraception: A History of Its Treatment by the Catholic Theologians and Canonists* (Harvard University Press, 1966), pp. 25–27, 44–45, 98.

[3]Peter Brown, *The Body and Society: Men, Women and Sexual Renunciation in Early Christianity* (Columbia University Press, 1988), p. 95. For extreme asceticism in late antiquity, see Brown, pp. 92–100, and Robin Lane Fox, *Pagans and Christians* (Alfred A. Knopf, 1986), pp. 356–77. For the misogynism of the period, for women as "the gate of Hell," see Chapter 4 below. Brown (p. 166) indicates that the fear and hatred of sex led to many more self-castrations than the famous one of Origen.

[4]The "normal" position (*Commentary on the Sentences of Peter Lombard*, 4.31) "reflected a belief in the natural superiority of man to woman" (Noonan, op. cit., p. 239), and the inces-

tuous union at least retained the integrity of the sex act (fertilization) according to ST 2-2, q 154, 11r.

[5]Noonan, op. cit., pp. 196–99. Twelfth-century theologians backed themselves into this odd view in order to defend earlier teachings on the marriage "debt" (*debitum*). Since one partner has to honor the debt of sexual response to another, even though he/she does not want to commit the sin of sex without procreation, the male may give in to the wife's desires so long as he does not spill his seed like Onan. One of the bases for this aberration was the patristic view that women, as the weaker sex, are more the prisoners of lust than men are (see Chapter 4).

[6]Ibid., p. 28. For contraceptives in the time of Jesus, see Soranus, *Gynecology*, translated by Owsei Temkin (Johns Hopkins University Press, 1956).

[7]James Neuchterlein, "Catholics, Protestants, and Contraception," *First Things*, April 1999, pp. 10–11, and "Correspondence," *First Things*, August/September 1999, pp. 2–6.

[8]See Chapter 6, on John Ford, S.J., and Germain Grisez.

[9]Noonan, op. cit., pp. 419–26.

[10]Pius XI, *Christian Marriage*,Vatican translation (Pauline Books and Media, n.d.), p. 28, citing Augustine, *Adultery* 2.12.

[11]Claude F. Mariotini, "Onan," ABD 5.20–21.

[12]Pius XI, op. cit., p. 29, citing Mt 15:14.

[13]Ellen Chesler, *Woman of Valor: Margaret Sanger and the Birth Control Movement in America* (Simon & Schuster, 1992), p. 203.

[14]Ibid., pp. 345–46.

[15]Robert McClory, *Turning Point: The Inside Story of the Papal Birth Control Commission* (Crossroad, 1995), p. 1.

[16]John C. Ford, S.J., quoted in Robert Blair Kaiser, *The Politics of Sex and Religion* (Leaven Press of *The National Catholic Reporter*, 1985), p. 145.

[17]Noonan, op. cit., p. 120.

[18]Gerald P. Fogarty, "The Council Gets Underway," in Giuseppe Alberigo, *History of Vatican II*,Vol. 2, translated by Joseph A. Komonchak (Orbis, 1997), p. 69.

[19]Ambrogio Valsecchi, *Controversy: The Birth Control Debate, 1958–1968*, translated by Dorothy White (Corpus Books, 1968), p. 120.

[20]Charles Moeller, "Pastoral Constitution on the Church in the Modern World: History of the Constitution," in Herbert Vorgrimler (editor), *Commentary on the Documents of Vatican II*, Vol. 5 (Herder and Herder, 1969), p. 13.

[21]Bernard Häring, "Fostering the Nobility of Marriage and the Family," in Vorgrimler, op. cit., p. 225.

[22]Andrea Riccardi, "The Tumultuous Opening Days of the Council," Alberigo, op. cit., pp. 27–32.

[23]Noonan, op. cit., p. 473.

[24]F. X. Murphy ("Xavier Rynne"), *Vatican Council II* (Farrar, Straus and Giroux, 1968), p. 555, Häring, op. cit., p. 228; Kaiser, op. cit., pp. 116–17.

[25]Häring, op. cit., pp. 228–45.

6.

The Tragedy of Paul VI: Encyclical

Pope Paul's action in the years leading up to *Humanae Vitae* (1968) looked so contradictory as to seem perverse. On the one hand, he sided with the minority in the Council to inhibit any talk of change on contraception—even intervening directly at the last minute, when there was no indirect way left him, to thwart the will of the majority. Yet, at the same time, he was expanding the Pontifical Commission on birth control that Pope John had set up, making its membership more inclusive, watching as it widened the scope of its deliberations. What can explain such behavior?

I think that only a combination of the calculating and the sincere can solve this mystery. On the calculating side, Paul's treatment of the commission subtly deflected it from its original purpose. Cardinal Suenens suggested the commission to Pope John to get an independent source of information *for use in the Council*. It would provide fresh material for the bishops to reflect on in their final debates. When Paul widened the commission's mandate, he said that its findings might be helpful to him in considering papal response to a 1964 UN conference on family planning. When that conference passed without the commission's being able to reach any useful conclusions before it convened, Paul's continuation of the commission's work for his own purposes made sure that its views were kept entirely apart from what was occurring at the Council. If he had lost his bid to reinsert *Casti Connubii* doctrine into the decree on the church in the modern world, he could have removed the whole subject of birth control from the Council's consideration, saying that it was being handled for him by the commission. The very existence of the commis-

sion seemed to give him options for maneuver. Yet the commission is
what sealed him into his doom on contraception.

He could not have suspected any such outcome—for one thing, because the commission was a papal secret, and the Vatican had lived for
decades with the assurance that it could contain its secrets. Even when
the Pope conceded the commission's existence, he left its composition
and function mysterious. All the participants were ordered to keep their
actions strictly hidden. There would be no official publication of minutes
or results. When a news photographer infiltrated one meeting, he was
chased down and his film was destroyed.[1] Even its own members could
not take informal pictures of each other while the commission was in existence. (A few snapshots were made after the dissolution of the body.)
Everything they said or did was to be turned over confidentially to the
Pope, who could use or suppress it at his discretion. If this original plan
had been followed, and the Pope wanted to ignore what the commission
did, it would no more exist on the record than had Pius XI's secretly
drafted encyclical on the Jews. The idea of a "runaway" commission was
remote from Paul's mind. What he wanted was one that would not affect
the debates of the Council fathers.

But Paul was a sincere believer, not a mere ecclesiastical politician, and
I think he was so convinced that church teachers could not have erred
that he hoped a broader look at the subject would end up confirming
Casti Connubii, perhaps on new grounds. He was no doubt encouraged
to think along these lines by John Ford, the preferred expert of the Curia,
who had decided that old natural law arguments against contraception
were weak, but the church could not have erred, so new grounds must
be found for bolstering the truth. If the Onan story could be sacrificed,
then so could conventional (Thomistic) views on natural law, so long as
the church remained consistent in its condemnation, on whatever
grounds. Ford brought to Rome a Catholic philosopher, Germain
Grisez, who helped him develop a new "will to life" argument.[2] The
Pope probably hoped this prefigured the outcome of the commission's
reflections. He was no doubt stunned when the commission attacked the
entire *Casti Connubii* position. And he was especially angered when the
commission's rejection of the past was leaked to the press. What he

thought he was fostering as a shrewd way of containing a problem had backfired, making the task of drafting *Humanae Vitae* more difficult than he had ever anticipated. Yet it must be drafted.

Humanae Vitae

The Pontifical Commission met five times, at first in the fall of 1963—six men convening at Louvain. The second meeting (like all subsequent ones) was in Rome, in the spring of 1964, attended by thirteen men. The number was increased to fifteen for a meeting that summer. Up to this point, no one had presumed to recommend altering the church's teaching on contraception. Things changed at the fourth session, held in the spring of 1965, when the size of the commission jumped up to fifty-eight, with five women among the thirty-four lay members. An expert called in for consultation was John T. Noonan, from Notre Dame in Indiana, whose study of the church's changing positions on usury had won scholarly acclaim. He was working on a similar study of changes in the prohibition of contraception—a book that would appear just as the commission was disbanded. Noonan opened the members' eyes to the way that noninfallible papal teaching can develop.

Another eyeopener was the result of a questionnaire brought to Rome by the lay couple Pat and Patty Crowley. They had long been active in the international Christian Family Movement, and they had surveyed their members—devout Catholics all—on their experience of the rhythm method of contraception. They found it far from natural. Since a woman's period fluctuates with her health, anxieties, age, and other influences, establishing the actual infertile period in any cycle required daily chartings of her temperature and close comparative reading of calendars—and even then the results were not sure. The most conscientious Catholics, who followed this nervous procedure with precision, found that it was not certain—which left them in great fear until the next menstruation (which might not occur). And in this concentration on the wife's physical conditions, her psychological patterns—of fondness, need, crises, travel—had to be ignored or repressed. The comments of the couples surveyed made riveting reading in the commission. A husband, a scholar, wrote:

> Rhythm destroys the meaning of the sex act; it turns it from a spontaneous expression of spiritual and physical love into a mere bodily sexual relief; it makes me obsessed with sex throughout the month; it seriously endangers my chastity; it has a noticeable effect upon my disposition toward my wife and children; it makes necessary my complete avoidance of all affection toward my wife for three weeks at a time. I have watched a magnificent spiritual and physical union dissipate and, due to rhythm, turn into a tense and mutually damaging relationship. Rhythm seems to be immoral and deeply unnatural. It seems to me diabolical.

His wife gave her side of the story:

> I find myself sullen and resentful of my husband when the time of sexual relations finally arrives. I resent his necessarily guarded affection during the month and I find I cannot respond suddenly. I find, also, that my subconscious dreams and unguarded thoughts are inevitably sexual and time consuming. All this in spite of a great intellectual and emotional companionship and a generally beautiful marriage and home life.[3]

The commission was hearing that rhythm made people obsessed with sex and its mechanics while minority members at the Council were arguing that rhythm allows people to escape the merely animal urges and enjoy the serenity of sexuality transcended. The commission was also hearing from doctors that nature, of course, provides women with their greatest sexual desire at just the fertile times that rhythm marked off bounds.

The combined impact of Noonan's history and the Crowleys' empirical findings made the commission members—good Catholics all, chosen for their loyalty to the church—look honestly at the "natural law" arguments against contraception and see, with a shock, what flimsy reasoning they had accepted. Sex is for procreation, yes—but all the time, at each and every act? Eating is for subsistence. But any food or drink beyond that necessary for sheer subsistence is not considered mortally sinful. In fact, to reduce eating to that animal compulsion would deny symbolic and spiritual meanings in shared meals—the birthday party, the champagne victory dinner, the wine at Cana, the Eucharist itself. Integrity of the act? Is it sinful to be nourished intravenously when that is called for? Does that violate the integrity of the eating act? The more the assembled members looked at the inherited "wisdom" of the church, the more they saw the questionable roots from which it grew—the fear and hatred of sex, the feeling that pleasure in it is a biological bribe to guarantee the race's perpetuation, that any use of pleasure beyond that purpose is shameful. This was not a view derived from scripture or from Christ, but from Seneca and Augustine.

The commission members, even trained theologians and spiritual counselors who had spent years expounding the church teachings, felt they were looking at reality for the first time. A cultivated submission to the papacy had been, for them, a structure of deceit, keeping them from honesty with themselves, letting them live within a lie. To their shared surprise they found they were not only willing to entertain the idea of the church's changing, but felt that it *had* to change on this matter, that the truth, once seen, could no longer be denied. When the nineteen theologians on the commission, convened for a separate vote, were asked whether church teaching could change on contraception, twelve said yes, seven no (including John Ford, who had joined the commission at this meeting).[4]

This set off alarm bells in the Vatican. For the next meeting, the last and the longest, from April into June of 1965, the members of the commission were demoted to "advisers" (periti) and the commission itself was constituted of sixteen bishops brought in to issue the final report. They would listen to those who had done the actual conferring, and theirs would be the final verdict. Debate before them would be presided over by Cardinal Ottaviani of the Holy Office. This bringing in of the big guns would have cowed the members in their first sessions. But things had gone too far for such intimidation now. The Crowleys brought another survey with them to the showdown, this one of 3,000 Catholics—

including 290 devout subscribers to the magazine *St. Anthony's Messenger*—of whom 63 percent said that rhythm had harmed their marriage and 65 percent said that it did not actually prevent conception, even when the right procedures were followed exactly (even neurotically).[5] Dr. Albert Gorres spoke of the self-censorship Catholics had exercised over themselves—something the members recognized in their lives when it was pointed out.[6] The Jesuit priest Josef Fuchs, who had taught *Casti Connubii* standards for twenty years, said he was withdrawing his moral textbook and resigning his teaching post at the Gregorian University in Rome now that he could no longer uphold what he was asked to profess.[7] The vote of the theologians who were presenting their findings to the bishops was now fifteen to four against the claim that contraception is intrinsically evil.[8] The vote of the larger group was thirty to five.[9]

Here was a perfect laboratory test of the idea that contraception is against nature, as that can be perceived by natural reason alone. These people were all educated, even expert. They were Catholics in good standing (they had been chosen on those grounds). They had been conditioned all their lives to accept the church's teaching—in fact they *had* accepted it in the past. They of all people would entertain the official case with open minds. They had no malice against church authorities—most of them had devoted much (if not all) of their lives to working with them. Most had entered the project either agreeing with the papal position or thinking that it was unlikely to change. Now they found themselves agreeing that change was not only necessary but inevitable. They had trouble imagining how they had ever thought otherwise. Cardinal Suenens explained how they had been conditioned to have a double consciousness, to live a lie:

> For years theologians have had to come up with arguments on behalf of a doctrine they were not allowed to contradict. They had an obligation to defend the received doctrine, but my guess is they already had many hesitations about it inside. As soon as the question was opened up a little, a whole group of moralists arrived at the position defended by the majority here . . . The bishops defended the classical position, but it was imposed on them by authority. The bishops didn't study the pros and cons. They received directives,

they bowed to them, and they tried to explain them to their congregations.[10]

As soon as people began to think independently about the matter, the whole structure of deceit crumbled at a touch. The past position could not be sustained, even among these people picked by the Vatican itself, much less among Catholics not as committed as these were. And it was absurd to speak of the non-Catholic world as ever recognizing this "natural law of natural reason."

The need to face the prospect of change was impressed on the people in the commission by the arguments of the five theologians defending *Casti Connubii*. They reduced their own case to absurdities. John Ford said that intercourse is not necessary for marital love: "Conjugal love is above all spiritual (if the love is genuine) and it requires no specific carnal gesture, much less its repetition in some determined frequency."[11] Ford also liked to say that, if the teaching on sexual activity only for procreation were changed, people could masturbate with impunity. Dr. Gorres quoted the Melchite Patriarch, Maximos IV, who said in the Council deliberations that priests display a "celibate psychosis" in the area of sex.[12] The Crowleys had learned about that mindset when they arrived for the fourth commission session at an empty seminary where the members would be staying. Patty was not allowed to stay in the same room with her husband, but had to go away at night to a convent down the road.[13] Sex could not occur in the confines of a seminary, even with no seminarians in residence.

The climactic vote of the commission—the one of the sixteen bishops—was nine to three for changing the church's position on contraception, with three abstentions. An agreement had been reached before the vote was taken to submit only one report for the commission, but Cardinal Ottaviani and Father Ford, seeing how things were going, had prepared a document of their own, which would later be misrepresented as an official minority document. There was only one official document, the sole one voted on by the bishops who had authority to report the body's findings. (Ottaviani was the one who had brought in these officials, hoping to get the result he wanted. When he failed to, he ignored his own device.)

The Ford "report," drawn up with Germain Grisez, said that any change was inconceivable. This was not because there were rational arguments against change: "If we could bring forward arguments which are clear and cogent based on reason alone, it would not be necessary for our Commission to exist, nor would the present state of affairs exist in the Church." No, the real reason to keep the teaching was that it *was* the teaching: "The Church could not have erred through so many centuries, even through one century, by imposing under serious obligation very grave burdens in the name of Jesus Christ, if Jesus Christ did not actually impose these burdens."[14] As a priest had put it in earlier debate, if the church sent all those souls to hell, it must keep maintaining that that is where they are.

This was not an argument that made sense, at this point, to the commission—to bishops any more than to the theologians or lay experts. But it was the one argument that, in the end, mattered to Paul VI. He took advantage of the so-called "minority report" to say that he could not accept the commission's findings since there had been disagreement with it.[15] Nine of the twelve bishops, fifteen of the nineteen theologians, and thirty of the thirty-five nonepiscopal members of the commission were not enough for him. Votes on the decrees in the Council had not been unanimous either, but he did not call them invalid for that reason. Paul's real concern was with the arguments that Ottaviani brought to him after the report was submitted. He knew what was worrying the Pope, and could play on that. F. X. Murphy had observed one thing about Paul's behavior throughout the meetings of the Council:

> The Pope was a man obviously torn by doubts, tormented by scruples, haunted by thoughts of perfection, and above all dominated by an exaggerated concern—some called it an obsession—about the prestige of his office as Pope. His remarks on this score at times displayed an almost messianic fervor, a note missing in the more sedate utterances of his predecessors. His innumerable statements on the subject were made on almost every occasion, from casual week-day audiences or Sunday sermons from the window of his apartment to the most solemn gatherings in season and out of season. Since it was part of the strategy of the [conciliar] minority to accuse the majority of disloyalty toward the Holy Father, Paul's constant harping in-

evitably caused the majority to think that he perhaps did share these misgivings, at least to a certain extent. It was noticed by students of Paul's remarks that while he showed an open-mindedness about almost any other subject, on the single theme of the papacy his mind remained strangely closed to analysis.[16]

Those words were written before *Humanae Vitae* was issued, but they explain the letter entirely.

The commission members left their work convinced that the Pope could no longer uphold a discredited teaching. When the report was leaked to the press, Catholics around the world took heart at the signs of change. So far from upsetting their faith, as the Pope feared, it heartened them. What would unsettle their faith was what Paul did next—issue *Humanae Vitae*, with its reiteration of *Casti Connubii*'s ban: "The church, calling men back to the observance of the natural law, as interpreted by its constant doctrine, teaches that each and every marriage act must remain open to the transmission of life."[17] Catholics responded with an unparalleled refusal to submit. Polls registered an instant noncompliance with the encyclical. At a previously scheduled Catholic festival of devout young Germans at Essen, a resolution that those attending could not obey the encyclical passed through a crowd of four thousand with only ninety opposing votes.[18] A simultaneous poll among German Catholics at large found that 68 percent of them thought the Pope was wrong on contraception.[19] Similar findings rolled in from around the world.

What were bishops to do? The encyclical itself had ordered them to explain and enforce the Pope's decision, along with all priests:

> Be the first to give, in the exercise of your ministry, the example of loyal internal and external obedience to the teaching authority of the Church . . . it is of the utmost importance, for peace of consciences and for the unity of the Christian people, that in the field of morals as well as in that of dogma, all should attend to the magisterium of the Church, and all should speak the same language.[20]

But for the first time in memory, bishops' statements, while showing respect for the encyclical, told believers they could act apart from it if they felt bound by conscience to do so. The assembly of bishops in the Netherlands put it most bluntly: "The assembly considers that the encyclical's total rejection of contraceptive methods is not convincing on the basis of the arguments put forward."[21] Other episcopal panels were more circumspect, but signaled that they would not consider those disobedient to the encyclical to be separating themselves from the sacraments. The Belgian bishops put it this way: "Someone, however, who is competent in the matter under consideration and capable of forming a personal and well-founded judgment—which necessarily presupposes a sufficient amount of knowledge—may, after serious examination before God, come to other conclusions on certain points." In other words: do not treat the Pope's words lightly, but follow your conscience after taking a serious look at them. That was the position taken by bishops in the United States ("the norms of licit dissent come into play"), Austria, Brazil, Czechoslovakia, Mexico, the Philippines, West Germany, Japan, France, Scandanavia, and Switzerland.[22] The Scandanavian statement was typical:

> Should someone, however, for grave and carefully considered reasons, not feel able to subscribe to the arguments of the encyclical, he is entitled, as has been constantly acknowledged, to entertain other views than those put forward in a non-infallible declaration of the Church. No one should, therefore, on account of such diverging opinions alone, be regarded as an inferior Catholic.[23]

The Pope was stunned. He would spend the remaining ten years of his pontificate as if sleepwalking, unable to understand what had happened to him, why such open dissent was entertained at the very top of the episcopate. Four years after the publication of *Humanae Vitae*, when the Pope looked "cautious, nervous, anxious, alarmed," he deplored the defiance of church teaching in a sermon at Saint Peter's, and this was the only explanation he could come up with for the defiance: "Through some crack in the temple of God, the smoke of Satan has entered."[24] He was increasingly melancholy and prone to tears.[25] Had he opened that crack in the temple of God? Even as a nagging suspicion this was a terrible burden to bear. It explains the atmosphere of darkening tragedy that hung

about his final years. He would not issue another encyclical in all those
ten years. He was a prisoner of the Vatican in a way that went beyond his
predecessors' confinement there. He was imprisoned in its structures of
deceit. Meanwhile, Father Ford, who had assisted his fellow Jesuit Gustave Martelet in drawing up *Humanae Vitae* under Cardinal Ottaviani's direction, went back to the seminary where he had taught moral theology
for years and found that the Jesuit seminarians there refused to take his
classes, since they knew from others in the Order what he had done in
Rome.[26] As a result of what he considered his life's great coup, his teaching career was over.

The whole Catholic attitude toward authority in general shifted with
the allowed dissent on *Humanae Vitae*.[27] What could be done about that?
Paul's hands, by his own act, were tied. Were those of future Popes as
well? Paul's immediate successor, John Paul (Albano Luciani) seemed to
signal that he would move away from the *Casti Connubii* ban. When the
world's first test tube baby was born, the Pope took the extraordinary step
of sending his congratulations, even though *Humanae Vitae* condemned
in vitro fertilization. He told newsmen:

> I send the most heartfelt congratulations to the English baby girl
> whose conception was produced artificially. As for her parents I have
> no right to condemn them . . . They could even deserve great
> merit before God for what they wanted and asked the doctors to
> accomplish.[28]

This was the kind of warm pastoral statement John XXIII was known for,
and Luciani disturbed some in the Curia with the fear that they were in
for another Johannine papacy. But Luciani died after a mere month in office, to be succeeded by a man who took his name from him, but little
else. Pope John Paul II, Karol Wojtyla of Poland, quickly showed by his
words and actions that he was even more strict on contraception than Paul
had been. He mounted a sustained conceptual and disciplinary defense of
Humanae Vitae, insisting on its strict acceptance in his world travels. He
solemnly celebrated the encyclical's tenth anniversary in 1978. The following year he launched a long series of discourses on sex published as
The Theology of the Body.[29] He quashed all dissent on *Humanae Vitae* at the

1980 Synod of Bishops meeting to discuss the family.[30] In 1981 he issued a long (120-page) document on the same subject, the Apostolic Exhortation *Familiaris Consortio*. In 1992, he followed that up with an equally long encyclical (*Veritatis Splendor*) reasserting the teaching power of the church in this and other areas. Besides, he has shown a clear determination to appoint only bishops who will back him up on contraception—though the body of the faithful has drifted farther away from him, on this point, all through his time in office. The double consciousness of Catholics is increasingly being stratified, the hierarchy accepting the papal view and the laity ignoring it. Only priests, caught between the two strata, are expected to incorporate both views in their conduct.

Familiaris Consortio

W hy would Pope John Paul II make the most controversial part of his office the central point of its discipline? In a world torn apart by so many serious issues of life and death, war and peace, why does he drive down the number of people wanting to be priests and nuns, why hammer away at an issue on which he daily loses ground? Even Pope Paul seemed to waver in his certainty on *Humanae Vitae*, muting the issue, suggesting there might be room for further thought on the matter. Four days after the encyclical was released, Paul met the wave of resistance with a placatory gesture—the encyclical, he said, "is not a complete treatment of marriage, the family and their moral significance. This is an immense field to which the magisterium of the church could and perhaps should return with a fuller, more organic, and more synthetic treatment."[31]

Paul was not concerned with sex in itself when he condemned contraception—there is nothing in his record to suggest a preoccupation with sex. It was authority that he cared about, and its undermining that he feared. He was obsessive about the papal record for consistency. With John Paul it is *both* authority *and* sex that are crucial. He fancies himself an expert, psychological as well as theological, on sex. Though he was appointed as one of the bishops called to vote in the final session of the

Pontifical Commission on contraception, he did not attend that meeting.[32] He channeled his views on the matter to the Pope, sending him a translation of his first published book, *Love and Responsibility* (1960). This grew out of his sessions with the youth group he led, as a priest, on mountain hikes, engaging the members in "surprisingly frank" discussions of sex, with a constant emphasis on *askēsis* (self-control). Another source of his interest and expertise on this matter was Dr. Wanda Poltawska, a Catholic concentration camp survivor who led a group of doctors in the study of sexual practices in Krakow. While the Crowleys were learning that the rhythm method led to "unnatural" frustration, Dr. Poltawska claimed to have established empirically that practicing contraception breeds neuroses, guilt, frigidity, and impotence. Karl Wojtyla drew on her findings for *Love and Responsibility*, which not only praised the rhythm system of family control, but supplied charts to make monthly observance of it look easy.[33]

As Pope John Paul II, Wojtyla claims that the church's teaching has always been the same on contraception, but he also feels he has new "personalist" insights to bring to that teaching. He presents his own views, especially in *Familiaris Consortio*, as continuing a train of thought highlighted by the Council document *Gaudium et Spes* and his predecessor's encyclical, *Humanae Vitae*. All three put a new emphasis on the marriage act as an act of love. This was a subject feared by the conservative minority in the Council. They knew that people like John Noonan had pinpointed a shift in emphasis in the twelfth and following centuries, when the sex act—presented as bestial or degrading in earlier church teaching—was accepted as noble if tied to married love and procreation. The Council minority feared that if the expression of love was put on a par with the aim of procreation, the former could be indulged without keeping every single act of intercourse "open to life." (That, in fact, was where Noonan thought his reading of history was bound to carry the magisterium.) Pope Paul shared the minority's concern, as he showed in his last-minute *modi*, one of which was aimed at removing a single word, *etiam* ("as well as"), which might suggest that procreation is just one end of marriage. The majority dodged that bullet. Even though *Gaudium et Spes* obliged the Pope by citing (in a footnote) *Casti Connubii* as binding, it was more positive about sex than most authoritative pronouncements had been. It especially emphasized that the married sex act is a matter of the partners' "mutual self-gift."[34]

In his own encyclical, *Humanae Vitae*, Paul VI seemed to abandon his concern with procreation as the "primary end" of marriage. He cited the "unitive" and the "procreative" aims of intercourse without ranking them.[35] This is because Germain Grisez had convinced John Ford and others responsible for the Pope's position that the emphasis on the mechanics of procreation ("the integrity of the act") was a losing argument. Grisez preferred to say that God is the giver and enhancer of life, and to oppose life is to oppose God. John Paul's *Familiaris Consortio* develops this approach, condemning contraception as expressive of "an anti-life mentality."[36] He also picks up the Council's language on self-giving. Now, instead of degrading the sex act, the Pope comes close to flattering it to death. It is so wonderful that it must always be perfect:

> Thus the innate language that expresses the total reciprocal self-giving of husband and wife is overlaid, through contraception, by an objectively contradictory language, namely, that of not giving oneself totally to the other. This leads not only to a positive refusal to be open to life but also to a falsification of the inner truth of conjugal love, which is called upon to give oneself in personal totality.[37]

In sex, you see, it is all or nothing. Unless the act expresses all values possible to it all the time, it is immoral. It would be hard to find a parallel in the moral world for this principle. Can we say that, unless one's charity is perfectly motivated, you sin by giving alms from lesser motives (e.g., to bolster self-esteem)? If alms-giving were banned unless its motive was a perfect charity, the church's donations would fall off sharply.

In order to be entirely perfect, in the Pope's eyes, the sex act must express its apparent opposite—continence and abstinence. A man comes back to his wife purified and improved after refraining from intercourse with her. He can only give himself when he has earned a self worth giving. "Man is precisely a person because he is master of himself, and has self-control. Indeed, insofar as he is master of himself, he can give himself to the other."[38] This is not a matter of absence making the heart grow fonder. The periodic continence imposed by rhythm is a good in itself:

"The mastery of self corresponds to the fundamental constitution of the person; it is indeed a 'natural' method."[39]

Logically, this should mean that everyone should periodically refrain from sex, even apart from any effort at birth control—and that is what John Paul is getting at. Unless one is willing to perfect oneself by periodic abstinence, it is possible to commit adultery with one's own wife. John Paul came up with this extraordinary view of concupiscence toward one's own wife in his address of October 8, 1980. After citing Christ's saying that "everyone who looks at a woman lustfully has already committed adultery with her in his heart" (Mt 5:28), he went on:

> Christ did not stress that it is "another man's wife," or a woman who is not his own wife, but says generically, a woman . . . Even if [a man] looked in this way at the woman who is his wife, he could likewise commit adultery in his heart.[40]

Such a person has not achieved the purity and selflessness necessary for the perfect self-giving that intercourse must be, when "freed from the constraint and from the impairment of the spirit that the lust of the flesh brings with it, the human being, male and female, finds itself mutually in the freedom of the gift."[41] John Paul makes the sex act so holy that only monks are really worthy of it. He even finds a way to personalize the menstrual cycle, saying that respect for the woman's natural rhythms shows that her partner is aware of her dignity.

> The choice of the natural rhythms involves accepting the cycle of the person, that is the woman, and thereby accepting dialogue, reciprocal respect, shared responsibility and self-control. To accept the cycle and to enter into dialogue means to recognize both the spiritual and corporal character of conjugal communion and to live personal love with its requirement of fidelity.[42]

The women whose anguish was spelled out in the Crowleys' survey are not likely to feel dignified by this mystical approach to menstruation.

For John Paul, sex is only holy when you have proved you can give it up, can remain free of concupiscence toward the partner, preserving a pure heart, a kind of would-be virginity, even in marriage. Here we reach the psychological source of John Paul's mystical certitude on the doctrine that even Paul advanced with hesitation and few Catholics are willing to accept, including those who admire John Paul in other areas. We shall find the same certitude on other matters—the necessity for priestly celibacy, the superiority of virginity, the reduction of the beatitude "Blessed are the pure in heart" to sexual purity (against the biblical scholarship on that verse). All of these are involved with the total devotion John Paul has to the virginity of Mary. He wants to introduce the aura of virginity even into marriage, where concupiscence toward one's own wife is forbidden. His pontifical motto *Totus Tuus* (Entirely Yours) is dedicated to Mary. His pilgrimages to all the Marian shrines continued his youthful submission to the Black Madonna of Czestochowa.[43] All the arguments of natural reason, all the consultations of theologians, all the misgivings of the world's bishops—none of these can alter the way one man's devotion now poses as the measure of divine truth. The rest of the church must live in structures of deceit because this one man is true to his intensely personal vision.

[1] Robert Blair Kaiser, *The Politics of Sex and Religion: A Case History in the Development of Doctrine, 1962–1984* (Leaven Press of *The National Catholic Reporter*, 1985), pp. 95–96.

[2] For the Grisez rejection of Thomistic arguments in favor of a new approach, see Janet E. Smith, *Humanae Vitae: A Generation Later* (Catholic University of America Press, 1991), pp. 340–70.

[3] Kaiser, op. cit., p. 95.

[4] Robert McClory, *Turning Point: The Inside Story of the Papal Birth Control Commission* (Crossroad, 1995), p. 71.

[5] Kaiser, op. cit., pp. 135–36.

[6] Ibid., p. 138.

[7] McClory, op. cit., p. 122.

[8] Ibid., p. 99.

[9] Kaiser, op. cit., p. 147.

[10] McClory, op. cit., p. 125.

[11] Kaiser, op. cit., p. 144.

[12] Ibid., p. 139.

[13] Ibid., p. 78.

[14] McClory, op. cit., pp. 110–11.

[15] Paul VI, *Of Human Life (Humanae Vitae)*, paragraph 6 (Pauline Books, 1968), p. 3.

[16] F. X. Murphy ("Xavier Rynne"), *Vatican Council II* (Farrar, Straus and Giroux, 1968), p. 429.

[17] Paul VI, op. cit., paragraph 11, pp. 5–6.

¹⁸John Horgan (editor), *"Humanae Vitae" and the Bishops: The Encyclical and the Statements of the National Hierarchies* (Irish University Press, 1972), pp. 15–16.

¹⁹Ibid., p. 16.

²⁰Paul VI, op. cit., paragraph 28, p. 14.

²¹Horgan, op. cit., p. 192.

²²Ibid., pp. 276, 81, 61, 73–74, 99, 205–6, 309–10, 169–70, 127, 238, 260.

²³Ibid., p. 238. Of course, some episcopal bodies accepted the papal teaching without expressly allowing for exceptions—England, Ireland, Italy, Korea, Spain, Yugoslavia, and a dozen or so others. But the departures from former compliance are what startles. Besides, while the number of conforming statements by national bodies is impressive, the actual number of dioceses represented by them is much smaller than those bodies with reservations. By breaking down the bishops' statements into actual dioceses represented by them, the Benedictine priest Philip Kaufman showed that only 17 percent worldwide accepted the encyclical without suggesting that Catholics could entertain doubts about it, while 56 percent did leave room for questioning by individuals' conscience, and 28 percent were equivocal. See Kaufman, *Why You Can Disagree and Remain a Faithful Catholic* (Crossroad, 1991), pp. 72–83.

²⁴Peter Hebblethwaite, *Paul VI: The First Modern Pope* (Paulist Press, 1993), p. 595.

²⁵Ibid., p. 594.

²⁶Ibid., p. 488 (on Martelet); Kaiser, op. cit., pp. 214–15.

²⁷This is the theme of several books by the sociologist Andrew Greeley. See, for instance, *Crisis in the Church: A Study of Religion in America* (Thomas More Press, 1979).

²⁸Jonathan Kwitny, *Man of the Century: The Life and Times of Pope John Paul II* (Henry Holt and Company, 1997), pp. 286–87.

²⁹John Paul II, *The Theology of the Body: Human Love in the Divine Plan* (Pauline Books, 1997).

³⁰Jan Grootaers and Joseph A. Selling, *The 1980 Synod of Bishops "On the Role of the Family": An Exposition of the Event and an Analysis of Its Texts* (Biblotheca ephemeridum theologicarum Lovaniensium, 64).

³¹Kaiser, op. cit., p. 200.

³²He said later that he would not travel when his senior bishop was forbidden to, though he found reasons to travel on other occasions.

³³Kwitny, op. cit., pp. 159–66.

³⁴*Gaudium et Spes*, paragraphs 48, 51, Walter M. Abbott, S.J. (editor), *The Documents of Vatican II* (Herder and Herder, 1966), pp. 250, 251, 256.

³⁵Paul VI, op. cit., paragraph 12, p. 6.

³⁶John Paul II, *The Role of the Christian Family in the Modern World (Familiaris Consortio)*, Vatican translation, paragraph 30 (Pauline Books, 1997), p. 48.

³⁷Ibid., paragraph 32, pp. 51–52.

³⁸John Paul II, *The Theology of the Body*, p. 398.

³⁹Ibid., p. 397.

⁴⁰Ibid., p. 159.

⁴¹Ibid., pp. 158–59.

⁴²*Familiaris Consortio*, paragraph 32, p. 52.

⁴³Kwitny, op. cit., pp. 37–38, 52, 83, 120, 132, 326–27, 435.

7.

Excluded Women

When Pope John Paul II visited the United States in 1979, he was met everywhere with enthusiasm verging on adulation. But when he reached Washington, and spoke to a gathering of nuns, he was met also with respectful dissent. Sister Theresa Kane was no young hothead or rebel, but the superior of the Sisters of Mercy and the elected head of the Leadership Conference of Women Religious (not a wild or radical group). Appointed to greet the Pope, she took the occasion to make a public request that "half of humankind" be recognized as worthy to be "included in all the ministries of the Church." The Pope answered that the Virgin Mary should be the nuns' model, and Mary was not a priest.[1]

Elsewhere the Pope gave the reasons for women's exclusion that Paul VI had written four years earlier, objecting to the Anglicans' decision to ordain women priests, an objection that the Congregation for the Doctrine of the Faith (the old Holy Office) followed up with a solemn declaration, *Inter Insigniores* (1976). The church has no power to ordain women, that document said, because Christ made only men his original apostles. Despite an official position that now welcomes scriptural scholarship, the Vatican can revert, when that is useful, to biblical fundamentalism of the most simpleminded sort. The twelve apostles were men, so all priests must be men. But the twelve apostles were married, and the church authorities decided they could change that—in fact, John Paul says that the church cannot go back to the original situation on this point. Saint Peter had a wife, but no modern Pope or priest can. Are we to say that all priests must be converted Jews? The twelve were. Are they all to speak Aramaic? For that matter, if we are to make the gospel situation binding now, we should observe that the apostles were not priests themselves (see below). And there was at least one woman apostle in the New Testament, Junia (Rom 16:7).[2]

The declaration, as if hesitant to rely on such a weak argument, tried to prop it up with two others, which had the opposite tendency. They dragged further down what had been shaky before. The first new argument had the merit of being quickly stated. Women do not *look* like Jesus:

> When Christ's role in the Eucharist is to be expressed sacramentally, there would not be this natural resemblance which must exist between Christ and his minister if the role of Christ were not taken by a man. In such a case it would be difficult to *see* in the minister the image of Christ. For Christ himself was and remains a man.[3] [Emphasis added.]

We must return to that point about playing "the role" of Jesus (see Chapter 6). Not much else can be said about such a bizarre argument. Is the other one any better? It runs this way: Because of the church's medieval reliance on the "Solomonic" Song of Songs to signify the mystical marriage of Christ with his church, the priest must play the male bridegroom, representing Christ, while the church is the female bride. When the congregation has to admit, in the course of this tortuous argument, that the priest also represents the church, the female partner, the congregation plunges into this bit of Lewis Carroll logic—the priest is the church only because he is the head of the church; and therefore the priest can only be the bridegroom even when he is the bride. Got it?

> However, it will perhaps be further objected that the priest, especially when he presides at the liturgical and sacramental functions, equally represents the Church: he acts in her name with the "intention of doing what she does." In this sense, the theologians of the Middle Ages said that the minister also acts *in persona Ecclesiae*, that is to say, in the name of the whole Church and in order to represent her . . . It is true that the priest represents the Church, which

is the Body of Christ. But if he does so, it is precisely because he first represents Christ himself, who is the Head and Shepherd of the Church.[4]

So even Christ is the church, as its head—he is the bride, and the Father is the bridegroom. Getting tired of this circularity? So were some scripture scholars, who gently tried to remind the congregation that the Song of Songs has nothing to do with priesthood, that its "mystical" applications are usually based on bad exegesis, fuzzy analogies, and outmoded social assumptions.[5] When is the last time you heard a sermon based on Bernard of Clairvaux's theology of the Song of Songs? Besides, when the prophets of Israel denounced male priests and rulers as violating Israel's "marriage bond" with Yahweh, there was no difficulty in seeing those males as part of the "bride."[6] Sexual stereotyping is not the content of revelation. Besides, the ecclesiologists were as unhappy with this passage as the exegetes. To say that a priest is above the church is not anything most theologians of the church would consider orthodox teaching.

Naturally, Catholics in general found these arguments about as convincing as the same teachers' "natural law" case against contraception. Before the declaration appeared, 29 percent of Catholics supported the idea of women priests. It was to contain a tendency in this direction that Paul VI had acted. But he accelerated the process, in dizzying ways. A month after the declaration became known in the United States, the approval was at 31 percent; three weeks later, 36 percent; two weeks later, 41 percent.[7] A favorable opinion that had been gradually solidifying shot up 10 percent in five weeks as a response to the declaration. It has been going up ever since. By the 1980s it was over 66 percent.[8]

And what was John Paul's reaction to this problem left over for him by Paul VI? It was to say that Paul VI had been too soft on the issue. That was the opinion of Joseph Ratzinger, who had worked on the document as a professor of theology at Regensburg, and whom John Paul would appoint to fill Cardinal Ottaviani's old post at the renamed Holy Office. Ratzinger would have made *Inter Insigniores* even tougher in terms of the command given to Catholics—as John Paul did in his own Apostolic Letter of 1994, *Sacerdotalis Ordinatio.*[9]

Wherefore, in order that all doubt may be removed regarding a matter of great importance, a matter which pertains to the Church's divine constitution itself, in virtue of my ministry of confirming the
brethren, I declare that the Church has no authority whatsoever to
confer priestly ordination on women, and that this judgment is to
be definitively held by all the Church's faithful.[10]

The Pope prompted the same kind of response that he had when he
strengthened *Humanae Vitae* with *Familiaris Consortio.* The rebellion was
intensified. The *National Catholic Reporter's* story was headlined, "Catholics Try to Digest Papal Bombshell." The theological faculty at Leuven
University expressed "consternation" at the letter. Belgian bishops
agreed to register their doubts in Rome. Individual theologians and
some bishops publicly questioned the Pope's reading of the Bible. The
editor of *Commonweal* said the Pope had opened rather than closed the
matter.[11]

How could the Vatican offer such weak reasons for retaining its male-
only rule? They were all that was left the authorities, since they were deprived of the original arguments for the rule, which had become too
disreputable for Rome to continue voicing them. There were, over the
centuries, only two reasons given for excluding women from the priesthood—that they were inferior beings unworthy to hold that dignity, and
that their ritual impurity kept them from the altar. The first argument
came mainly from pagan antiquity, the second from Jewish temple practice. *Inter Insigniores* (paragraph 6) admitted that such views had been expressed in the past, but denied that they had any effect on the church's
discipline—which is a demonstrable falsehood, a deceit that structures all
the papacy's current statements on the matter.

Thomas Aquinas was not a lone voice but the articulator of a consensus, when he gave the primary motive for refusing ordination to women:
"Since any supremacy of rank cannot be expressed in the female sex,
which has the status of an inferior, that sex cannot receive ordination"
(ST Suppl. q. 39r). Saint Bonaventure agreed: since only the male was
made in the image of God, only the male can receive the godlike office
of priest.[12] Duns Scotus said that women as the successors of Eve, through
whom man fell, cannot be the officers of man's salvation.[13]

Why were these men so sure that women are inferior? Aquinas had Aristotle's assurance:

> In terms of nature's own operation, a woman is inferior and a mistake. The agent cause that is in the male seed tries to produce something complete in itself, a male in gender. But when a female is produced, this is because the agent cause is thwarted, either because of the unsuitability of the receiving matter [of the mother] itself or because of some deforming interference, as from south winds, that are too wet, as we read in [Aristotle's] *Animal Conception* (ST 1 q 92, 1 ad 1).

In Aristotle's physiology, the male seed is the formal cause of conception; it is active, with the noble elements prevailing (fire and air). Woman is only the material cause of conception, passive, with the lower elements prevailing (water and earth). When the formal cause succeeds, it produces a male that looks like the father. When it flounders in the passive receiving muck (which Aristotle associates with menstrual blood), it produces (in descending order) either a male that looks like the mother, a female that looks like the father, or a female that looks like the mother.[14] Since the female, when she is conceived, is actually a failed male, a deformity (*anapēria*), it takes longer for her to be formed in the womb, yet she emerges from this longer process smaller and weaker than the male, and she ages faster and declines when freed from the womb.[15] Her very makeup makes her less capable of reason and virtue and discipline than the male—in Aristotle's words, "more shameless, lying and deceptive"— leaving her unstable and inconstant, a prey to the passions, less able to control herself or others.[16] Saint John Chrysostom said women are just not smart enough to be priests.[17]

Aristotle's was not the only classical form of misogynism that Christianity inherited, but it was a pervasive one because it was so impressively argued. It was based on scientific experiments like the dissection of pregnant animals. This led to its being echoed, implicitly if not expressly, in part if not in whole, by a vast range of ancient authors. It was passed to the Eastern church through Clement of Alexandria (c. 150–c. 215) and to the Western church through Tertullian (c. 155–c. 220).[18] Clement wrote that "A woman, considering what her nature is, must be ashamed of it."[19] Tertullian said that women, continuing the role of Eve the temptress, are "the gateway through which the devil comes."[20]

The general classical view of woman's sexuality was the opposite of Victorian sentiment about the blushing and shy woman preyed on by brutal men. Given the looser control of reason and the unintegrated passions implicit in classical theories of her nature, Greek and Roman authors thought women were voracious in their sexuality. Here, too, Aristotle led the way, with claims about the sexual appetite of female animals in general.[21] Folklore support for this observation came in part from the fact that women can have intercourse at any time, since they need no erection or ejaculation (as the aging Mark Twain said, ruefully, "They are capable as candlesticks"). This led to fearful views of men's inability to satisfy such unremitting demands. In the *locus classicus* of Roman misogynism, Juvenal's Sixth Satire, a man is advised to stick with boys, not women, since a boy will not rail as a woman does when you do not keep up with her sexual urges (6.36–37). The Empress Messalina is described by Juvenal as going to a brothel to be drudged all night and still returning "with unsated vulva engorged and burning" (6.129). The medical writer Soranus (first century CE) described nymphomaniacs as having "an irresistible desire for sexual intercourse and a certain crazed lack of shame (from the sympathetic reaction of brain tissue to the uterus)."[22]

These sexual vampires haunted the nightmares of celibate Christians, so that Epiphanius, the bishop of Cyprus, wrote: "Women are easily seduced, weak and lacking in reason. The devil works to spew his chaos out through them" (PG 42.740). Women were more vulnerable to demoniac possession.[23] In the thirteenth century, Albert the Great (Thomas Aquinas's teacher) was still saying things like this:

> The woman contains more liquid than the man, and it is a property of liquid to take things up easily and to hold onto them poorly. Liquids are easily moved, hence women are inconstant and curious . . . Woman is a misbegotten man and has a faulty and defective nature in comparison with his. Therefore she is unsure in herself. What she herself cannot get she seeks to obtain through lying and diabolical deceptions. And so, to put it briefly, one must be on guard with

every woman, as if she were a poisonous snake and the horned devil.[24]

The friability of women's nature made the strength of virgin martyrs all the more amazing for Christians—they were said to have made themselves male.[25]

Strong as these arguments for barring women from the priesthood were felt to be, there was an even stronger one in most men's eyes—women's ritual impurity. In the New Testament itself, there is no ordination to a ritual priesthood. As the distinguished Dominican theologian, Yves Congar, put it:

> Here are the facts. The word *hiereus* (priest, sacrificer) appears more than thirty times in the New Testament, and the word *archiereus* more than one hundred and thirty times. The use of these words is so constant that it clearly shows a deliberate and highly significant intention, especially as the writers of the first Christian generation very carefully follow the same line. With them, as with the New Testament, *hiereus* (or *archiereus*) is used to denote either the priests of the levitical order or the pagan priests. Applied to the Christian religion, the word *hiereus* is used only in speaking of Christ or of the faithful. *It is never applied to the ministers of the Church's hierarchy.*[26] [Emphasis added.]

But when an echo of the Temple priesthood returned to Christianity, so did the ritual taboos around it. Bishops were told that they, like Jewish priests, could not sleep with their wives on the eve of offering sacrifice.[27] This taboo would play its part in the gradual extension of a priestly obligation not to have wives in the first place. Jerome and Origen thought even the laity should refrain from sexual congress on the eve of receiving the sacrament.[28] The priest was given a monopoly on the administration of sacraments, and especially on the consecration of the Eucharist—an act hedged off from ordinary life in ways that made the church's sanctuary a kind of mini-Temple, with mysteries penetrated only by the initiates. In time, the "rood screen" would block the view of the laity, and sacerdotal Latin would insure that even hearing would not reveal much of what went on in the Holy of Holies. The priest now had specially chrismed consecrating fingers—lack of the forefinger or thumb was enough to bar a man from ordination, no other digits seeming pure enough for the task. The laity, of course, were not allowed to touch the consecrated host with anything but the tongue (and innards). In the eleventh century, after priestly celibacy had become obligatory in the Western church, Saint Peter Damian wrote that Christ, since he was born of a Virgin, should be touched only by virginal hands.[29]

As soon as the demand for ritual purity arose, woman was bound to be disqualified for the sacred service. She is ritually impure because of her menstruation. She would profane even the inner court of the Jewish Temple, much less the Holy of Holies. Though the Jews did not live in quite the panicky dread over women's menstruation that other cultures have, their concern with it was still enough for the Bible scholar Jacob Milgrom to say that the general "attitude to the menstruant continued to be dominated by fear."[30] The female as such was so impure that a woman who bore a girl child was impure for twice the length of days, afterward, as one bearing a male. She was not allowed to touch any consecrated thing or enter the sacred precinct for thirty-three days after bearing a boy, but for sixty-six days after bearing a girl (Lev 12:1–5).[31] The sequestration of women in the outer parts of synagogues, behind screens, expressed the same view—that they could not deal with things holy. Christians applied the same restrictions after they created a ritual priesthood of their own. During menstruation, according to Patriarch Dionysius of Alexandria (third century CE), "pious, devout women would never even think of touching the sacred table or the Body and Blood of the Lord" (PG 10.1281). Even when not menstruating, women were not allowed to enter the sanctuary, approach the altar, or touch the sacred vessels. The Council of Laodicia (fourth century) decreed, "It is not permitted women to enter the altar areas."[32] In the ninth century, Bishop Haito of Basle included this in his enactments:

> Everyone should take care that women do not approach the altar;
> even women consecrated to God may not intrude into any kind of
> altar service. If altar linens must be washed they should be removed

by clerics, given over at the altar rails, and also be taken back that way. And likewise offertory gifts, if they are brought by these women, are received by priests there and brought to the altar.[33]

When even to get near the altar was forbidden to women, so unhallowed were they and alien from the sacred, ordaining them priests was of course unthinkable. Nor are such notions entirely dead even now. As recently as 1917 Canon Law (Canon 813.1) said, "Female persons may in no case come up to the altar, and may give responses only from afar." Women were not allowed inside the sanctuary in the days when I was growing up, and the Vatican ruled in 1980 that "Women are not allowed to act as altar servers [acolytes]."[34] Since women were not allowed in the choir space, which was behind the sanctuary in medieval cathedrals, the all-male choir became the rule—leading to the acquisition of sopranos in the form of castrati (for which the Vatican choir was famous). Males, even when mutilated, were less unclean than women.

All such ritual requirements are very far from the New Testament situation in which the Pope tells us we shall find male-only priests. The problem is that when we look at the New Testament we find no priests at all, female *or* male. As Raymond Brown, the conservative Catholic scholar, wrote:

> Did the historical Jesus think about ordination? He chose the Twelve, but they were to sit on thrones to judge the twelve tribes of Israel (Luke 22:30). There is no biblical evidence that he thought about any of his followers, male or female, as priests, since there were already priests in Israel . . . From the New Testament it appears that the clear conceptualization of the Christian priesthood came only after the destruction of the Jerusalem Temple in AD 70.[35]

Emerging from all the later crazed talk of female inferiority and impurity, we breathe a cleaner world in the New Testament. In fact, one of the earliest Christian documents we have is a baptismal hymn quoted in the second earliest New Testament text (Paul's letter to the Galatians—only his letter to the Thessalonians is earlier). This denies all inequality between men and women.

> Baptized into Christ,
> you are clothed in Christ,
> so that there is no more
> Jew or Greek,
> slave or free,
> man and woman,
> but all are one, are the same
> in Christ Jesus.[36]

The astonishing thing, given the pagan and Jewish attitudes toward women, is that the Jesus of the gospels lives that baptismal vision. He mixes with women, even unclean women, even prostitutes, even outcasts like the Samaritan woman, as well as with other "low life." This shocked not only his opponents but his own followers (Jn 4:27).

> There is little reason to question the authenticity of the information that women traveled with and served Jesus and the disciples, as this was conduct which was unheard of and considered scandalous in Jewish circles . . . For a Jewish woman to leave home and travel with a rabbi was not only unheard of, it was scandalous. Even more scandalous was the fact that women, both respectable and not, were among Jesus' traveling companions.[37]

Jesus healed the woman with a discharge of blood (Mk 5:25-34)—even though she had touched him and made him unclean. Irregular blood issues were even more polluting than regular menstruation, as we learn from Leviticus 15:25–30, and that is why the woman approached Jesus stealthily and touched his garment before she could be stopped.[38] There were no medieval canonists around, the kind who prevented women from touching an altar, to keep her from touching the Lord himself. Jesus' willingness to deal with outcasts, with those who had unclean spirits (the kind fit only to be cast into unclean pigs), with tax collectors (dealers in the profane), may show up even in the genealogy given him by Matthew's gospel, where—unusually for any genealogy of the time—there are four women progenitors, and all of them with some "hint of scandal" in their lives.[39]

The women followers of Jesus "followed along with him" (*synakolou-thousai*, Lk 23:49) all the way from Galilee to Jerusalem, and they were the ones who stayed with him to the end, standing by the cross in John's gospel when all men but one had fled. In three gospels, the Galilean women were the first to discover the empty tomb (they alone were tending it), and they were charged to bring the good news—to evangelize—that the Lord is risen. Even Augustine, not always a praiser of women, said in his Sermon 232:

> Here we should ponder the providential aptness of Our Lord's work. For this is how the Lord Jesus Christ arranged that women should be the first to proclaim that he had risen. Because man fell by a woman, and because the virgin Mary bore Christ, women were now to proclaim that he had risen. Through woman, death? Through woman, life! (PL 38.1108.)

So there is nothing in the gospels to indicate that Jesus himself could have held any of the vile attitudes about female inferiority and impurity that we have seen the church's teachers displaying through the centuries and imposing in his name. Those views were foisted on him—by bishops, and theologians, and saints who thought they knew better than the gospel. They were preaching Aristotle, not Christ.

Still, it can be objected, if Jesus had such a high opinion of women, why didn't he make even one of them a priest? Well, as Raymond Brown has reminded us, he did not make any man a priest either. Why should he do for a Mary Magdalen what he did not do for a Peter? We have very full lists of all the church ministries in the earliest days of the church—ten of them in the first letter to the Corinthians, six in the letter to the Romans, five in that to the Ephesians. We hear of emissaries (*apostoloi*), workers for the gospel (*kopountes*), prophets, ministers (*di-akonoi*), elders (*presbyteroi*), evangelists, teachers, shepherds, guides, exhorters, miracle workers, healers, tongue-speakers, tongue-interpreters, spirit-distinguishers.[40] Every one of these functions could be exercised by women, and there were no other functions to exercise. We do not hear of individual priests, only of the priesthood of the whole Christian community (I Peter 2:5). No people exercise separate functions as baptizers, Eucharist officiators, mass celebrators, ministers of sacraments. We do not hear of office itself, only of people with various functions. This is surprising, says Wayne Meeks in his study of the early communities' structure, because the Christian gatherings resemble very closely Hellenistic clubs—and those clubs abounded in nicely gradated offices (*archai*).[41] Christian leadership, by contrast, was charismatic, dynamic, non-hierarchical. Arlo J. Nau has even argued that the treatment of Peter in Matthew's gospel was meant to inhibit any hierarchical notions.[42] Leaders were not to be appointed by human authority but by the promptings of the Spirit.

Paul goes out of his way to say that his work was not authorized by the church in Jerusalem, or the Twelve, or anyone but the Lord (Gal 1:1–20). He calls himself a worker, and addresses his fellow workers, "Andronicus and Junia, who have shared my [Jewish] background and my imprisonment, highly distinguished apostles who came before me to Christ" (Rom 16:7). By the ninth century, it shocked misogynist-conditioned Christians that Junia, a woman, was called an apostle—so they marked a different accent on the word to change her into a man, Junias, though that name is attested nowhere else.[43] They also toned down the warm descriptions of women's place in Paul's ministry, as when he says that Euodia and Syntyche "strove alongside me (*synēthlēsan*) for the gospel" as "partners in my effort" (*synergoi*) at Philippians 4:2. In Romans 16, he greets ten women, including not only the apostle Junia but Mary, "a hard laborer" (*kopiousa*) for the church there—*kopiao* is the verb he uses of his own efforts for the gospel. Elizabeth Castelli notes that it has, for him, "a near-technical sense that refers to missionary work."[44]

Andronicus and Junia seem to be one of those missionary teams we hear of elsewhere—Prisca and Aquila, another team Paul worked with, were wife and husband, so Junia and Andronicus (both called apostles) were probably married as well.[45] There are five mission teams of two that have women in them—Prisca and Aquila (Rom 16:3), Andronicus and Junia (16:7), Philologus and Julia (16:15), Nereus and his sister (16:15), Euodia and Syntyche (Phil 4:2–3).[46] When Paul refers to Prisca and Aquila, he puts the wife's name first, which indicates the leader of the team (e.g., Barnabas and Paul, when Barnabas was the older apostle).[47] We are also told that Peter traveled with his wife (I Cor 9:5). Were those two a missionary team as well? Was Mrs. Peter an apostle? Can we entertain that idea, even as a possibility?

"Definitely not!" say the Pope's men (who would no doubt like to see Mrs. Peter lose her lodging in scripture at Mark 1:29–31 and I Corinthians 9:5). They can make this assertion on the basis of their two false equations: first, that the Twelve means the apostles, and second that apostle means priest. The Twelve are contrasted with the apostles by Paul (I Cor 15:5–7), though the Twelve were *also* apostles and (according to Matthew's gospel) learners ("disciples").[48] But these last two terms had a wider meaning than that of the Twelve, who were symbolic of the twelve tribes who will be judges in the eschatological time of trial.[49] The Twelve do not ordain any (nonexistent) New Testament priests. Paul was not commissioned by the Twelve. After his baptism by Ananias (not one of the Twelve), his only commission was from God and from the church at Antioch when it made him a fellow emissary (the literal meaning of apostle) to Jerusalem. The emissaries who went out from the churches were contrasted with those performing the internal functions of the household (prophecy, for instance, and instruction).

Since the basic early unit of the church, as it emerged from the synagogues, was the household, the presider over the communal meal there would be the house's host.[50] Or, often, hostess—like Phoebe in Cenchreae, who is Paul's fellow minister (*diakonos*) and "a leader (*prostatis*) to many, including myself."[51] Or Lydia at Philippi (Acts 16:14–15). Or Chloe in Corinth (I Cor 1:11). Or Appia in Philemon's city (Phlm 1:2). The synagogues denied women the right to speak or play a role in services. But when the church moved to households, women not only prophesied and led prayers (I Cor 11:4) but could be the "founding members" of the local churches.[52] When Prisca and Aquila welcomed Paul into their home, Prisca was the superior. Does that mean she was the "celebrant" of the communal meal (the agape feast)? No, but only because there was no one celebrant. The priesthood was of the whole body.

The multiple roles of the leaders seem to break down into two main groups—the teachers/prophets and the ministers/housekeepers. We tend to think of the former as the "real" ministry, the priestly one, and the latter as the work of "the good nuns" or of lay boards handling the finances of a parish. But what we today call sacramental life—communal

observances like the agape meal—were probably part of the housekeep-
ing side of the early communities. Paul's idea of teaching did not seem to
have much to do with sacramental administration. He says he baptized
few even in the church he established at Corinth (I Cor 1:14). "For
Christ did not send me to baptize but to bear the revelation" (I Cor
1:17). As Markus Barth demonstrates, there is no mention of anyone ef-
fecting Christian marriage in the early communities but the partners
themselves.[53] There is no reason to think these communal activities were
segregated by gender, any more than the teaching ones were. It is significant that women are called prophets, since that was a high office. It did
not mean a predictor of the future, but—in the line of ancient
prophets—one speaking by divine mandate to warn, rebuke, or comfort.[54] Prophets were especially good at rebuking authority. There were
apparently Theresa Kanes in the early church.

The daring equalities of the Christian assemblies—which got out of
hand in Corinth—led to the imposition of self-discipline, bringing them
into accord with "table codes" of the Hellenic world by the end of the
century, as we see in the post-Pauline "pastoral" letters—e.g., I Tim 2:8
(c. 90 CE?).[55] These restrictive epistles would later be cited as the role of
women was brought into accord with the world into which Christianity
was expanding.[56] A misogyny out of keeping with the original gospel was
absorbed by the church as it acquired new disciplines and structure. It is
rightly argued that the church had to develop new disciplines, and new
doctrines to support them, as it grew out of its informal and charismatic
early days. Fair enough. But two things should be observed. The Popes
have not said they were defending a development from the first situation,
but a literal (indeed, fundamentalist) confinement to that first situation—
that is, we must stay at just the level of the first choice of men by Jesus
to be his apostles. But if we actually look at that moment of the church's
life, we do not find priests at all, and we see women playing very active
roles in the informal ministry. The second thing to observe is that, no
matter what legitimate developments took place under the breathings of
the Spirit, we cannot impute to that Spirit the inhalation of misogynist
stains from the circumambient culture.

Yet that inhalation occurred. Thus began a long process of leaching
women out from the gospel story. Preaching and iconography would re-

duce or eliminate all but the most obtrusive presences (episodes like
those with the Samaritan, the woman with the hemorrhage, the prostitutes). The mass of women quietly following Jesus ("attending" him,
akolouthein) was shoved aside or shown only at the edge of a male coterie
close to the Lord. The Last Supper, for instance, has only males at table in
the many paintings of the event. It is significant that most of the great
frescoes and murals of the Last Supper were created for the refectories of
monasteries or chapter houses (e.g., Leonardo's) or for the side walls of
the church sanctuary (e.g., Tintoretto's famous series)—i.e., in male domains. Not only that, the men in the painting are only twelve in number—as if there were no other followers but they.

Actually, women were constant in their attendance on Jesus throughout his career and were the least likely to desert him as the crisis approached. They are censored out of the Last Suppers because they were
not worthy to be at the creation of the Mass—as they would be unworthy of celebrating it, or even approaching the altar on which it was celebrated, for centuries of Christian history. The women in Jesus' company
were not isolated behind a screen, or cloistered in their own company, a
group of proto-nuns. Nor were they virgins wandering loose in Palestine. They were no doubt married, like most of the disciples, including
the apostles. They were with their men in the upper room just before the
Pentecost event (Acts 1:14). But in the paintings they are magically swept
away before the descent of the Spirit at Pentecost. Only the Twelve—and
sometimes the Virgin Mary—are worthy to receive that charism.

Earlier, when the disciples were scattering in despair after Jesus' death,
a man fell in with two disciples going off to their home (Lk 24:15). They
stopped to eat at Emmaus. Only one of the two disciples is named, and
he is male. The natural supposition would be that his wife was the other.
But have you ever seen a picture of the supper at Emmaus that contains
a woman at table with the risen Jesus for the breaking of the bread? The
whole way of imagining the gospel has falsified women's role in the life
of Jesus and the founding of the church. The long working of poisonous
notions—of women's inferiority and impurity—has conditioned our
heritage in ways hard to trace and difficult to extrude. That is why the
ban on women priests matters. It is not so much that women are clam-
oring to become priests (especially as the priesthood currently exists), but

the perpetuation of this ban keeps alive the whole ideological substructure on which it is based. It is the last fierce bastion where the great Christian lie about women has entrenched itself. Pope Paul's Congregation said that whatever odd notions about women existed in the past had no real practical influence on the church's actions:

> It is true that in the writings of the Fathers one will find the undeniable influence of prejudices unfavorable to women but, nevertheless, it should be noted that these prejudices had hardly any influence on their pastoral activity, and still less on their spiritual direction.[57]

It is an odd thing for a Pope to say that doctrine—what one thinks—does not matter. This resembles the attitude of those who said that a belief in black inferiority did not lead Southerners to any real acts of injustice toward the blacks. It is like saying that holding Jews to be Christ-killers could not have contributed to pogroms, to persecution, to the Holocaust. Justice can never be done to women—or to anyone—until the injustices perpetrated against them are recognized as such. Those past injustices were not papal sins, since those who committed them—our thinkers like Albert the Great, our saints like Aquinas—did not realize they were doing wrong. But not to realize it now, when the evidence is so overwhelming, when the opportunities for redress are available—to perpetuate the wrongs to women as a way of maintaining that the church could not have erred in its treatment of women—that is the modern sin, and it is a papal sin. The structure upholding the legacy of wrong is not invincible ignorance but a cultivated innocence, *ignorantia affectata*.

[1]Jonathan Kwitny, *Man of the Century: The Life and Times of Pope John Paul II* (Henry Holt and Company, 1997), p. 340.

[2]For Junia see note 3.

[3]Congregation for the Doctrine of the Faith, *Inter Insigniores*, 1977, paragraph 27, in Leonard and Arlene Swidler (editors), *Women Priests: A Catholic Commentary on the Vatican Declaration* (Paulist Press, 1977), pp. 43–44.

[4]*Inter Insigniores*, paragraph 32 (p. 45).

[5]Dorothy Irwin, "Omnis Analogia Claudet," in Swidlers, op. cit., pp. 271–77.

[6]Carroll Stuhmueller, "Bridegroom: A Biblical Symbol of Union, Not Separation," ibid., pp. 278–83.

[7]Leonard Swidler, "Roma Locuta, Causa Finita?" ibid., p. 3.

[8]Kwitny, op. cit., p. 637.

[9]Peter Hebblethwaite, *Paul VI: The First Modern Pope* (Paulist Press, 1993), p. 667.

[10]John Paul II, *On Reserving Priestly Ordination to Men Alone (Sacerdotalis Ordinatio)*, Vatican translation (Pauline Books, 1997), p. 7.

[11]Peter Hebblethwaite, *Pope John Paul and the Church* (Sheed and Ward, 1995), pp. 276–78; Kwitny, op. cit., pp. 666–67.

[12]Bonaventure, *Commentary on the Sentences* IV, distinction 25, article 2, question 1.

[13]John Duns Scotus, *Commentary on the Sentences* IV, distinction 25, article 2, question 2.

[14]Aristotle, *Animal Conception (De Generatione Animalium)* 766–68. See Lesley Dean-Jones, *Women's Bodies in Classical Greek Science* (Oxford University Press, 1994), pp. 176–99.

[15]Aristotle, op. cit., 775a.

[16]Aristotle, *Animal Investigations (De Historia Animalium)* 68a11–12.

[17]John Chrysostom, *De Sacerdotio* 2.2 (PG 48.633).

[18]Emanuela Prinzivalli, "Donna e generazione nei Padri della Chiesa," in Umberto Mattioli (editor), *La donna nel pensiero cristiano antico* (Marietti [Genoa], 1992), pp. 79–94.

[19]Clement, *The Educator (Paedagogus)* 2.33 (PG 8.430).

[20]Tertullian, *Female Fashions (De Cultu Feminarum)* 1.1 (PL 1.1418).

[21]Aristotle, *Animal Investigations (De Historia Animalium)* 572. See classical passages cited in R. A. B. Mynors, *Virgil, Georgics* (Oxford University Press, 1990), p. 224.

[22]Soranus, *Gynecology* 3.3.

[23]Peter Brown, *The Body and Society: Men, Women and Sexual Renunciation in Early Christianity* (Columbia University Press, 1988), pp. 150, 153.

[24]Albertus Magnus, *Commentary on Aristotle's "Animals"* 15, q. 11, cited in Uta Ranke-Heinemann, *Eunuchs for the Kingdom of Heaven* (Penguin Books, 1990), p. 108.

[25]Jerome and Ambrose in the West, Basil and Gregory of Nyssa in the East, all say that the heroic virgin becomes a kind of honorary man—see Haye van der Meer, S.J., *Women Priests in the Catholic Church? A Theological-Historical Investigation*, translated by Arlene and Leonard Swidler (Temple University Press, 1973), pp. 78–80, and Susanna Elm, *"Virgins of God": The Making of Asceticism in Late Antiquity* (Oxford University Press, 1994), pp. 91, 101, 120–21, 134.

[26]Yves Congar, O.P., *Priest and Layman*, translated by P. J. Hepburne-Scott (Darton, Longman & Todd, 1966), pp. 74–75.

[27]Edward Schillebeeckx, *The Church With a Human Face* (Crossroad, 1988), pp. 240–44.

[28]Jerome, *Epistle 48.15*; Origen, *Commentary on Ezechial*, Chapter 7.

[29]Peter Damian, *On the Dignity of the Priesthood*, cited in Ranke-Heinemann, op. cit., p. 108.

[30]Jacob Milgrom, *Leviticus 1–16* (AB, 1991), pp. 948–53.

[31]The rabbinical literature has some even harsher things to say about women. The Talmud bShabbath 152a says: "A woman is a pitcher full of filth, with its mouth full of blood, yet all run after her." Cited in Leonard Swidler, *Biblical Affirmations of Woman* (Westminster Press, 1979), p. 156.

[32]Van der Meer, op. cit., p. 92.

[33]Ibid., p. 95.

[34]Sacred Congregation for the Sacraments and Divine Worship, *Instruction Concerning Worship of the Eucharistic Mystery (Inestimabile Donum)*, confirmed by His Holiness Pope John Paul II, Vatican translation, paragraph 18 (Pauline Press, 1994), p. 8.

[35]Raymond E. Brown, S.S., *Biblical Reflections on Crises Facing the Church* (Paulist Press, 1975), pp. 53–54.

[36]Gal 3:26–28. Scholars isolate this as a hymn on the basis of its verse form and parallels in other parts of the New Testament. J. Louis Martyn, *Galatians* (AB, 1997), pp. 374–83.

[37]Ben Witherington III, *Women in the Ministry of Jesus* (Cambridge University Press, 1984), p. 117.

[38]Vincent Taylor, *The Gospel According to St. Mark* (Macmillan, 1966), p. 290. See Barbara E. Reid, *Choosing the Better Part?* (The Liturgical Press, 1996), pp. 135–43, and Elaine J. Lawless, "The Issue of Blood," in Beverly Mayne Kienzle and Pamela J. Walker (editors), *Women Preachers and Prophets Through Two Millennia of Christianity* (University of California Press, 1998), pp. 1–18.

[39]Karl P. Dornfried, "Mary in the Gospel of Matthew," in Raymond E. Brown et al., *Mary in the New Testament* (Fortress Press, 1978), pp. 77–83.

[40]I Cor 12:8–30, Rom 12: 6–8, Eph 4: 11. These kinds of leaders are listed and discussed by Wayne A. Meeks, *The First Urban Christians: The Social World of the Apostle Paul* (Yale University Press, 1983), pp. 131–36.

[41]Ibid., pp. 134–39.

[42]Arlo J. Nau, *Peter in Matthew: Discipleship, Diplomacy, and Dispraise* (The Liturgical Press, 1992).

[43]Joseph A. Fitzmyer, *Romans* (AB 33, 1993), pp. 737–38. Peter Lampe, "Andronicus" (ABD 1.248–49) and "Junias" (ABD 3.1127).

[44]For instance, at II Cor 6:5, Ph 2:16. Elizabeth A. Castelli, "Paul on Women and Gender," in Ross Shepard Kraemer and Mary Rose D'Angelo (editors), *Women and Christian Origins* (Oxford University Press, 1999), p. 225.

[45]Reflecting the practice of the church he wrote for, Mark (6:7) has Jesus send out missionaries "by twos." There was Jewish precedent for this according to Joachim Jeremias, "Paarweise Sendung im Neuen Testament," in A. J. B. Higgins (editor), *New Testament Essays* (Manchester University Press, 1959), pp. 136–41.

[46]On the teams, see Margaret Y. MacDonald, "Reading Real Women Through the Undisputed Letters of Paul," in Kraemer and D'Angelo, op. cit., pp. 204–7.

[47]Peter Lampe, "Prisca" (ABD 5.467–68) and "Aquila" (ABD 1.31920).

[48]Raymond F. Collins, "Twelve" (ABD 6.670–71).

[49]Ibid., p. 671.

[50]Meeks, op. cit., pp. 75–80.

[51]On Phoebe (Rom 16:1–2), see Fitzmyer, op. cit., p. 731.

[52]Ben Witherington III, "Lydia" (ABD 4.422–23).

[53]Markus Barth, *Ephesians 4–6* (AB 34a, 1974), pp. 774–53.

[54]M. Eugene Boring, "Early Christian Prophecy" (ABD 5.495–502).

[55]Kathleen E. Corley shows how the pressures to conform to Hellenistic table codes are registered in the gospels written in the period of the pastoral epistles (post-80 CE): *Private Women, Public Meals: Social Conflict in the Synoptic Tradition* (Hendrickson Publishers, 1993).

[56]There is one intrusion of the later conduct codes (Haustafeln) in the genuine letters of Paul, the command that women keep silent in the gatherings (I Cor 14:33–36). Since this clashes with Paul's own words in the same epistle urging women to be veiled *while they prophesy and pray publicly*, many have suspected there is an interpolation here to bring Paul into accord with the pastoral epistles. But William E. Orr and James Arthur Walther, among others, argue that Paul is referring to some specific abuse in the embattled Corinthian situation, one that involved bringing marital disputes into the gathering. See Orr and Walther, *I Corinthians*, AB 32 (1976), pp. 311–13. Also, to similar effect, Ben Witherington III, *Women in the Earliest Churches* (Cambridge University Press, 1988), pp. 90–104.

[57]*Inter Insigniores*, paragraph 6 (p. 38).

8.

The Pope's Eunuchs

Pope Paul VI intervened in the Second Vatican Council to affect its deliberations on the family with his "adjustments" (*modi*) on contraception. The Council fathers were able to water down those suggestions. Paul had taken no such chances, earlier in the fourth session, on the question whether Catholic priests should be allowed to marry. On October 12, 1965, *Le Monde* published the leaked draft of a speech by Bishop Koop of Brazil, in which Koop planned to ask the Council to allow married priests to supplement the short supply of clergy for his people. This was just one of many such requests being prepared, or so the staff of the Vatican feared. Therefore, one day before *Le Monde* could get its story into print, the Council was stunned by a letter addressed to it by Pope Paul and read aloud before the assembled fathers. In the letter the Pope said he did not want to take away the Council's freedom to deliberate under the guidance of the Holy Spirit—and then he did just that:

> We have learned that certain Fathers intend to discuss the law of ecclesiastical celibacy in the Council as it is observed in the Latin Church. Therefore, without infringing in any way on the right of the Fathers to express themselves, we make known to you our personal opinion which is, that it is not opportune to have a public discussion of this topic, which demands so much prudence and is so important. [So the Council cannot exercise prudence or deal with important things?] We not only intend to maintain this ancient, holy and providential law to the extent of our ability, but also to reinforce its observance, calling on all priests of the Latin Church to

recognize anew the causes and reasons why this law must be considered most appropriate today, especially today, in helping priests to
consecrate all their love completely and generously to Christ in the
service of the Church and of souls. If any Father wishes to speak
about this matter, he may do so in writing by submitting his observations to the Council Presidency which will transmit them to us.[1]

In other words: "If you want to speak, don't—write it down and give it
over for the Pope's perusal only."

Father Murphy, writing as "Xavier Rynne" in *The New Yorker*, passed
on this information:

According to René Laurentin [writing in *Le Figaro*], the problem of
a married clergy for Latin America and other areas, along the lines
of the Eastern discipline, had been before the Holy See since the
days of Pope Pius X, but the Roman authorities had always felt that
any concession here would inevitably lead to reconsideration of the
status of those living in clerical concubinage in Italy and other
countries, estimated variously in the thousands, and this they were
not prepared to face.[2]

That was the real danger, according to Murphy. If the missions were allowed to have married priests, as the Eastern churches recognized by
Rome were, then priests all over the world would want to marry their
mistresses. The dam would break. The line must be held, even though this
made nonsense of the claim that priestly celibacy is freely chosen and not
imposed.

Vatican anxiety on this subject was indirectly confirmed by a spokesman for the papal secretariat of state, Monsignor Paul Poupard, who tried
to explain the Pope's action this way:

Their motive [that of Curia members asking the Pope to close off
discussion] was the fear of allowing the public appearance of division which would have serious consequences for priests who were
rather shaky [Poupard was speaking in French, and used the words
souvent fragiles]; and also the fear that, in view of the pressure from

the mass media, their [the fathers'] interventions on this subject would not be free.[3]

The Pope, in other words, was not taking away their freedom—the press was. It might report on the discussions, and therefore there could be no discussion. (The press was reporting, quite successfully, on all other matters. If this rule applied across the board, the Council would have to be sent packing.) The idea that priests' own commitment to celibacy could not survive public discussion of it was also a sign of anxiety verging on panic. Poupard was undoubtedly right when he said that the papacy feared "the appearance of division." That is the source of much if not most of the deceptiveness of the office.

The Pope assured those around him that he would solve the problem by writing an encyclical on it. That was to be the solution on contraception, too. It is the regular way the modern papacy has compounded its problems. A dubious heritage is fumbled at in a first document or discussion. Paul VI says he will remedy things with a papal statement, which proves a disaster. Then John Paul nails the worst aspects of the encyclical into place, unbudgeable. We have seen this sequence on the subjects of contraception and women priests. Something similar occurred on the Holocaust, except that Paul VI did not intervene between the Council's statement and John Paul's *We Remember*. Now we shall see the same process running its familiar course on the problem of celibacy.

Paul released his encyclical, *Priestly Celibacy (Sacerdotalis Caelibatus)*, on June 12, 1967. His difficulty here was even greater than it would be in his contraception encyclical, *Humanae Vitae* (1968). There, at least, he could appeal to a steady record of condemnation (though for differing reasons) across the history of the church. But in early centuries of Christianity in the Western church, and up to this minute in the Eastern churches, priests were allowed to marry. That also meant that Paul's problem was greater than his Congregation would face in the document against women's ordination, *Inter Insigniores* (1976). Paul, when it came to endorsing that product of his Curia, could fall back on biblical fundamentalism, on the fact that the apostles were male. Now he must cope with the fact that the apostles were also married.

The importance of this problem can be seen in the most glaring omission from *Sacerdotalis Caelibatus*. If you look at its footnotes, you find a continual stream of citations from the New Testament. But only three places in the New Testament directly address the subject of this encyclical. Two of them are cited, not quoted, in a single footnote of the encyclical.[4] The third, the most relevant, is nowhere even mentioned. The first two say this: "A bishop must be irreproachable, the husband of only one wife" (I Tim 3:2), and "[a presbyter should be] a man unimpeachable, the husband of only one wife, with children of the faith" (Tit 1:7). When it serves its purpose, the Vatican equates the New Testament word "presbyter" with priest.

But the third passage is the one that of itself should have precluded Paul VI's trying to write this encyclical in the first place. Saint Paul (the Pope's namesake, to whom he felt a special devotion) is telling the Corinthians that he has not imposed on them—in fact, he has not even claimed all his rights "as an apostle." He says to them: "Have I not the right [*exousia*] to take a Christian wife about with me, like the rest of the apostles and the Lord's brothers, and Stone [Cephas]?"[5] The Pope would naturally be reluctant to quote anything reminding people that Peter (his putative forebear and model) was married. But the point truly embarrassing to his argument is that word *exousia* (prerogative, or power). This is not a matter of permission or mere concession given to the apostles. It is a *right* that Paul possessed without exercising and Peter (Cephas) possessed and exercised—part of what Paul goes on to call "the right given me by my preaching" (I Cor 9:18). If that was an apostolic prerogative, what right has anyone later to take away the right? Omission of this most relevant text, just because it is inconveniencing, is an example of the intellectual dishonesty this book is studying.

Those three New Testament passages, the hardest ones for the Pope, the encyclical must scant. It prefers to dwell on two others that have nothing to do with ministry or the priesthood. His favorite passage, cited four separate times, is the reference to eunuchs (Mt 19:11–12). In Matthew's gospel, Jesus has just forbidden divorce, which prompts the disciples to say, "If this is the rule for husband and wife, better not marry at all" (verse 10). Jesus says that it is not so easy. If you do not marry, you must live as a eunuch, since fornication is also forbidden by the law. That is the logic connecting their objection with what he says next. He puts the matter provocatively, since the eunuch was ignoble or even repulsive. A man born as a eunuch, even into the priestly (Levite) tribe, could never be a Jewish priest—deformity was an impurity, and procreation was a man's duty and pride. So why would one *choose* an impurity, and defy family duty?

The words should be translated to bring out their shocking nature, in which the words "eunuch" or "eunuchize" are almost cruelly dwelt on five times in one verse: "Some of the sexually maimed come out of their mother's womb that way, and others are sexually maimed by men who sexually maim them, and still others are sexually maimed because they sexually maim themselves for the heavenly reign. If a man can yield to this, let him yield to it." The verb for yield (*chorein*) is literally "clear space for it." It was used of armies falling back from assault. Jesus' words attack a man's pride and integrity. It is typical of our softening translations that even this passage has lost its rebarbative nature in its reading from the pulpit. The passage itself would seem an *attack* on eunuchizing except for the final words about the heavenly reign (*basileia*) for whose arrival we pray in the second petition of the Paternoster.

> The structure of this saying on eunuchs from a Jewish perspective proceeds from least objectionable (eunuchs by nature) to more objectionable (man-made eunuchs whether by crime or as punishment for a crime), to most objectionable (self-made eunuchs). The saying builds to a climax, and the third group of eunuchs is marked in a special way from the other two groups. When Jesus says, "The one who is able to accept this," he implies that his words are addressed to those who have an option, unlike the eunuchs of verse 12a and 12b.[6]

Why would Jesus be so sensationalistic in this verse? He speaks elsewhere of maiming or mutilation: "I tell you anyone who looks at a woman with lust for her has at that point (*ēdē*) debauched her in his heart. And if your eye makes you stumble, dig it out and fling it away" (Mt 28–29). Here, too, the language is harsh and extreme—to treat as an adulteress is to debauch. He goes on to say that if a sin is committed with the (ritually favored and therefore precious) right hand, you must chop it off (*ekkoptō*, verse 30). If priests were legally bound to this as the Pope now binds them to the eunuch passage, a number of them might have to go without their blessing and consecrating right hands.

These passages belong to that body of sayings that proclaims a transvaluation of all values at the arrival of the reign (*basileia*) of God. Thus we hear of a disciple having to hate his father and mother (Lk 14:25), just as Jesus refuses to acknowledge his mother (Mk 3:33). We hear you must give a bandit the things he forgot to ask for (Lk 6:29). The Vatican tries to soften most of these "hard sayings" by calling them counsels of perfection rather than commandments of obligation—but it is precisely as a mark of "perfection" that hating one's parents would be most revolting as a moral ideal. Unless Jesus was talking here about the clean break with the past order, in provocative symbols, he was talking nonsense. But Pope Paul wants to take one of these mysterious eschatological signs—the sign of the eunuch—and make it a law for ministers of the gospel. (Church teachers have even tried to use the eunuch passage to justify nuns' virginity, though women cannot be eunuchized, that word whose ugly reality Jesus stressed.) Why does the Pope not put it into canon law that priests must hate their fathers and mothers?

Whatever the eunuch passage means, it cannot refer to the ministry. It is not addressed to any *class* or group, not even to disciples at large, but to individuals who can "yield" to this strange charismatic calling. The proof that this has nothing to do with ministry is that the apostles did not "yield to it." They were married. That in itself shows that the gospel makes no connection of Matthew 19:11–12 with the ministry—much less with the priesthood, which does not even exist in the gospel accounts. Whatever else the apostles were, they were clearly not eunuchs for heaven's reign. Yet this is the main text the Pope relies on to establish a scriptural basis for priestly celibacy. He cites it four times, after refusing to cite at all the one New Testament passage that has most to do with the idea of apostleship and marriage (I Cor 9:5).[7] This parody of exegesis shows a profound disrespect for the revealed word itself. New Testament passages are twisted, omitted, extended, distorted, perverted to make them mean whatever the Pope wants them to mean.

Such a procedure poses a severe test to any priest's intellectual integrity. Is he meekly to accept a ludicrous and compromising argument? Is he to live by it as if it were the real meaning of the gospel he is serving? Is he to pass it on to his congregation with a straight face? Is he to ask *them* to swallow anything—even disrespect for the Bible—in the name of respect for the papacy? Is he to become a eunuch, not for the heavenly reign, but for the Pope's dominion? Popes in the past had their castrati, convenient for singing in the Sistine choir. Is he now to have a guard of eunuchs meant to show that papal teaching was right on the subject of celibacy, no matter what scripture says? As we have seen, he turned even the Council's bishops into intellectual eunuchs when he said that they could not question the celibacy ordinances, they must wait for his pronouncement—and then, when the pronouncement comes, it is this shabby raid on the Bible.

It was said above that he had two main passages in scripture that he preferred, to the exclusion of the truly relevant ones. Beyond the eunuch text, cited four times, there is another passage, cited three times: Paul's argument in the seventh chapter of I Corinthians (verses 7–40) that he would prefer for all those who are unmarried to remain unmarried, like him. Since Paul was a zealous Pharisee before his call from Christ, and a mature man by then, it is presumed that he was married, as was expected of his sect. That means that his wife must have been dead, or otherwise separated from him, by the time of this letter. Clement of Alexandria (second century) was followed by others in thinking that Paul's wife was alive, but in agreed-on separation from him, during his apostolate.[8] In the earliest church, the normal expectation was that a man would be married. Celibacy was the odd thing that needed explaining. That is why Paul is so cautious and undemanding as he recommends a course that the other apostles did not follow. After all, he could not take away what he calls their right to marry in a later part of this very letter (9.6). Everything he says is therefore hedged and deferential. He semi-retracts his statements even as he makes them:

I give this as a recommendation, not a directive: I prefer that all men be as I am. But each has his own spiritual gift from God, so one will act this way, another that way (7:6–7).

This is I speaking, not the Lord (7:12).

I have received from the Lord no requirement concerning virgins, but I offer my opinion as one in a position of trust by the mercy of the Lord (7:25).

I suppose (*nomizō*), then, that it is a good thing in this imminent crisis, that it is good, for a man to remain in the same condition [neither to dissolve a marriage nor to undertake one] (7:26).

I say this for your benefit, not to tie you in a rope (7:35).

This is just my opinion, though even I have the spirit of God, too (8:40).

Paul cannot say often enough that *this is not a rule*. It is not a rule from God. It is not even a rule (as opposed to an opinion) from Paul. Others have different charisms. Other apostles *are* married. He grants their opinion and gift. He offers a variant position for consideration. He presents it not as a demand (6) but as a "benefit" (35). He argues for it on practical grounds (to face an "imminent crisis" without distraction). This is a matter of prudential judgment, open to debate, not a revelation or obligation or exaction.

William Orr and James Walther, in their comment on verse 25, say:

> It is clear that Paul does not think that the Spirit had bestowed upon the church the creative power to produce ad hoc sayings of Jesus to fit the situation in the life of the church—as is sometimes assumed in modern scholarship . . . If any early Christian prophet or enthusiast would have been so empowered, certainly Paul would have been.[9]

Paul had many directives from the Lord, and he was not hesitant to announce their origin. In this very chapter, when he is speaking of marital fidelity, he says, "I bring this proclamation, not I, but the Lord" (7:10). But he knew the difference between such directives and his own opinion. Pope Paul does not have such scruples. When he prefers that "others be as I am," he enforces it as a divine command. He presumes to have more authority than his namesake.

Even if Paul's recommendation were to be read as a requirement, it was not addressed specifically to ministers of the gospel but to everyone in Corinth. He is saying that he wishes everybody to stay married or to stay unmarried. This is an important point, because the Pope uses one of Paul's practical arguments for celibacy as applying specifically to priests—

that it frees them to be more attentive to the church's affairs than to a family. But this is not offered by Paul as a *clerical* code. It is for all the people in Corinth:

> I prefer you to have no worries. The unmarried man worries only about the Lord's affairs, how he may please the Lord. But the married man worries about worldly affairs, how he may please his wife. And he is torn apart. As for the woman, both the unmarried and the virgin, she worries about the Lord's affairs, how she may be consecrated in body as well as spirit. But the married woman is worried about the worldly affairs, how she may please her husband. I say this for your benefit, not to tie you in a rope (7:32–35).

In making his tentative suggestion that others be like him, Paul is certainly not offering a profound theology of marriage. For that we must look to Ephesians 5:9–6:9, whether that is by Paul (as Markus Barth argues) or by a brilliant Pauline thinker. Here there is a more pragmatic consideration of a specific situation (the imminent crisis). This time of stress makes Paul call on everyone to hold his or her current station, which is almost a battle station. He says, for instance, that slaves should remain slaves right after saying that the married and unmarried should hold to their condition (7:21). This is an intimate part of the argument—yet Pope Paul does not import the priesthood into *this* verse, saying that priests should be either slave or free according to their past condition. We shall have to consider later whether lack of a family actually makes a priest more free. But here Paul's argument is meant to apply, not to priests (who did not yet exist) but to everybody, and it is not applied to them today. We do not tell teenagers, "If you are still unmarried, stay that way." The situation has changed for Christians in general. The whole argument is, therefore, inapplicable.

Though he has only these two main passages to rely on in a serious way, the Pope cites peripherally some other places in the New Testament, as if they could lend support to his shaky position—e.g., Christ's call to disciples to leave all and follow him (not directed to ministers specifically but to all disciples—and, besides, the apostles did not leave their wives), or the saying in Matthew's gospel that there will be no marriages in heaven (but priests are on earth with the rest of us). He also makes a general appeal to the New Testament, not tied to any one passage, by saying that priests should resemble Christ, and since he was a virgin they should be too.[10] This is like his argument that women cannot be priests because they do not look like Christ. The symbolism of Christ's virginity is a subject to be taken up later. All that need be said here is that the imitation of Christ, so far as that is proposed in essentials (not accidentals), is a gospel call to all Christians, not in any exclusive way to gospel ministers. If it were tied specifically to the ministry, in the Pope's concentration on Christ's virginity, then the apostles would have had to be virgins.

But, of course, this whole charade of scriptural appeal is not what Paul VI is really interested in. He is concerned with the long practice of the church (at least of the Western church, at least in Christianity's second millenium). He wants to assure others that the church cannot have been wrong here, any more than it could have been wrong on the Jews, or contraception, or women priests. But it *was* wrong on those, and if we turn, in the next chapter, to the actual practice Paul is defending, we shall see that it was wrong on this point as well.

---

[1] "Xavier Rynne," *Vatican Council II* (Farrar, Straus and Giroux, 1968), p. 520.

[2] Ibid., p. 521.

[3] Peter Hebblethwaite, *Paul VI: The First Modern Pope* (Paulist Press, 1993), p. 442.

[4] Paul VI, *The Celibacy of the Priest (Sacerdotalis Caelibatus)*, Vatican translation, papal website, footnote 2.

[5] I Cor 9:6. The text says literally "a sister wife," where the sisters and brothers of the Christian brotherhood are meant. (Not all the apostles could have had actual sisters with them, and would not have passed them off as wives.) The wife of an apostle must be one of the fold, as the elders' children must be "of the faith" at Titus 1:7. I use here the translation of the New English Bible. Cephas is normally translated "rock" in English, but Peter is the foundation of the church (Mt 16:18)—we do not say the foundation rock.

[6] Ben Witherington III, *Women in the Ministry of Jesus* (Cambridge University Press, 1984), p. 31.

[7] The four citations are at *Sacerdotalis Caelibatus*, footnotes 2, 5, 35, 36.

[8] Eusebius, *History of the Church*, 3.39.1. For Paul's marriage, see Jerome Murphy-O'Connor, O.P., *Paul, A Critical Life* (Oxford University Press, 1996), pp. 62–65 and Joseph A. Fitzmyer, S.J., *Jerome Biblical Commentary* (Prentice-Hall, 1968), Vol. 2, pp. 217–18.

[9] William F. Orr and James Arthur Walther, *I Corinthians* (AB 32, 1976), p. 218.

[10] Lk 18:19–30 (cited in *Sacerdotalis Caelibatus*, footnote 33); Mt 2:30 (cited in footnote 66).

9.

Priestly Caste

aul VI's encyclical on celibacy admits that priests were married in the early church, but says that later experience, under the guidance of the Holy Spirit, led to "a deeper penetration of spiritual things."[1] He admits that it took some time for experience to show the spiritual wisdom of priestly celibacy. The church began to pass serious legislation on the matter only in the fourth century, and even then there was wide disagreement on the policy and practice of marriage among bishops and priests. Late in the fourth century, Augustine is still in friendly correspondence with a married bishop, Memor of Capua, giving him advice on the education of his son, who also became a married bishop, and whose wife was the daughter of a bishop. The saintly Paulinus of Nola wrote a wedding hymn for that son and hoped that there would be a long line of bishops in the heirs of such pious families.[2]

Since priests and bishops were already married in the fourth century, there was no question of declaring such marriages invalid. Some argued that it would be immoral to put away a wife taken in good conscience according to longstanding church practice. The first efforts at celibacy were, therefore, legislation to prevent priests from having intercourse with their wives, either before celebration of the Eucharist, or when they were promoted to bishop or after the birth of an heir. Only much later (in the twelfth century) would clerical marriages themselves be declared invalid.[3]

The grounds for male celibacy were like those for female exclusion from the ministry—a requirement of ritual purity modeled on that of the Levitical priesthood. Ambrose said that priests who continued having intercourse "pray for others with unclean minds as well as unclean bodies."[4] Saint Peter Damian said that since a virgin brought forth Jesus as a baby, only virgins should bring him forth on the altar in the Eucharist.[5] This remained the rationale for priestly celibacy until this century. In 1054, Cardinal Humbert, Pope Leo IX's delegate to Byzantium, condemned the Eastern churches for allowing priests to marry:

> Young husbands, just now exhausted from carnal lust, serve the altar. And immediately afterward they again embrace their wives with hands that have been hallowed by the immaculate Body of Christ. That is not the mark of a true faith, but an invention of Satan.[6]

Pope Innocent II declared at the Synod of Clermont in 1130: "Since priests are supposed to be God's temples, vessels of the Lord and sanctuaries of the Holy Spirit . . . it offends their dignity to lie in the conjugal bed and live in impurity."[7] So strong was this tradition of ritual purity that Edward Schillebeeckx, a specialist on church documents, says that the Matthew passage on eunuchs (19:11) was never officially cited as a reason for celibacy until the Second Vatican Council, when it was rushed in to take the place of the untenable old argument from Leviticus. Why did it take four centuries for celibacy to become a major concern?

A little historical empathy makes the development look more sensible than it would at first glance appear. The fourth century was a time of tremendous upheaval. The Emperor Constantine made Christianity the recognized religion of the empire after his conversion in 312—which might seem a solution to the problems of a church intermittently persecuted in its early days. But the immediately post-Constantinian time was a period of stressful growth for Christianity, which was torn by heresies, unsure of its own internal authorities, and launched on a new course of make-or-break ascetical adventures. At the very moment when Christianity seemed to have won worldly success, the spiritual leadership of that church became dramatically and intransigently otherworldly. While previously unexpected order was being imposed from the top down by Constantine—who ran church councils as his political right, broke heresies, and installed bishops—a different kind of authority was surging up from below, to heady acclaim from ordinary people. Priests and bishops were caught between these totally different impulses. If they aligned themselves too simply with one of the two dynamics, they could suffer defeat from the other. An imperial discipline derived from the Roman state could leave them open to charges of corruption in the eyes of the purists of the desert communities. On the other hand, an alignment with the unruly monks and mystics of Syria could lead to Roman repression, to a bishop's loss of patronage, including his revenues and his see itself.

We can see different stages of this struggle when Athanasius of Alexandria hid among the desert communities while on the run from the imperial police in the 360s.[8] Another stage was marked when Theophilus of Alexandria and John Chrysostom of Constantinople used a band of insurgent monks as pawns in their own power game, bargaining for the best way to present the treatment of them to the emperor in the early fifth century.[9] These are just two better-known cases of the problem posed to bishops by the adventurous ascetics at the time of their greatest popular appeal. The authorities did not know how to deal with people who were outside the normal parish structure, and who felt that they were too pure themselves to submit to compromising clerics who were married, or tainted by political power, or so far below them in the Lord's favor that to move down toward them rather than farther up toward God was to betray the ascetic calling itself.

The man who has made it possible for us modern folk to understand the extraordinary power of the ascetics of the fourth and fifth centuries is Peter Brown. In his *The Body and Society* (1988) and other works, he has described how these daring souls commandeered the imagination of their time. They were the astronauts of a spiritual space haunted by demons, people who tortured themselves into an entirely new state of being.[10] David Brakke has compared them to those "technicians of the self" conceived by Michel Foucault, men who make of their own bodies and psyches the laboratories of a new anthropological era.[11] Their celebrity, earned paradoxically far off the ancient urban map, drew crowds to them for adulation and consultation, for the aura of wisdom that no longer shone upon mere priests or politicians. The difference in moral authority between priests and ascetics can be seen from this: Gregory Nazianzus later denounced his own Christian parents for persuading him to renounce ascetic life to become a priest.[12] John Chrysostom only became a priest after his health broke in the desert, forcing him to give up the ascetic life.[13]

One way to reduce the gap between priestly and ascetic authority was for the priests to imitate the ascetics, trying to regain lost ground by becoming celibate themselves, by fasting in the city as well as in the desert. An even quicker solution might be to co-opt the ascetics, making them priests or bishops, so people could not so easily contrast the two orders to the detriment of the priests. But the desert saints resisted this tactic. To leave the desert, to give up the utopian egalitarianism of the monasteries or the splendid isolation of the hermitages, would be a descent to the ordinary after the long struggle up onto rarified heights. It would, in Gregory Nazianzus's words, be a surrender of the ascetic's dangerous glamour for "the drudging commerce in souls."[14] Athanasius had to beg the desert stars to become bishops, and he sometimes failed.[15] When the famous monk Ammonius was summoned to take on his duty as a bishop, he sent back his left ear, and threatened to send his tongue if asked again—thus disqualifying himself for ordination.[16]

Consecrated female virgins were also a potential power in the fourth century, as the Arians proved by giving them teachers who recruited them for the conflict with orthodox trinitarians like Athanasius.[17] Athanasius responded in his own see of Alexandria by creating a body of writings that proved from scripture that women must be docile, unlearned, and sequestered.[18] He could not use that approach to the male heroes of the desert. He wooed them instead with campaigns to integrate them into the life of the laity and parish churches, curbing their penitential excesses with scriptural arguments, encouraging them to be politically active (but on his side), and subtly reshaping the image of their great symbolic leader, Saint Antony.

Athanasius's *Life of Antony* is one of the spiritual classics. It would play a role in Augustine's conversion. It helped to spread the monastic ideal. But Athanasius inflated the reputation of the saint while reducing his prickly individuality to manageable dimensions. He played down, for instance, the learning that Antony displays in his surviving letters, making him a docile follower of Athanasius in his own attacks on the learned pretensions of Arians.[19] In the biography, Antony is made to tell Neoplatonist philosophers:

> We Christians acquire secret wisdom not by skill in Greek arguments but by the power of faith dispensed to us through Jesus Christ . . . You cannot by your verbal enticings halt the advance of Christ's teaching, whereas we, by calling on the crucified Christ, can disperse those demons you revere as gods. Through the symbol of the cross, your magic becomes impotent, your potions ineffectual.[20]

The power of the ascetic came through prayer, which worked miracles. Athanasius, even while celebrating this cleansing holiness, had to control it. In a typical contest between charismatic and institutional leadership, he won the contest by not claiming a total victory for his side. Instead, he relativized the differences between the two groups. Sometimes, he said, even bishops work miracles.[21] And sometimes, by his careful promptings, even monks can submit to organizational disciplines. He made the monks more ecclesial and the priests more ascetical. This was an important step along the path to an entirely celibate priesthood. After all, some monks had refused to take the Eucharist from bishops they considered too worldly.[22] One remedy for that was to make the priests more ritually pure.

What gave the ascetics their renown, as Peter Brown emphasizes, was the perception of their spiritual powers—to heal, to foresee, to exorcise, to defy the devil.[23] Athanasius could not compete in this arena, miracle by miracle, but he could emphasize what power the priest had and the ascetic did not—the miraculous power to consecrate bread and wine and make it become the Lord. "Monks participated in the unity through receiving the sacraments at the hands of the bishops."[24] By using this maneuver, Athanasius helped promote the idea of the priest as a person whose power resides in his eucharistic consecration. The Eucharist was Athanasius's trump card. If the monks would not be ordained themselves, they remained dependent on the bishops for "the celebration of Lent and Easter, because the Christian Pasch was an epitome of the Christian life," no matter what other rites the ascetics could invent.[25] Spiritual power surged up from below in the monks' triumphs over the body. But another kind of power struck from above, like lightning, and was distributed out through the consecrating hands of priests. This view would help along the tendency to focus authority at the top of the hierarchic structure, where the power to ordain channeled power to consecrate out among the priests. In time this power to consecrate would be seen as the essence of the priesthood. For many it still is. Paul VI speaks in his encyclical of "the ministry of the Eucharist, in which the whole spiritual good of the Church is contained."[26]

The danger of such an approach is that it separates the priest from the community whose joint meal was the original condition of the Eucharist. We see that in the way the priest eventually began to celebrate the Eucharist by himself—after all, what really mattered was just his consecration of the sacred elements. Everything else could be dispensed with. This one power of the priest was the source of awe he could elicit from the faithful; it became a kind of magic potency. Folk legend among Catholics told of weird uses the power could be put to. We heard such stories from the nuns. A fallen priest had only to pronounce the magic words over a bakery window, and all the bread would be turned to the Lord—so a pious priest would have to eat every last crumb in order to prevent others from desecrating the Lord's body. If a hurried communicant leaves the church with the Lord's body still undigested in him, an acolyte hurries along with a lighted candle to show that the Lord is still present.

When I was young I used to serve a private Mass for a priest who was either so scrupulous or so pious that when he came to the purported words of consecration he sounded out each consonant and vowel separately, as if making sure the magic formula was given all its force: *"Hoc est e-nim cor-pus me-um."* A quantifying of the miracles arose, in which it was considered "wasteful" for priests to celebrate the Eucharist together since they could each consecrate that much more of the Lord if they said their separate Masses.[27] The original sign of union had become a means of separation. The priest's private business at the altar was something the laity could only behold from afar, if at all, as the sanctuaries became a reserve for the priestly caste. The priest turned his back on the laity, as if huddled over his private mystery. Rood screens, or (later) communion rails, fenced the vulgar multitude off from the sacred proceedings.

The sacral language, Latin, had more efficacy because the faithful did *not* understand it. Ornate vestments, from a distant culture no longer alive, marked the priest at the altar as standing outside his own time, the time inhabited by the ordinary mortals outside the communion rail. In a later effort to align the priest with more ascetical sources of authority, every priest was made to read on his own a daily selection of the canonical hours sung by cloistered orders, as if he were a part-time monk. This hour or so spent in reading the Latin "breviary" caused a withdrawal from the ongoing life of those around him, as I realized when the priest who was our debate coach in high school had to stop the car he was driving us in and go off to finish his duty before midnight. Hedge after hedge was added to isolate the physical reality of the eucharistic host. Every move toward the priest's monopolistic control of this sacred transaction went along, pari passu, with the need for ritual purity in the administrant.

Since the power of the priest depended on this summoning of a separate physical reality in the Eucharist, stories were invented to make that physicality more evident. When the host at Bolsena was "wounded," it bled—Raphael painted the miracle in the Vatican's Stanza of Heliodorus. The host's (but not the wine's) divine reality, even apart from the eucharistic meal, was demonstrated by reservation of consecrated hosts after the Mass, display of them in monstrances at Benediction, and the delivery of them to people in hospitals. Since Christ was present in all particles of the host, so that a communicant receives him no matter how small the segment eaten, a strange technology in bakery made eucharistic hosts resemble a new kind of plastic that would not fragment when broken, leaving clean edges and no crumb problem. To this day, that ideal is preserved in church legislation. In a Vatican instruction approved by John Paul II in 1980 we read: "The preparation of the bread requires attentive care to ensure that the product does not detract from the dignity due to the Eucharistic bread, can be broken in a dignified way, *does not give rise to excessive fragments*, and doesn't offend the sensibilities of the faithful when they eat it." [Emphasis added.][28]

Given the tremendous emphasis later focused on the power of the priest to consecrate, it is odd that the New Testament—despite its long list of various functions and ministries in the Christian community— never mentions this at all. Recent Catholicism would make this the major power passed down from the apostles. It was even said that this proves the Catholic church is the only valid Christian sect, since it alone gives its priests the consecrating power. Other services are merely human, a matter of talk and commemoration. In fact, when I mentioned to a parish priest in the 1960s that a visiting priest had given a good sermon, he said, "You shouldn't come to Mass just to have your curiosity tickled." He thought Protestants gave good sermons because they did not have anything truly divine going on at the altar. The transformation of the host makes Mass *the* divine event, a literal repetition of the Last Supper. But the apostles are never described as having that power to consecrate, in the New Testament itself or in the early Christian literature. In fact, no one—apostle or not—is described as presiding over the communal meal. As Raymond Brown says:

> There is simply no compelling evidence for the classic [Catholic] thesis that the members of the Twelve always presided when they were present, and that there was a chain of ordination passing the power of presiding at the Eucharist from the Twelve to missionary apostles to presbyter-bishops . . . Some have suggested that the prophets [who included women] regularly presided at the Eucharist. Acts 13.1-2 has prophets "liturgizing," and *Didache* 10.7 would permit prophets to give thanks (*eucharistein*); the "ministry (*leitourgia*) of prophets" in *Didache* 15.1 is related to celebrating the Eucharist on the Lord's day in 14.1.[29]

Brown, as we saw earlier, says there is no priesthood in the New Testament, since the first disciples still went to the Temple (Acts 21:26), where God's priesthood was still in effect.[30] What would a Christian priest have done in the original eucharistic meals? It is hard to imagine any disciple doing what Paul VI imagines: taking on the role of Jesus as his dramatic representation (*eikon*).[31] Did the disciples reenact the Last Supper, with one of them playing the role of Jesus? If so, did the priest not eat or drink the bread and wine himself? It is hard to imagine Jesus saying that bread and wine were his body and blood and then eating his own body, drinking his own blood.[32] Where did the playacting aspect of this ceremony end? If the priest played the role of Jesus, did someone else play that of Judas, or of the "beloved disciple" who leaned on Jesus' breast? If the latter, there is a problem for later iconography, which makes the beloved disciple one of the Twelve—a thing modern scholars no longer believe.[33] If the priest has some magic words to say in the persona of Jesus, why do the words of consecration come down to us in different versions in the New Testament and early Christian writings?

Since it is the Spirit, acting through the whole community, that consecrates, Western theologians are more and more agreeing with Eastern ones that the actual consecrating words are the call (*epiklēsis*) on the Spirit to "come upon these gifts and make them holy," not the words quoted from the Last Supper.[34] In fact, the words of Jesus, "Take this and eat, it is my body," are, on the face of them, words of *distribution,* which probably followed on his own prayer to the Father, which were the true consecrating words at the Last Supper. As Bernard Häring says: "It is not we priests who consecrate, such that what was bread becomes the presence of Christ. This mystery takes place on the occasion of *epiklēsis,* by the power of the Holy Spirit."[35] Even if one does not accept this interpretation of the sacrament, it is clear that the Spirit's presence in the community is what consecrates, so all those stories of priests changing bread and wine with a magic formula, even in a bakery or a bar, are nonsense. They have no such magic, and the Spirit would not act apart from the community.

Since the Spirit consecrates within the community, if one person presides at the Eucharist, it is simply as the community's representative, not as Christ's. The first letter of Peter (2:5) refers to Christians as "living stones assembled into a spiritual temple, formed into a holy priesthood to offer spiritual sacrifices." That is the way, early in the second century, Ignatius of Antioch—usually the first witness called for a belief in Christ's real presence in the Eucharist—talks of the community. Instead of being fenced off from the altar, the faithful *are* the altar, just as *their* flesh is the temple: "You sustain God in you, the altar in you, Christ in you, and holiness in you . . . Guard your flesh as God's temple."[36] It is more the faithful who become the body and blood of Christ than bread and wine do.

Within the congregation there is "a union of the flesh and spirit of Jesus Christ."[37] The faithful are "created again in faith, which is the Lord's flesh, and love, which is Jesus Christ's blood."[38] It makes no sense to form a sacred area away from the faithful, who are the real altars and temples and bearers of Christ's flesh and blood. They are not distant from the mystery. They *are* the mystery. For Ignatius, the Eucharist was the full realization of that "one-ing" (*henōsis*) among themselves he urges on all the communities he addresses.

Almost three centuries later, Augustine was still talking of the faithful as the stuff that is transformed by the Eucharist. He never mentions (any more than the New Testament did, or Ignatius did) the power of the priest to consecrate. He says it is the faithful recipients who make the body of Christ present by *becoming* it. Over and over he places the validity of the sacrament in the recipient's unity with God and each other, not in any preceding words or magic of the priest. He denied that Christ's risen physical body could be in more than one place. When Christ is said to be in several different places, it is the members of his body in the Christian community that are referred to.[39] How, he asks, can the body of Christ, which died and went to heaven, be in the Eucharist, and he answers:

> If you want to know what is the body of Christ, hear what the Apostle [Paul] tells believers: "You are Christ's body and his members" (I Cor 12:27). If, then, you are Christ's body and his members, it is your symbol that lies on the Lord's altar—what you receive is a symbol of yourself. When you say "Amen" to what you are, your saying it affirms it. You hear [the priest say] "The body of Christ," and you answer "Amen," and you must *be* the body of Christ to make that "Amen" take effect. And why are you a bread? Hear the Apostle again, speaking of this very symbol: "We, though many, are one bread, one body (I Cor 10:17)."[40]

Augustine rejects the idea that teeth and chewing and swallowing make one receive the body and blood of Christ:

> "This then is the bread that comes down from heaven, so that the one eating it shall not die" (Jn 6:50). But these words apply only to the

validity of the mystery, not to its visibility—to an inner eating, not an external one; to what the heart consumes, not what the teeth chew.[41]

Augustine says that we cannot take Christ into us. "The symbol is received, it is eaten, it disappears—but can Christ's body disappear, Christ's church disappear, Christ's members disappear? Far from it."[42] We must be taken into Christ's body, not he into ours: "We abide in him when we are his members, and he abides in us when we are his temple. And for us to become his members, unity must bind us to each other."[43] The eucharistic transformation is, for Augustine, a change of the community into a single thing, and the symbolism that he finds in the Eucharist is not of the physical body of Christ but of the mystical union of his members under the sign of bread, made a unit from many grains of wheat, and wine, made a unit from many grapes. Explaining the meaning of the Eucharist to newly baptized Christians, he says:

> This bread makes clear how you should love your union with one another. Could the bread have been made from one grain, or were many grains of wheat required? Yet before they cohered as bread, each grain was isolated. They were fused in water, after being ground together. Unless wheat is pounded, and then moistened with water, it can hardly take on the new identity we call bread. In the same way, you had to be ground by the ordeal of fasting and exorcism in preparation for baptism's water, and in this way you were watered in order to take on the new identity of bread. But bread must be finished by baking in fire. In this way you were being ground and pounded, as it were, by the humiliation of fasting and the mystery of exorcism. After that, the water of baptism moistened you into bread. But the dough does not become bread until it is baked in a fire. And what does fire represent for you? It is the [post-baptismal] anointing with oil. Oil, which feeds fire, is the mystery of the Holy Spirit . . . The Holy Spirit comes to you, fire after water, and you are baked into the bread which is Christ's body. That is how your unity is symbolized.[44]

So clearly is the bread a sign of the unity of Christians that it was customary in Augustine's time to send some of the bread left over from the eucharistic meal to other communities, expressing a general oneness.[45] That would never happen today, when people think the host could be desecrated if handled by anyone but a priest. Candles were not carried alongside the *eulogion* (as it was called). The only effect of an unbeliever's eating the bread is that he or she does not become a member of the body of Christ. There is no actual body in the host to bleed or be abused.

It has scandalized many Catholics that, as the Augustinian scholar F. van der Meer had reluctantly to admit, in all of Augustine's hundreds of sermons delivered at the eucharistic meal, "he does not speak of a real presence" in the bread and wine.[46] Augustine in the fourth century, just as Ignatius in the second, would never have thought that reverence to the Eucharist involved removing its mystery from the midst of the believers. They would not have fenced off the altar, since the people *were* the altar, just as they were the bread lying on it. They would not have used a language the people could not understand. Augustine often spoke as if the homily were the most important part of the service. He used the phrase "breaking the bread" to mean breaking open the meaning of the saving scriptures, which he was there to study with his fellow believers.[47] He repeatedly described the beloved disciple as "drinking truth" at the Last Supper, not when he drank the cup but when he leaned on the Savior's breast.[48] Christ's words were the mystery for Augustine. He wanted no adventitious mystification. He did not wear altar vestments at the eucharistic meal, but his everyday clothes.[49] He had no taste for pomp. He melted down the precious metals of communion vessels to ransom prisoners.[50] His fellows in Christ were the real vessels of Christ's body. He agreed with Saint Paul, who said that mystery for its own sake, like speaking in tongues that no one could interpret, was not a service to the community: "Where there is no interpreter, let no one speak in tongues before the gathering—speak rather to yourself and to God" (I Cor 14:28). Yet the priest muttering Latin before modern communities was in effect just speaking to himself and God. The original language of the Mass was whatever tongue the community spoke—Aramaic in Jerusalem, Greek in the diaspora, Latin only after a while in Rome. At the Last Supper Jesus did not speak in some exotic tongue his disciples could not understand. When Peter and Paul went to Rome, the Jewish communities there would have used Greek, the lingua franca of the empire, the language of the New Testament, which made it unnecessary for the apostles to learn Latin at an advanced age.

Partly by accident, the liturgy was the first major topic taken up for discussion at the Second Vatican Council. It surprised some observers that bishops could disagree so heatedly on what seemed to them a mere point of church practice, not of high dogma—use of the vernacular instead of Latin. After all, Eastern churches in communion with Rome use Greek at the Mass. Why should it be so odd to return to the practice of the early church? The observers did not realize that the whole ritual purity of the priesthood and the sacramental system was felt to be at risk. To turn the priest around and make him face the community instead of the wall, to have the laity respond to the priest's words in a language they share, to express the unity of the body of Christ in greetings and handshakes, to sing in terms of the culture you belong to (instead of in medieval Latin chants)—all this offended the jealous guardians of the Eucharist as a mystical rite that takes place only in the traffic between the priest and God. Where would it end? Would the practice of a priest saying Mass all by himself be abolished?

The need to keep Latin as a mark of caste was demonstrated at the Vatican Council, where bishops could not express themselves spontaneously or with subtlety because they were forced to use Latin, yet many begged to keep the dead language that sealed them off from the laity in their church rituals. It was most telling that Cardinal Spellman of New York got up to defend the use of Latin, but spoke it so barbarously that people could not understand him.[51]

Many in the laity were offended by the changes, which they said reduced the Mass, took away its aura of mystery, put it on a level with a "hoedown" or jamboree. A silent privacy had grown up on the laity's side of the communion rail, to match foreign language on the priest's side. Unable to participate in a single activity as one body with the celebrant, Catholics meditated in seclusion, said the rosary, read prayers, and did not want their neighbors intruding on what was essentially a private exercise. They treated the Eucharist as if they were making a silent visit to the chapel or attending Benediction with the host in a monstrance. William Buckley shared Evelyn Waugh's disdain for the liturgical changes, and reflected, after Waugh died, that "no imagination is so vivid as to visualize

Mr. Waugh yanked from prayerful thought to clasp the hand of the pil-grim to his right, to his left, ahead, and behind him."[52] Buckley would have agreed with Cardinal McIntyre of Los Angeles, who told the bish-ops at Vatican II that letting lay people participate in the Mass would just distract them.[53]

Vatican officials feared change in the liturgy for a very real and prac-tical reason. If you take away the magical aura from the Mass, the exis-tence of a priestly caste with ritual purity is hard to justify. If a privileged entree to sanctuaries from which the laity are excluded is gone, what happens to the rules of Leviticus? That is why Pope Paul VI was forced back on weaker and weaker arguments for preservation of the caste's celibacy. He tried to say that asceticism is itself a witness to the purity of a person's dedication. That was true of the desert fathers. But they did not minister to a community—they went off on their spiritual adventure to avoid the duties and entanglements of the priests. Besides, their asceticism was part of an integral life pattern. They fasted, punished their bodies, ab-stained from company and entertainments and pleasures. The modern priest is not in general terms an ascetic. An ascetic like the Dalai Lama does impress people by the monkish discipline he observes. He is not only celibate. He does not drink alcohol, smoke tobacco, play games, go to the movies.

Priests may today be celibate; but—with some honorable excep-tions—they usually maintain a comfortable life style, especially as com-pared with the poor they profess to be serving. We all know priests with refined tastes in food and drink, nice cars, expensive stereos. In the 1950s, Pope Pius XII and the General of the Jesuits, looking after the health of the priests as well as the costs of medical insurance and treatment, com-manded all Jesuits to stop smoking—and the order known for its obedi-ence simply ignored the command. It was felt to be asking too much. Some talked as if the very fact that they observed celibacy gave priests a compensatory right to all other legitimate pleasures. Pope John XXIII knew his assembled clergy at Vatican II well enough that he had a coffee bar set up at a side entrance to Saint Peter's for smokers to escape to dur-ing the sessions—otherwise, he said, "the bishops will be puffing under their mitres."[54] They may be estimable men, but they are not convincing as desert fathers.

In fact, priests indulge openly in pleasures far less innocent than smoking. As P. T. van Asten, the Superior General of the White Fathers, said at the 1971 synod in Rome:

> What witness is given by a celibate priest, consecrated to God, if he has not renounced riches, ambition, or honors? Would the care of children and the love of a woman be more dangerous for a priest than the care of riches or the smoke of incense? Why this strange lenience toward ambition, honor, or riches . . . and this strictness over marriage?[55]

If priests are so ready to indulge in other pleasures, then why is celibacy their one abstention? It is not the witness of asceticism in a broader sense that can justify this, but only the sneaking, no longer confessed heritage of the Stoics and Leviticus that makes sex of itself somehow unclean and debasing. The Pope can no longer say that, but his actions reveal his instincts in the matter. Unable to give the real reason, he constructs defenses like this argument from, of all things, efficiency:

> The consecration to Christ under an additional and lofty title like celibacy evidently gives to the priest, even in the practical field, the maximum efficiency and the best disposition of mind, mentally and emotionally, of the continuous exercise of a perfect charity . . . It also guarantees him a greater freedom and flexibility in the pastoral ministry.[56]

So the celibacy that was originally intended to draw the priest away from other people into a sacral sphere is now called a tactic to achieve availability and access. Pursuing this argument to a point verging on the ludicrous, he joins withdrawal and availability, saying that the priest's very separateness will bring him closer to people who do not share his celibacy:

> If this means that the priest is without a direct personal experience of married life, he nevertheless will be able through his training, his ministry, and the grace of his office, to gain even deeper insights

into every human yearning. This will allow him to meet problems of this kind at their source and give solid support by his advice and assistance to married persons and Christian families. For the Christian family, the example of the priest who is living his life of celibacy to the full will underscore the spiritual dimension of every love worthy of the name, and his personal sacrifice will merit for the faithful united in the holy bond of matrimony the grace of a true union.[57]

People cannot have a true union in marriage unless it is graced for them by someone else's nonmarriage! Here, subtly, the old disparagement of marriage reasserts itself almost against the Pope's conscious intent. Only the nobler life can bless the less noble one, the one not able to maintain itself in terms of its own value and dignity.

In practical terms, just how true is the Pope's "greater availability" argument? Do any of us feel we must find an unmarried doctor, since no other will be able to give our health his full attention? Do we seek out unmarried counselors, teachers, leaders? Is a President of the United States shirking his tremendous responsibilities if he has a wife and children? If we want uncompromised service to the nation, should we require celibacy of those seeking high political office? The emptiness of the service argument is clear from a thousand examples of generous devotion given to their calling by married men and women. For that matter, can we honestly claim that married Protestant ministers, Orthodox priests, or rabbis are less caring than are Catholic priests? Are they less available, accessible, committed, successful in dealing with people? Most of them seem more open and approachable. Many priests have an instinctive preservation of caste wrought in them by their training, a standoffish and authoritarian bearing that impedes communication—as we saw for years in the low esteem they put on their preaching skills, degraded by comparison with their emphasis on sacramental power. If celibacy is supposed to give the priest more time and energy to spend on the faithful committed to his care, empirical evidence proves that the priests are either not spending their time and energy that way, or that they have not acquired the basic skills for communicating their concern. In a major report by the National Opinion Research Center's Social Study Survey, it was found that fewer than half of Catholics in 1974 thought their own parish priest was very understanding of practical problems, and only a third of those under the age of thirty-four thought so—despite the fact that parish priests received higher general approval ratings than bishops or the Pope.[58] People think they get more understanding from their (married) individual doctor or congressman. Priests get low ratings for their sermons, a basic tool for teaching or conveying sympathy, and most people's only way of rating their priest. In Chicago, only 15 percent of German Catholics thought sermons were excellent—22 percent of Irish Catholics thought they were.[59]

Most bishops conduct their lives sequestered from the people. I had occasion, at one time, to seek a bishop's attention. It was easier to get that of my senator. If addressing the needs of the faithful were the real concern, access to them would be more readily achieved by, for instance, having women priests in whom other women could confide more easily. And how is it addressing the needs of the laity to sustain a caste system that drastically reduces the number of priests? With the best will in the world to serve, the fewer and older priests who are facing their task these years cannot be accessible to all. The priest-to-parishioner ratio was 1 to 1,100 in 1970, it was 1 to 2,200 in 1990, and it will be 1 to 3,100 in 2005.[60]

Paul VI says that the priest should resemble Christ. Well, where is Christ to be found on earth these days? A theologian priest I know tells the community when he preaches that he comes to Mass to find Christ, and that he finds him by looking out at the faces before him. The Christ to be resembled is there, in the members of his body. That man over there is Christ. So is this woman over here. So, at that moment, are we all. This priest also uses the Augustinian formula when he gives out communion: "Receive what you are, the body of Christ."

---

[1] Paul VI, *The Celibacy of the Priest (Sacerdotalis Caelibatus)*, Vatican translation on the papal website, paragraph 18.

[2] Peter Brown, *Augustine of Hippo* (University of California Press, 1967), pp. 381–82. The son of Memor, Julian of Eclanum, became Augustine's harshest critic during the Pelagian controversy.

[3] Hans-Jürgen Vogels, "The Community's Right to a Priest in Collision with Compulsory Celibacy," in Edward Schillebeeckx and Johann-Baptist Metz (editors), *The Right of the Community to a Priest* (Seabury Press, 1980), pp. 88–90.

⁴Ambrose, *On the Duties of the Servants of the Church* 2.249, cited in Uta Ranke-Heinemann, *Eunuchs for the Kingdom of Heaven*, translated by Peter Heinigg (Viking, 1990), p. 103.

⁵Peter Damian, *On the Dignity of the Priest*, cited in Ranke-Heinemann, op. cit., p. 108.

⁶Ranke-Heinemann, op. cit., p. 107.

⁷Ibid., p. 110.

⁸David Brakke, *Athanasius and the Politics of Asceticism* (Oxford University Press, 1995), pp. 129–41.

⁹J. N. D. Kelly, *Golden Mouth: The Story of John Chrysostom—Ascetic, Preacher, Bishop* (Cornell University Press, 1995), pp. 191–229.

¹⁰Peter Brown, *The Body and Society: Men, Women and Sexual Renunciation in Early Christianity* (Columbia University Press, 1988), pp. 213–40.

¹¹Brakke, op. cit., pp. 142–44.

¹²Gregory Nazianzus, *Oration* 18.37 (PG 35.1035).

¹³J. N. D. Kelly, op. cit., p. 34.

¹⁴Gregory of Nazianzus, op. cit., p. 1035.

¹⁵Athanasius finally won over Dracontius but could not land the bigger catch, Pachomius. Brakke, op. cit., pp. 99–120.

¹⁶Ibid., p. 109.

¹⁷Ibid., pp. 65–66.

¹⁸Ibid., pp. 139–40.

¹⁹Ibid., pp. 213–14.

²⁰G. J. M. Bartelink, *Athanase d'Alexandrie, Vie d'Antoine* (Editions du Cerf, 1994), paragraph 78, pp. 332, 334.

²¹Ibid., p. 105.

²²Ibid., p. 81.

²³Peter Brown, "The Holy Man in Late Antiquity," in *Society and the Holy in Late Antiquity* (University of California Press, 1982), pp. 1121–52.

²⁴Brakke, op. cit., pp. 109–10.

²⁵Ibid., p. 144.

²⁶*Sacerdotalis Caelibatus*, paragraph 29.

²⁷A theologian advised American bishops at the Second Vatican Council that "when 100 priests concelebrated, the Church was 99 masses short," according to F. X. Murphy ("Xavier Rynne"), *Letters from Vatican City* (Farrar, Straus & Company, 1963), p. 114.

²⁸*Instruction Concerning Worship of the Eucharistic Mystery (Inestimable Donum)*, issued by the Sacred Congregation of the Sacraments and Divine Worship, Approved and Confirmed by His Holiness Pope John Paul II (Pauline Books, 1994), paragraph 8, p. 7.

²⁹Raymond E. Brown, S.S., *Priest and Bishop* (Paulist Press, 1970), p. 41.

³⁰Ibid., pp. 16–17.

³¹*Sacerdotalis Caelibatus*, paragraph 31.

³²Joachim Jeremias, *The Eucharistic Words of Jesus*, translated by Norman Perrin (Fortress Press, 1977), p. 212.

³³Raymond E. Brown, Karl P. Donfried, Joseph A. Fitzmyer, and John Reumann, *Mary in the New Testament* (Fortress Press, 1978), p. 211.

³⁴Yves Congar, *I Believe in the Holy Spirit*, translated by David Smith (Crossroad, 1997), Vol. III, p. 233.

³⁵Bernard Häring, *Priesthood Imperiled* (Triumph Books, 1996), p. 131.

³⁶Ignatius of Antioch, *Letter to the Ephesians* 9:1; *Letter to the Philippians* 7:2.

³⁷Ignatius, *Letter to the Magnesians* 1:1. Also, *Letter to the Trallians*, Induction.

³⁸Ignatius, *Letter to the Trallians* 8:1.

[39] Augustine, *Interpreting John's Gospel* 30.2, 28.2.

[40] Augustine, Sermon 272 (PL 38.1247).

[41] Augustine, *Interpreting John's Gospel* 26.12.

[42] Augustine, Sermon 227 (PL 38.1101).

[43] Augustine, *Interpreting John's Gospel* 27.6.

[44] Augustine, Sermon 227 (PL 38.1100).

[45] Augustine, *Letters* 24.6, 31.9, 32.3.

[46] F. van der Meer, *Augustine the Bishop*, translated by Brian Battershaw and G. R. Lamb (Sheed and Ward, 1961), p. 284. Marie-François Berrouard thought he could establish that one text in Augustine affirmed the real presence, but Edward J. Kilmartin, S.J., shows how flimsy his case is. See Berrouard, "L'être sacramental de l'eucharist selon saint Augustin," *Nouvelle revue théologique* (1977), pp. 702–21. Kilmartin, "The Eucharistic Gift: Augustine of Hippo's Tractate 27 on John 6.60–72," in David G. Hunter (editor), *Preaching in the Patristic Age* (Paulist Press, 1989), pp. 162–81.

[47] For scripture as bread see Augustine, *Interpreting John's Gospel* 34.1, 41.3.

[48] Ibid. 16.2,18.1, 20.1.

[49] Van der Meer, op. cit., p. 317.

[50] Ibid.

[51] Murphy, op. cit., p. 99.

[52] William F. Buckley, Jr., *Nearer, My God* (Doubleday, 1997), p. 103.

[53] Murphy, op. cit., p. 125.

[54] Ibid., p. 118.

[55] Edward Schillebeeckx, *The Church With a Human Face* (Crossroad, 1988), p. 226.

[56] *Sacerdotalis Caelibatus*, paragraph 32.

[57] Andrew Greeley, *Crisis in the Church; A Study of Religion in America* (The Thomas More Press, 1979), p. 157.

[58] Ibid., p. 192.

[59] Ibid., p. 158.

[60] Chester Gillis, *Roman Catholicism in America* (Columbia University Press, 1999), p. 246.

10.

Shrinking the Body of Christ

In 1981, a Jesuit priest, John Coleman, wrote in the Jesuit journal, *America*:

> Any profession for which the following facts are true—declining absolute numbers in the face of growth of the large population, significant resignations, a declining pool of new recruits and an aging population—can be referred to as having a deep-seated identity crisis, whatever the internal morale of the group.[1]

Yet the Vatican continues to deny that there is a major problem in the recruitment or retention of priests—just as they denied the problem of disappearing nuns, though they are all but gone now. In 1965, the year the Vatican Council ended, there were almost 50,000 seminarians training for the priesthood in America. By 1997, a tenth of that number was enrolled.[2] Two years later, that number was halved, making for a 70 percent drop-off in a decade.[3] While fewer priests are being ordained, those who have been ordained continue to leave—the younger ones going faster, pushing up the average age of the dwindling supply that remains. One out of every ten parishes lacks a resident priest.[4] The hierarchy tries to hide the crisis, even from itself. The archbishop of Omaha calls the crisis "artificial and contrived," played up by Catholics who are not "loyal to the magisterial teaching of the Pope."[5] The National Catholic Directory understates the changes by new methods of reporting priests' numbers in America, including those who are missionaries abroad in the domestic count.[6] Great Britain does not supply the numbers of resignations.[7]

When the facts and figures of decline are presented to them, members of the hierarchy respond, with Bishop G. M. Carter of Ontario, "We don't make moral decisions on the basis of surveys."[8]

The drastic shortage has led dioceses to admit into the priesthood some who would not have been considered eligible in the past—older men, who will not be able to serve long; widowed and divorced men; Episcopalian priests who convert.[9] Other bishops hope that the American church can go back to its way of importing priests, as in the days of the church's immigrant status. Now they want to bring in priests from Nigeria, since African seminaries still have high enrollment (largely from rural districts, though the continent itself is undergoing rapid urbanization). But that would drain priests from a continent that is itself short of priests—mainly because colonial missionaries are not being replaced, or have withdrawn, or are dying. In the 1970s, 70 percent of the priests in Africa were missionaries, and the continent still had 38,138 mission churches without resident pastors.[10]

So American hopes of replenishing the priesthood from abroad are illusory. In the third world, half the mission posts have no resident priest.[11] In the developed world, America's own problems are occurring. Replacement rates tell the story. For every 100 priests who died or resigned, Italy had just 50 to take their place, Spain 35, Germany 34, France 17, Portugal 10.[12] In the United States, the average age of diocesan priests was fifty-eight in 1999, and roughly 25 percent of the total were over seventy.[13] The priesthood is on the way to the condition of convents, where nuns are in their seventies, and any young woman foolhardy enough to join an order would spend most of her own time tending to her retired or ailing or dying sisters.

In the narrowing circle of priests, what is the morale? What can it be when 80 percent of young priests think the Pope is wrong on contraception, 60 percent of them think he is wrong on homosexuality, yet the Vatican keeps up the pressure to have them voice what they do not believe?[14] It is one thing to make brave sacrifices for a cause you can proclaim wholeheartedly. It is another thing to be trapped in equivocation or evasion about one's convictions. Besides, the demands on time, energy, and composure intensify as the supply of priests shrinks while the Catholic population continues to grow. A study commissioned by the United

States bishops in 1985 found that 40 percent of priests had "severe personal, behavioral or mental problems in the previous twelve months."[15] When it became clear that the findings would be so dismal, the bishops withdrew from it, and some of them denounced the published findings that appeared.[16]

Who goes into the seminaries, then, when this is the prospect for priestly life? One answer was given in a *New York Times Magazine* article on the "new breed" of priests-in-training, men chosen at the insistence of Rome for their subservience to the kinds of argument we have been considering as the Vatican's product on contraception, celibacy, and women. The sincere idealists discovered at Mount Saint Mary's Seminary in Maryland believe that the only trouble with the church is that its full message is not being preached—especially on matters like masturbation. Tom Holloway, twenty-nine, says that he intends to preach on that unpopular subject. As his classmate, Brian Bashista puts it, "We're the John Paul II generation."[17] They prove that in various ways. Some of them went to confession for having read the Starr Report on President Clinton's sexual wrongdoing. Another says he had to give up watching his favorite TV show, "Seinfeld," because he suspected that "Jerry was contracepting."[18] Serious men might well hesitate before joining this company, putting themselves under Rome's discipline with enthusiastic enforcers as their colleagues. Meanwhile, the number of parishes without priests is growing.

This situation could not have arisen in the early centuries of the church. Then a community did not wait for some higher authority to drop a priest down out of the hierarchical heaven, accepting what it was given (if anything). Communities voted for their own priests, who were committed to staying with the community that chose them. There was no candidate list submitted by Rome. Anyone could be chosen, so long as the community wanted that person. That was the proof of a vocation. In fact it *was* the vocation, the calling by the Christian body of Christ for a leader of its own desire. When Ambrose was elected bishop of Milan, he was not even baptized yet.

A man was obliged to accept this call, out of duty to the Christian community which was Christ's body. Augustine protested that he was a recent convert, but the community at Hippo prevailed on him anyway.

Even a mere visitor to a town could be dragooned. Married men were chosen if the community wanted them. We saw in the previous chapter that monks of the desert resisted the call to become bishops or priests—that was the measure of their daring new independence. John Chrysostom, by contrast, had to make an elaborate defense of his first resistance to the priesthood, a resistance put up when he still aspired to be an ascetic.[19] Ambrose protested that he had a valid excuse for not serving—he was a civil magistrate, and such officers had been excluded up to this point. The community overruled him by appealing for an exemption—not to the Pope or a council, but to the Christian Emperor Valentinian (who was resident in their city of Milan).[20]

Once a man was chosen, he was not advanced to the priesthood as an independent status. He was the priest *of the community that chose him.* He could not leave that community on his own initiative. Even deacons were similarly bound to their place. When a deacon in Augustine's diocese was seen away from his town, he was rebuked with these words: "You are tied to a wife [the community], do not seek a divorce."[21] A priest could be expelled or removed only for some grave sin—in 335 the Emperor Constantine exiled Athanasius from his see at Alexandria on suspicion of heresy.[22] Here we can identify the seed of later developments that would lead papal Rome to acquire a monopoly over priestly ordination. That power was seized not from the people themselves but from political rulers who had, in time, assumed ever greater control over the nomination and acclamation power of Christian communities. This political control was first asserted as a peacekeeping measure, when communities were riven by factions, either heretical or schismatic. Constantine had established a precedent for the encroachment when he removed Donatist bishops from office in Roman Africa. When "lay investiture" controversies arose, in later centuries, the power to ordain did not return to its original locus, the people of each community, but was wrested from secular rulers by an expanding and aggressive papacy.

But this monopoly was a late development, after centuries in which priests were chosen by local communities, political authority, or some combination of the two. And once a man was installed in his see or parish, he was responsible to it. When Augustine wanted to take some time out from his episcopal duties for deep study or writing, he had to ask the community's permission.[23] When he tried to prevent his congregation from choosing a reluctant man as one of its priests, it ignored his desires and continued its demands—Augustine had to work out a compromise binding the man to the place even without ordination (epp. 125, 126). When, in failing health, he expressed a preference about his successor, he had to submit his choice to the congregation's vote.[24] This mutual responsibility to each other was so intimate in the early days that we hear nothing of "massing priests"—men ordained to dispense sacraments without being tied to a particular community—until the fourth century, when they are called "visitors" to distinguish them from the normal (stationary) priests.[25]

It was unthinkable in those days that a settled congregation would lack a priest. They would simply choose one. If he had been a layman up to that point, their choice made him a priest from then on. As Raymond Brown writes of the New Testament era that began this practice:

> A more plausible substitute for the chain theory [of "apostolic succession"] is the thesis that sacramental "powers" were part of the mission of the Church and that there were diverse ways in which the Church (or the communities) designated individuals to exercise those powers—*the essential element always being church or community consent (which was tantamount to ordination,* whether or not that consent was signified by a special ceremony such as the laying on of hands). [Emphasis added.][26]

In fact, as Fritz Lobinger and others have argued, no one should have the authority to deprive a church of its right to a leader.[27] That right is a greater one than the later right of Rome to send only approved people to the churches, which means depriving many churches of the leadership that is the symbol of their unity, of that which makes them the body of Christ. Rome infringes that right when it says that only people authorized by it can administer the sacraments, then maintains a discipline and a set of teachings that limit the number of priests who can qualify. The requirements of Rome are put above those of the communities the priests are supposed to exist for and serve. Most churchmen now think that Rome abused its authority when, in the Middle Ages or Renais-

sance, it put whole communities or countries under an interdict (deprivation of all sacraments) in order to punish rulers at odds with the Vatican. But now the church is imposing a kind of creeping and quiet
interdiction when it makes communities do without priests. Bernard
Häring, the eminent moral theologian, noting that the Catholic Catechism makes it a grave sin not to receive the Eucharist on holy days, says
that the grave sin is in the authorities who make that impossible for so
many Catholics.[28]

How does modern Rome justify its control of the supply of priests? It
claims that only apostolic succession can give men the power to consecrate the Eucharist. But Raymond Brown notes that a fellow Christian
scripture scholar remarked to him that Catholic scholars were obviously
not being listened to when the Second Vatican Council declared bishops
the successors of the apostles.[29] Paul VI more specifically called them the
descendants of the Twelve, who ordained only men. Since, as we have
seen, there are no priests in the New Testament, there could be no ordination of priests. Indeed, as Markus Barth points out, the idea of a "laity"
separate from the church's authority is foreign to the New Testament (he
calls a section of his commentary on Ephesians 4–6 "The Church Without Laymen and Priests").[30] Where then did Rome get the notion that
apostles ordained priests? The text normally invoked is that place in the
Acts of the Apostles where deacons are chosen *by the entire congregation
(pas ho plēthos, 6:5)* for the laying on of hands by the Twelve. Even the idea
of electing people to this office originated in the whole body. Besides,
these deacons, we are expressly told in Acts 6:3–4, were chosen to dis-
tribute food to the needy, and were not teachers of the word—therefore,
not priests in any later sense. As Raymond Brown says,

> The theory about passing on powers through ordination faces the
> serious obstacle that the New Testament does not show the Twelve
> laying hands on bishops either as successors or as auxiliaries in ad-
> ministering sacraments. A possible partial exception is the laying of
> hands on the Hellenist leaders in Acts 6:6, but even there it is not
> clear who lays hands, the Twelve or the community as a whole. And
> if we confine ourselves to the idea of succession, we may assert that
> according to New Testament thought *there can be no successors to the*

Twelve as such . . . The symbolism of the Twelve is associated with
the idea that the Christian movement represents the renewal of Israel. Thus, just as at its founding Israel consisted of twelve tribes descended from the twelve sons of Jacob-Israel, so at the moment
when Jesus renews Israel there are his Twelve disciples to proclaim
the good news of what has happened. By this symbolism *the Twelve
are unique.* When Judas betrays Jesus and reduces the number to
eleven, someone has to be elected to fill out the Twelve. But when
the individual members die, they are not replaced; rather, as the
founders of the renewed Israel, they are immortalized. According to
Revelation 21:14, the twelve foundations of the city that is the
heavenly Jerusalem have on them "the twelve names of the Twelve
apostles of the Lamb." Furthermore *they cannot be replaced* because,
precisely as the Twelve, they have an eschatological role to play: in
the judgement scene they have been appointed to sit on twelve
thrones judging the twelve tribes of Israel (Lk 22:30, Mt 19:28).
[Emphasis added.][31]

The laying on of hands is a gesture used for many purposes in the Jewish and Christian scriptures—blessing, healing, invoking the spirit over
sacrificial victims, baptizing. There is no specific ordination rite involved
in the gesture. After all, the Twelve claim their authority from Jesus, and
no mention is made of his laying his hands on them when they were
chosen. The adoption of the gesture with hands in a Christian rite for
priests probably came from a Jewish practice of laying hands on rabbis
when they are appointed—a practice not reported until late in the first
century, and one that did not imply any rabbinical "succession."[32] The
same is true of the early Christian formula of ordination when we first
encounter it after the New Testament period. The late first-century baptismal document, *Didache* (15.1) says that bishops are chosen when *the
local community* lays hands on the man it has elected.

There is no indication that the community thought it was replicating
some action taken by the Twelve. On the contrary, Paul and Barnabas,
neither of whom was one of the Twelve, nor were they appointed by the
Twelve, laid hands on those chosen to be elders in Asia Minor (Acts
14:21–23). This leads Brown to say that "there is some evidence that Paul

may have appointed presbyter-bishops, but *no evidence that the Twelve did.*" [Emphasis added.][33] Only Peter of the Twelve is said to have left Jerusalem. And the role of the Twelve in Jerusalem is so otherworldly that another figure entirely is presented, in the Acts of the Apostles, as the principal church authority there—James the brother of the Lord (who is neither James, son of Zebedee, nor James, son of Alphaeus, who are the Jameses in the Twelve).[34]

Well, if Peter alone of the Twelve left Jerusalem, can the chain of succession be derived from him as the bishop of Rome? So defenders of the papacy have claimed.[35] But Brown asserts that "Peter never served as the bishop or local administrator of any church, Antioch and Rome included."[36] And he quotes with approval this passage from D. W. O'Connor:

> That Peter founded the Church in Rome is extremely doubtful and that he served as its first bishop (as we understand the term today) for even one year, much less the twenty-five-year period that is claimed for him, is an unfounded tradition that can be traced back to a point no earlier than the third century. The liturgical celebrations which relate to the ascent of Peter to the Roman episcopacy do not begin to make their appearance until the fourth century at the earliest. Furthermore, there is no mention of the Roman episcopacy of Peter in the New Testament, I Clement, or the epistles of Ignatius. The tradition is only dimly discerned in Hegesippus and may be implied in the suspect letter of Dionysius of Corinth to the Romans (c. 170). By the third century, however, the early assumptions based upon invention or vague unfounded tradition have been transformed into "facts" of history.[37]

Even Catholic histories of the papacy no longer trace it back to Peter as bishop of Rome.[38] Clement of Rome was by later tradition called the third bishop of Rome (Pope), but Eamon Duffy says of the letter attributed to him (and called by some "the first papal encyclical"):

> Clement made no claim to write as bishop. His letter was sent in the name of the whole Roman community, he never identifies

himself or writes in his own person, and we know nothing at all about him. The letter itself makes no distinction between presbyters and bishops, about which it always speaks in the plural, suggesting that at Corinth [to which the letter is addressed] as at Rome the church at this time was organized under a group of bishops or presbyters, rather than a single ruling bishop. A generation later, this was still so in Rome. The visionary treatise *The Shepherd of Hermas*, written in Rome early in the second century, speaks always collectively of the "rulers of the church," or the "elders that preside over the church," and once again the author makes no attempt to distinguish between bishops and elders. Clement is indeed mentioned (if Hermas' Clement is the same man as the author of the letter written at least a generation before, which we cannot assume) but not as presiding bishop. Instead we are told that he was the elder responsible for writing "to the foreign cities"—in effect the corresponding secretary of the Roman church.[39]

Ignatius of Antioch, writing in the first decade of the second century, is the first author we know of to make a clear distinction between bishop and elders, but he describes the bishop's office as embattled, new, needing defense—and as not existing yet in Rome. In six of his seven letters he makes it a principal point to rally people to their bishop as the sign of church unity. Only when he writes to Rome does he omit any reference to a bishop, a thing that, given his urgency about the office, he would not have done if there had been a Roman bishop. This is especially true since he does refer to Peter and Paul when writing to Rome, where they died—and he would surely have referred to Peter as a bishop, to reinforce his campaign for that office's importance, if he thought that Peter had held the post.[40] Ignatius would not be so passionate about the bishop's authority if it had not been resisted. He tells us that people are not accepting the bishop in Magnesia because of his youth, in Ephesus because their man does not speak well, in Smyrna because the bishop there, Polycarp, is not aggressive enough.[41] Even more important, Ignatius too, who offers himself as a model bishop, has not been able to impose his authority in his own church at Antioch.

Ignatius wrote his seven letters in a passionate week or so as he was traveling toward his execution in Rome.[42] It used to be thought that, for some odd reason, the Romans had taken just this one man from this one city as part of a general persecution of Christians. But P. N. Harrison established, from the text of the letters themselves, that Ignatius had been arrested as the man responsible for civil unrest in a divided Christian community, and that Ignatius is pleading in his early letters for the help of other bishops and communities to restore him to the good graces of the Antioch Christians—a plea that was successful by the time he wrote gratefully to the Philippians and the Smyrnaeans.[43] Ignatius, so fiery in his language, must have had a knack for stirring up trouble. Even a brief stopover in Philadelphia led to bitter accusations against him. He was accused of arriving there with a concerted plan to help the local bishop by imposing his views. He writes apologetically afterward that he had engaged in no prior consultation with the bishop's party and just spoke his mind on the spur of the moment.[44]

Though Ignatius is the first and major author used to support the idea of an apostolic succession of bishops, he contrasted himself with the apostles—said he did not have their powers—in his letters to the Trallians (3:3) and Romans (4:3). His best modern student says that in his work "episcopacy does not seem to have been reinforced by the idea of succession . . . the apostles seem to be spoken of basically as figures from the past."[45] He does tell Christians to honor their leaders as they would the apostles—but when he says that he is not talking about the bishops. The role of the apostles is seen in *the elders*, the subordinates of the bishops (Smyrnaeans 81, Trallians 2:2 and 3:1). The bishops are not given an apostolic role. Christians are to honor them *as Jesus honored the Father* (Magnesians 7:1, Trallians 2:2). This makes the body of Christians Jesus, the superior of the apostles *and the equal of the Father he honors*. Ignatius uses this analogy because the Christian community is, first and foremost, the body of Christ, the locus of earthly holiness. The bishop, as a symbol of their unity, stands for Jesus' own concentration on his mission as endorsed by the Father. It is not so much the authority of the bishop that Ignatius is interested in as the oneness (*henōsis*) of the community that the bishop symbolizes. The profound element in the letters is not any theory of authority but the joint holiness of the congregation that is Christ. As he wrote to the Ephesians (9:1):

You are all shaped as stones for the temple of the Father, lifted on high through the scaffolding of Jesus Christ (which is his cross), winched upward by the Holy Spirit. Faith is your link, and love your course, up to God. This makes you fellows in the process, embodying God, temple, Christ, and sacred vessels in yourselves.

It is true that Ignatius repeatedly tells the Christians to do nothing without their bishop—including celebration of the Eucharist. But that does not mean that the bishop alone has the consecrating power. In fact, deacons seem to be the custodians of the sacramental action, as they are in Justin the Apologist.[46] Ignatius is using the symbol of the bishop to oppose factions in the churches (including his own) that have withdrawn from the main body to hold their own services, based on the docetist heresy (belief that Jesus' human nature was not real but a phantasm). Only when the Christians are united to their own one body are they Jesus, capable of celebrating their own reality. What makes the bishop the principal symbol of such oneness? *The fact that they elected him.* The contemporary document, *Didache*, the next-earliest text that speaks of bishops' authority, tells the community, "*You yourselves must lay hands on* bishops and deacons that are worthy of the Lord" (15:1). The Ignatian bishop is usually called "monarchical" because Ignatius wants him to be the single leader at the top of the community. But that is a misnomer. He is a democratic leader chosen by the people. All his authority comes from that election by Christ's body. Those who withdraw from the congregation into faction are rejecting the people's choice, the authority of the body that chose the bishop.

So Ignatius, far from endorsing an "apostolic succession," refutes it. The bishops are not chosen by the apostles to be over the community. They are elected by the community in their role as Christ, and then they are honored as Christ honored the Father, his equal. Jesus, though he followed the Father's will, was not subordinate to him. Neither is the community subordinate to the bishop. The recurrent formula in Ignatius is "do nothing apart from (*aneu* or *choris*) the bishop."[47] "Be at one with him," or "in harmony with him."[48] "Form ranks with (*hypotassein*) him *and with each other.*"[49]

The modern papacy claims to be descended from the bishop's office typified by Ignatius. Nothing could be further from the truth. Popes do not claim to derive their authority from the people but to be rulers appointed by apostolic forebears going back to the mythical laying on of hands by the Twelve or to the nonexistent episcopacy of Peter in Rome. And the Pope does not merely deny the authority of the people. Despite much talk of "collegiality" at the Second Vatican Council—of the Pope acting with and in the body of bishops—Paul VI and John Paul II refused to share any real power with them. As we shall see later, John Henry Newman, relying on the history of the church, said that church authorities should consult the laity on matters of doctrine and discipline.[50] The modern Popes refuse to consult even the clergy, or the bishops, or the national synods of the hierarchy.

When a post-Council synod of bishops met in 1971, there was great hope that it would open a channel for Catholic discontent to be addressed in Rome. Since the subject proposed to the synod was ministry, the shortage of priests was bound to come up, and a majority of bishops in the early rounds of discussion made it clear that they thought some relaxation of the celibacy requirement was needed. But manipulation of the issues as proposed and a covert change in the wording of the text for a final vote allowed the Curia to frustrate the will of the majority.[51] When another synod met in 1980 to deal with the subject of the family, Cardinal Ratzinger, who established the order of proceedings, simply refused to recognize the widespread resistance to *Humanae Vitae*, and debate was limited to degrees of rigor in enforcing that encyclical.[52] The whole farce of consulting the bishops has been carried out in an atmosphere of distrust and resentment, stage-managed by a papal Curia that did not want the procedure in the first place and has done everything possible to make it an empty sham. The Pope is put in the position of forcing unwanted things on his own clergy, driving a wedge of separation between them and their congregations, the original source of their—and his—authority.

Nor does the Curia wait for the bishops to come to Rome. It interferes with the efforts of bishops to respond to pastoral needs in their own domain, as we can see from the doomed letter on the status of women that American bishops labored for a decade to prepare. In 1983 they began a process of consulting women on their concerns (the process of consulting the faithful that Newman considered a duty of the church). After a first draft was presented to the bishops in 1988, expressing sympathy with the complaints of women who were consulted, John Paul issued a preemptive letter on women setting limits on what the bishops could say. The Virgin Mary was offered as the pattern of humility for women. A second draft of the bishops' letter tried to accommodate itself to the Pope's directive, citing his letter twenty times, but it was reported to leave some openings for change. The Pope forbade them to discuss this draft until they had consulted with him. A delegation to Rome was told that there was still insufficient emphasis on the Virgin's humility as the norm for women. A third draft was worked up, adhering even closer to the Vatican line. By now the women who had been supportive of this effort withdrew in protest from what was happening to their work (an echo of the treatment given the consultants on birth control two decades earlier). Liberal bishops gave up on the project, letting a conservative bishop draw up the fourth (final) draft. Archbishop Rembert Weakland of Milwaukee warned that passage of such a retrograde document would have an effect like the publication of *Humanae Vitae*. The conference of bishops voted down its own product—the first time that had happened in their history.[53]

The Pope alone, we are now asked to accept, is competent to tell Christian people how to live. No one else can have any say in the matter—not a Council, not the college of all bishops, not the national synods of bishops, not the Christian people. The Holy Spirit now speaks to only one person on earth, the omnicompetent head of the church, a church that is all head and no limbs. If that were so, then the body of Christ would be shamefully reduced.

---

[1]John A. Coleman, S.J., "The Future of the Ministry," *America*, March 28, 1981, p. 247.

[2]Chester Gillis, *Roman Catholicism in America* (Columbia University Press, 1999), p. 256.

[3]Jennifer Egan, "Why a Priest," *New York Times Magazine*, April 4, 1999, p. 30.

[4]Charles R. Morris, *American Catholic* (Times Books, 1997), p. 246.

[5]Gillis, op. cit., p. 249.

[6]Ibid., p. 246.

[7]David Rice, *Shattered Vows: Priests Who Leave* (William Morrow and Company, 1990), p. 23.

[8]Andrew M. Greeley, *Crisis in the Church: A Study of Religion in America* (Thomas More Press, 1979), p. 11.

[9]Ibid., p. 246.

[10]Jan Kerkhofs, "Priests and 'Parishes'—A Statistical Survey," in *The Right of the Community to a Priest* (Seabury Press, 1980), p. 3, and Fritz Lobinger, "The Right of the Community to Develop in Its Faith," ibid., p. 52.

[11]Kerkhofs, op. cit., p. 4.

[12]Rice, op. cit., p. 24.

[13]Egan, op. cit., p. 30.

[14]Morris, op. cit., p. 293.

[15]Rice, op. cit., p. 23.

[16]Thomas C. Fox, *Sexuality and Catholicism* (George Braziller, 1995), pp. 171–74.

[17]Egan, op. cit., pp. 33, 54.

[18]Ibid., p. 33.

[19]J. N. D. Kelly, *Golden Mouth: The Story of John Chrysostom* (Cornell University Press, 1995), p. 28.

[20]Neil B. McLynn, *Ambrose of Milan: Church and Court in a Christian Capital* (University of California Press, 1994), pp. 44–52.

[21]F. van der Meer, *Augustine the Bishop*, translated by Brian Battershaw and G. R. Lamb (Sheed and Ward, 1961), p. 228.

[22]Timothy D. Barnes, *Athanasius and Constantius: Theology and Politics in the Constantinian Empire* (Harvard University Press, 1993), pp. 23–25.

[23]Van der Meer, op. cit., p. 272.

[24]Ibid.

[25]Edward Schillebeeckx, *The Church With a Human Face: A New and Expanded Theology of Ministry*, translated by John Bowden (Crossroad, 1988), pp. 140–41.

[26]Raymond E. Brown, S.S., *Priest and Bishop: Biblical Reflections* (Paulist Press, 1970), pp. 41–42.

[27]Lobinger, op. cit., pp. 51–56.

[28]Bernard Häring, C.SS.R., translated by Joyce Gadoua, CSJ, *Priesthood Imperiled* (Triumph Books, 1989), p. 133.

[29]Brown, op. cit., pp. 47–48.

[30]Markus Barth, *Ephesians 4–6*, AB34A, pp. 477–84.

[31]Brown, op. cit., p. 58.

[32]Robert F. O'Toole, "Hands, Laying on of," ABD 3.47–49.

[33]Ibid., p. 43.

[34]Florence Morgan Gillman, "James, Brother of Jesus," ABD 3.620–21, and Donald A. Hagner, "James," ABD 3.616–18.

[35]Defenders of papal supremacy want to make Peter the Pope's predecessor as bishop of Rome since they would like to derive a papal claim from Matthew 16:18, "I declare that you are Stone (*Petros*), and on this stone (*petra*) I shall raise up my people's building, stronger than evil's fortress." But exegetes, Catholic as well as Protestant, no longer find a papal commission in this passage. Even Giacomo Martina, S.J., in defending the claim to papal infallibility, says that it can no longer be based on the First Vatican Council's argument from this passage, but only on the church's acceptance of the claim.

[36]Raymond E. Brown, S.S., *Biblical Reflections on Crises Facing the Church* (Paulist Press, 1975), p. 70.

[37]D. W. O'Connor, *Peter in Rome* (Columbia University Press, 1969), p. 207.

[38]See for instance, Richard P. McBrien, *Lives of the Popes* (HarperSanFrancisco, 1997), pp. 29–30, and Eamon Duffy, *Saints and Sinners: A History of the Popes* (Yale University Press, 1997), pp. 7–8.

[39]Duffy, loc. cit.

[40]Ignatius, Letter to the Romans 4:3.

[41]See the text and commentary in William R. Schoedel, *Ignatius of Antioch* (Fortress Press, 1985), for Ignatius to the Magnesians 3:1–2, to the Ephesians 15:1, to Polycarp 1:2 (Schoedel, pp. 77–78, 108–10, 259–60).

[42]For the rapidity of the letters' composition, see P. N. Harrison, *Polycarp's Two Epistles to the Philippians* (Cambridge University Press, 1993), pp. 111–12.

[43]Ibid., pp. 79–106. Cf. Schoedel, op. cit., pp. 212–13.

[44]Ignatius to the Philadelphians 7:11–12 (Schoedel, pp. 204–06).

[45]Schoedel, op. cit., pp. 22, 113. Though Ignatius is usually cited in support of the "monarchical" bishop, "there is a strong collegial element in Ignatius' view of the ministry" (p. 46).

[46]Ignatius to the Trallians 2:3 (Schoedel, p. 141).

[47]Ignatius to the Magnesians 7:1, to the Trallians 2:2 (*aneu*), to the Trallians 7:2, to the Smyrnaeans 8:2 (*choris*).

[48]Ignatius to the Philippians intro., Magnesians 6:1, 6:2.

[49]Ignatius to the Magnesians 13:2. Sometimes the Christians are told to "form ranks with the bishop and the elders" (Ephesians 20:1, Magnesians 2:1, Romans 13:2), or just "with the elders" (Trallians 2:3), or just "with the bishop" (Ephesians 2:1, Trallians 2:1).

[50]John Henry Newman, *On Consulting the Faithful in Matters of Doctrine* (Sheed and Ward, 1961).

[51]Schillebeeckx, op. cit., pp. 211–36.

[52]Jan Grootaers and Joseph A. Selling, *The 1980 Synod of Bishops "On the Role of the Family": An Exposition of the Event and an Analysis of its Texts* (Leuven University Press, 1983), pp. 84–88.

[53]Fox, op. cit., pp. 235–43.

11.

Hydraulics of Grace

CWhen Augustine asked himself what constitutes a valid marriage, he considered one situation in some detail, turning it over and over to form a number of hypotheses about the motives of those caught in such a situation. His close analysis takes its insight from the fact that he is describing his own union with the woman who bore his child when he was a teenager. He lived with that woman—"and with her alone, since I kept faith with her bed"—for fifteen years.[1] They had no more children after the first one. He practiced contraception, since he was a Manichean at the time, and that religion forbade procreation. Here is the account of his condition, along with its moral possibilities, taken from *The Good There Is in Marriage* (Chapter Five):

> It is often asked whether this is a true marriage—when a man and woman, he not another's husband nor she another's wife, live together solely out of desire for each other and not to beget children, but with this understanding: that he will not have sex with another, nor will she.

> [First Hypothesis]

> This could with some logic be called a marriage *if* they have agreed to live so till one of them dies, and *if*, though they do not intend to have a child, neither do they preclude that by an express decision or make use of forbidden means to assure that none is born.

[Second Hypothesis]

But if these conditions are not met, or even one is not, I cannot imagine how this could be considered a marriage. Say a man lives with a woman for a period, but only till he finds another, better suited to him in terms of rank or wealth, whom he will take as wife—he I say is an adulterer in his intent, not with the one he is looking for but with the one he currently sleeps with outside of marriage. And so is she an adulteress if, aware of this arrangement and consenting to it, she has mere sex with him nonetheless, outside the marriage bond.

[Third Hypothesis]

But if she remains faithful to his bed, and seeks no other partner after he has gone off to his bride, and is determined to abstain from sex, I could not with any assurance consider her an adulteress, though no one doubts that having sex with a man not her husband is sinful.

[Fourth Hypothesis]

In fact, if she had wanted to have children, so far as the decision was up to her, but unwillingly did whatever was done to prevent conception, I would think better of her than of many women, lawfully wed and therefore not adulteresses, who force reluctant husbands to render their sexual dues, not out of a desire for children but with a lustful excess in demanding what is their right.

[Fifth Hypothesis]

Yet even here there is some good, because at least they are married. For women marry to bring lust under a legitimate restraint, not letting it rove at large without focus (for it has no principle of restraint within itself), but making it stable in faithful companionship, where the boundless urge for sex is tempered by the chaste purpose of having children. So, though it is a low thing to have lust, even for a husband, still it is good to desire only one's own husband and to have none but his children.

After a general description of the relationship, considered from without, he goes into the internal attitudes of the partners. The first hypothesis describes what would have been a valid marriage if he and his partner had observed the two conditions of permanent fidelity and procreation. The second hypothesis describes what he actually was guilty of—adultery to his partner, since he observed neither of the two conditions. It may be asked how he could be adulterous if his attitude made the marriage invalid in the first place. He says that the adultery is not legal and literal but "in intent" (*in animo*). This is his way of stressing that he wronged the partner he left, not the woman he was planning to marry. His partner would have been equally adulterous in her intent if she had not observed lifelong fidelity and had prevented children's birth.

But in fact (Hypothesis Three) she did observe lifelong fidelity, not marrying again. She thus met one of the two conditions in the first hypothesis—so that, even though she was not legally married, Augustine hesitates to judge her. Meeting even one of the two conditions places her outside the normal condemnation of adultery. Yet the matter is not allowed to rest here. He goes on to say (Hypothesis Four) that she also met the other condition, in so far as she was able, wanting to have more children though he would not let her. That makes her even less an adulteress than she was felt to be in the former hypothesis. More than that, it makes her nobler than ("placed above," *anteponenda*) legally married women who separate sex from procreation in their marriages. These women are like Augustine when he practiced contraception in his illicit affair.

But Augustine, wanting to be fair even when he honors such women less than his former lover, says that at least they confined their sex within marriage, where the partner's "dues" have to be honored. And even if the married women have no children, they would have them with their husbands if with anyone, so long as they keep sexual activity confined to them. Such are the gradations of merit or guilt that can be involved inside as well as outside the marriage bond.

This is a sensitive treatment, a kind of masked tribute to the woman he wronged, exonerating her and condemning only himself. His Christian readers (of whom she could well have been one) knew of his affair, which he had openly described in his *Confessiones*, and would have understood what he was talking about. But what should surprise and interest us most about the entire discussion is what isn't there, what would have been there if a modern bishop were discussing valid marriage. There is no mention of wedding "in the church." Hypothesis One gives us a description of a valid marriage, though no priest is needed to perform it, no sacrament is entailed. In all Augustine's hundreds of sermons, there is none that was delivered at a wedding ceremony—for a quite simple reason: marriage was not, in the fourth century, a sacrament of the church.

It is true that Augustine says there must be three things in any marriage—offspring (*proles*), companionship (*fides*), and a symbolic bond (*sacramentum*). That term *sacramentum*, a favorite one with Augustine, never means what Catholics now call a sacrament, one of the seven authorized channels of grace administered by the church. "It is clear that for him the word *sacramentum* is still something very imprecise."[2] Used of marriage, *sacramentum* meant for Augustine the symbolic bond in the creation story, where God creates man and woman so that they shall become "one flesh" in marriage (Gen 2:24), making their union permanent. "every holy sign—every sign, that is to say, which the words either of Scripture or of the Church refer to things divine—he calls a 'sacrament.' "[3] Even when the New Testament talks about the permanence of marriage, it refers to the Genesis text (Mt 19:5, Mk 10:7, Eph 5:31). The New Testament saying that husbands should love their wives as Christ does the church (Eph 5:25) has been offered as a sacramental claim for marriage, but Markus Barth shows that the Ephesians passage is about a nonlegalistic love in perfect freedom of the Spirit.[4]

Since God established the nature of marriage at creation, the early church did not feel it had any jurisdiction over it. For Augustine, as we have just seen, it was the inner motives of the partners themselves that constituted the reality of marriage. In *The City of God* (6.9) he derides the pomp (and the obscenity) of pagan marriage rites. Legal marriage is necessary, to secure property rights and legitimacy of inheriting offspring. But the spiritual reality of "one flesh" can only be the product of the partners' *fides*, making each a trusty (*fidus*) companion. Thus the church council of Toledo (499 CE) recognized the validity of what we call "natural law marriages"—which is what Augustine's union would have been if he had met the two *internal* conditions of the first hypothesis above. Roman law at the same time recognized concubinage as a form of monogamy.[5]

It was not until the fifth century, after Augustine's death, that the church began to validate marriages on its own, stepping in to replace the diminishing authority of the state in the Christian empire.[6] The preeminence of the bride's father in Roman marriage yielded gradually to the authority of the priest. As the sacramental status of marriage made it a channel of grace, the proper church ceremony became the condition of legitimate cohabitation for Catholics. Omission of it made any intercourse sinful, even if it took place within a civilly sanctioned marriage. The Catholic who omitted this sacrament was precluded from receiving other sacraments. To be married "outside the church" resulted, that is, in de facto excommunication. One could not receive the Eucharist again until the sin was repented, until the false marriage was broken off or a real one performed by a priest.

The aim in creating this sacrament was to give marriage new force and spirituality, to make it a special source of grace to the married partners. But its paradoxical result was to cheapen all marriages but the new kind. Augustine's union, if he had observed the conditions described in Hypothesis One, would have been a sacred bond, just as it was described in Genesis. But now the church felt that it could demote this divinely sanctioned marriage and replace it with an ecclesiastically sanctioned one. Since other marriages are not real ones, they need not be permanent. The partners did not become "one flesh" because a priest did not bless them. The Catholic who sinfully contracts such a marriage, or the non-Catholic who does so innocently, can later leave the partner of such a union and enter the church to receive a "real" marriage.

Since only the church marriage need be permanent, there is no divorce from it. But the church has figured out a way to make even this sacramental marriage not real—if it can be established that one or both of the partners suffered some defect (physical, mental, or attitudinal) that disqualified them from marriage at that time. The marriage can be de-

clared null. There is no divorce, because the marriage never existed in the
first place. It was never really contracted. That is how Sheila Rauch
Kennedy, two years after her divorce from Joseph Kennedy, the nephew
of President John Kennedy, learned that her marriage, which had lasted
for twelve years and produced two children, had never existed. Her former husband wanted to remarry in the church, and the condition was
that she agree that there had been a defect in the first ceremony. She did
not think there had been. The two had known each other for nine years
before their marriage. They were both mature, responsible, in love, aware
of the church's requirements, and certain that they met them. Why
should she deny this now? Was she to claim, against her conscience, that
she brought children into the world without a due regard for the sacred-
ness of the union that produced them?

The church authorities she dealt with encouraged her to be complicit
in what she felt was a lie. In fact, they could not understand her obstruc-
tiveness. They even hinted that her attitude could itself be made a sign of
her defective attitude fourteen years earlier. She was shocked at her encounter with the structures of deceit. Her ex-husband could not understand why she was being so punitive to him and his new bride. She
reports him as saying: "Look, Sheila, get yourself under control. Of course
I took our marriage and the children seriously. And of course I think we
had a true marriage. But that doesn't matter now. I don't believe this stuff.
Nobody actually believes it. It's just Catholic gobbledygook, Sheila. But
you just have to say it this way because, well, because that's the way the
church is."[7]

If he did not say that, plenty of other Catholics do. The annulment
process has become so wholesale, perfunctory, and dishonest that it is
widely accepted as "Catholic divorce." In America alone there are over
sixty thousand annulments per year. Ninety percent of those who apply
for them receive them.[8] Oddly enough this situation is supported by
many "liberal" priests who think the church's requirement of lifelong fidelity is too hard. Instead of being able to say that honestly, they support
the lying fiction that marriages like that of the Kennedys never took
place. Since Sheila Kennedy would not cooperate with the deception,
Joseph Kennedy had to rely on testimony from political friends and supporters to "establish" that he had not been mature enough to take mar-

riage vows when he was twenty-seven—though of course he was qualified now to enter into a real marriage, having proved the unreality of the
first one.

It might surprise Catholics to know that the sacrament of penance did
not exist in Augustine's fourth century, any more than the sacrament of
matrimony did. In the early days of the church, it was felt that baptism
created a new person, incorporated into the body of Christ and filled
with the Holy Spirit. Sin was an entire way of life, lived under the domain of the devil. Lapses and squabbles within the loving community
could be borne by forgiving brothers and sisters—Saint Paul does not tell
the troublemakers in the Corinthian community that they must go to
confession, or perform any rituals of penance. A really serious offense led
to permanent expulsion from the body of Christ—as when Peter curses
Ananias for "lying to the Holy Spirit" (Acts 5:3–5). Ananias had cut himself off from the body of Christ, where the Spirit made all one. The example of Judas taught that one who had turned himself back to the devil
was lost.

When some Christians defected from fear or weakness during the
Roman persecutions, rigorists like the followers of Donatus in Africa felt
that the only way for these severed members to reunite with the body of
Christ was to start all over again, with a new baptism. Augustine and others opposed this repetition of initiation. They gave the egregious sinner
one chance to do public penance. They rejoined the body after a pre-
scribed period of humiliation and good behavior, with reduced status
where that was appropriate (priests lost their priesthood). If another offense occurred after that, the sinner was permanently excommunicated.

This early concept of penance was entirely communal. The sinner had
publicly withdrawn from the body of Christ, shamed his or her baptism,
broken the mystical solidarity with Christ's members. Though the bishop
set the terms for re-entry—which often involved months of public test-
ing and penitential acts—it was the whole community which accepted
the sinner back, restoring him or her to equality with it in the oneness
of the Savior's body. There was no private commerce with a priest, who
alone might claim the power to forgive sin in secret.[9]

The introduction of private penance for lesser sins was done, like the granting of annulments, for motives of compassion. But it went along with the sacralization of the priesthood, the monopolization of grace, and the severance of priest judges from lay sinners. Just as the priest alone came to consecrate the Eucharist, and withdrew into a sacred sanctuary sealed off from the layman, so did the priest become a judge of every aspect of a person's life in the confessional. There was a commerce in grace, which was conceived of as a quantifiable item. Mortal sin drained it totally from the soul. Venial sins lowered the level in the tank. Occasions of grace filled the tank back up. People were encouraged to go to confession frequently, even for minor sins, since more grace was poured in each time.

Grace could also be acquired by authorized devotions, including the grace of an early pass from purgatory if indulgences were earned. Instead of the Spirit as a continual presence in the church, variously manifested but always energizing the whole, grace became a private possession (or deprivation). Prayers were said to boost the private supply of grace. Saying the rosary earned an indulgence of specified days spared in purgatory (if the rosary was a properly blessed one). Indulgences could be earned by going to certain churches on certain feasts (some would pop in and out repeatedly to rack up a larger number). The clergy manned a hydraulic system pumping grace back into souls, or measuring its flow to this or that good cause.

The respected Dominican theologian, Yves Congar, asked why the Holy Spirit, continually referred to and invoked in the early history of the church, became a kind of forgotten person of the Trinity in more recent times. He suggests that there has been a substitution of human agencies for the free action of the Divinity. Instead of the presence of the Spirit, breathing where it will, in the interaction of the Father with the Son in His body, grace is made a stuff controlled by the papal system of spiritual aqueducts and storage tanks. In a new form of idolatry, the Pope becomes a substitute for the Spirit. Congar quotes Pope Pius IX making this claim in 1864:

The Catholic Church is one with a unity that is visible and perfect throughout the whole world and among all peoples, with a unity,

the beginning, the root and the indefectible source of which is the
supreme authority and the "excellent principality" of blessed Peter,
the prince of the apostles and of his successors in the Roman
throne.[10]

Pius XII said much the same in 1950, when he wrote that the
enlightener of the church is not the Spirit but the teaching office of the
Vatican:

Together with the sacred sources (Scripture and tradition), God has
given to his Church a living magisterium to throw light on and explain those matters that are contained in the deposit of faith only in
an obscure and so to speak implicit manner.[11]

This model of the Pope as omnicompetent oracle, replacing scripture
and the Spirit, is what John Paul II admires in his forebear Pius XII.

---

[1]Augustine, *Confessions* 4.2.

[2]F. van der Meer, *Augustine the Bishop*, translated by Brian Battershaw and G. R. Lamb
(Sheed and Ward, 1961), p. 280.

[3]Ibid., p. 298.

[4]Markus Barth, *Ephesians 4–6* (AB 34A, 1960), pp. 738–53.

[5]Antti Arjwa, *Women and Law in Late Antiquity* (Oxford University Press, 1996), pp.
205–10.

[6]Ibid., pp. 193–202.

[7]Sheila Rauch Kennedy, *Shattered Faith* (Pantheon Books, 1997), pp. 10–11.

[8]Ibid., p. 12.

[9]Van der Meer, op. cit., pp. 382–87.

[10]Yves Congar, *I Believe in the Holy Spirit*, translated by David Smith (Crossroad, 1983),Vol.
I, p. 162, quoting Pius's letter of September 16, 1864, rejecting union with any branch of
Christendom that does not recognize papal supremacy.

[11]Ibid., p. 162, quoting Pius XII's encyclical *Humani Generis*.

12.

Conspiracy of Silence

One of the most poignant things about cases of priests molesting children or youths is that they go, naturally, for their easiest targets—good Catholic families. As the report on a survey of clinicians dealing with child abuse put it: "Religious professionals' role as unquestioned moral leaders apparently gave them special access to children, much like the access that trusted family members have in incest cases."[1] Devout Catholic families will be the least suspicious of a priest's conduct and the most intimidated about challenging the church. They will also, precisely because of their faith and trust, be the most deeply seared by betrayal. The Miglini family of Dallas, Texas, is a good example. Pious people, more than tithing their worldly goods to the church, they had priests in their family and circle of friends. They felt grateful for the attention given their children by these eminent men of God. That is why it was such a shock for their older son, Mike, to wake up with a priest clawing his hips and trying to thrust his penis into his anus.[2]

In 1984, Mike had been invited to visit Father Robert Peebles at his chaplain's post, Fort Benning, Georgia. He knew the priest from the time when Peebles was the Miglinis' parish priest in Dallas, the scoutmaster of the diocese's Catholic Boy Scout troop. Mrs. Miglini had sewed Peebles's scoutmaster uniform. Mike was flattered to be invited to inspect the Fort Benning flight operation. But instead of giving him a tour of the base, Father Peebles took Mike straight to his room where they drank beer after beer while renewing their acquaintance. After Mike woke from a beer-induced stupor to feel the priest's assault he ran to the post's military police, who arrested Father Peebles. But, in accord with deference patterns that shelter priests, the arresting officers did not notify Mike's parents or take him to the civil authorities. Instead, they placed him in the custody of another priest.

That priest, they may have supposed, would surely think first of Mike's own needs, calling his parents, or taking the fifteen-year-old to a doctor, or both. That is what you or I would do, and we are not given that self-less concern for others that celibacy frees the priest to act on. No, this man—held, we have been taught, to a higher standard of compassion—called another priest at All Saints in Dallas to discuss damage control. His first thought was for the reputation of the assailant, not for the harm done to the one assailed. He was not himself a child molester, or a defender of molestation. He did not think of his action as protecting a criminal. He was protecting the church from imputations (true or false) of heartless-ness, and he was exemplifying that heartlessness as he tried to deny it. He did not have reason to fear a superior's rebuke for his conduct. He had more reason to suspect that he would be punished for not protecting the "good name" of a priest. He surely knew other priests that had happened to. He did not even have to give the matter much thought. Long habit, deep patterns of mutual "support," come automatically to priests in such a situation. The Pope's grand vision of men freed from families in order to be fearless and truthful in service to others can quickly be reduced, where "the good of the church" is concerned, to an incapacity for reach-ing up to the level, even, of common decency.

Mike was kept all the next day and night at the priest's rectory—hardly the most comforting atmosphere after his humiliating experience. The next day he was sent home, to be greeted at the airport, not by his par-ents (who had still not been informed), but by the priest who had been called the night before, who took him to All Saints parish. Only then were the parents informed of an "attempted" assault. The pastor, Mon-signor Raphael Kamel—who was chancellor of the diocese—told them this had never happened before. The parents then met with the judicial vicar of the diocese, Father David Fellhauer (later Bishop Fellhauer). He agreed that Mike should meet with a psychologist, one who helped the diocese (he would also, without the parents' knowing it, be Father Pee-bles' psychologist). This doctor said that the trauma of a trial would be injurious to their son. Meanwhile, Monsignor Kamel, a family friend, asked the parents to allow the military police not to bring Father Peebles before a court-martial. He needed counseling, not twenty years in prison at Fort Leavenworth. The parents did as they were asked, thinking of the scandal they might cause the church.

They did not tell their younger son, Tony, what had happened, not wanting to make him disillusioned with the church. That was unfortunate. If they had told him, Tony now says, he would have let them know something that he had been hiding from them in shame. He had been sexually abused by another priest at All Saints, Father Rudolph Kos. (A third priest resident at All Saints at the same time, Father William Hughes, would later face trial for sexual assault on a young girl.)

The parents did not realize that they had been made complicitous in a cover-up by Father Peebles's enablers. Their only fault was their devotion to the church. That was part of what inflamed Father Peebles, by his own later admission: "I never molested a stranger, or even a casual acquaintance. There always had to be that element of trust and even adulation on the part of both the boy and his parents."[3] He had been a sexual abuser at All Saints—he had been reassigned to Fort Benning after confessing that. His confessor told him to repent sincerely, but not to torture himself with guilt—the boys were young and would "bounce back." With the help of the Miglinis' letter, Peebles was allowed to leave the army with a less than honorable discharge and no court-martial. The diocese sent him to a counseling center, where—after a month—he was said to be cured, and reassigned to another Dallas parish, where he became pastor. When more charges against him arose, he was sent again to a counseling center, where his record showed that he admitted to molesting between fifteen and twenty boys in a seven-year period. The diocese now dismissed him, but gave him $22,000 for tuition at Tulane University Law School and supported him with $800 a month for two years.[4]

In a sense, Mike and Tony were the lucky ones. Mike suffered claw marks, Tony just had Father Kos take his foot and masturbate himself with it. Had they been around the priests longer, they would have been assailed anally and orally by the two priests, as other boys were. What saved Tony further molestation was his parents' refusal to let him stay overnight with the altar boys' club Kos kept at the parish. Kos urged other parents to let their boys stay over in order to keep his adopted son company. The "son" would not learn till he was thirty-one that he had never been legally adopted, though Kos had told his mother, a single working mother, that he was adopting him to "help bring the boy up." Kos ran a club for boys that supplied minors with alcohol, TV games, marijuana, and sex. Other priests in the rectory ignored this activity. (Two others, it later turned out, were also abusing minors.)

Only when Kos was moved to a new parish, in 1985, did the pastor there complain to the diocese of the way Kos kept boys in his room.[5] Monsignor Robert Rehkemper, the second highest official in the diocese, ordered Kos to stop the practice. When Kos did not desist, the pastor wrote again to Rehkemper, describing the number of boys still staying overnight. Nothing happened. The pastor wrote a third time. The diocesan personnel board now knew of the infractions, and instructed Rehkemper to write a stern order that it must stop. Rehkemper, instead of writing, gave Kos a vocal warning. Once again, the priest persisted. The pastor wrote to the bishop now, but heard only that Father Kos was being moved to Ennis, Texas, where he became pastor of his own church.

The next year, a couple in Kos's church wrote to the bishop complaining of his keeping boys in the parish house. Two years after that, an assistant pastor went to Monsignor Rehkemper to report on Kos's continued pattern of behavior. Kos was sent to a Catholic psychiatrist, who saw no reason to remove Kos (who kept up the abuse even as he was seeing the psychiatrist). But a social worker who had become familiar with the case wrote Rehkemper that Kos's behavior was that of a "classic pedophile." Now the alarmed assistant pastor wrote a detailed (twelve-page) letter to the bishop, Charles Grahmann. Kos was sent to a counseling center in New Mexico—from which he called one of his victims to have a rendezvous while he was on leave from the center.[6]

Finally, in 1993, first one boy, then several, and finally eleven boys— now men—brought suit against Father Kos for his long record of abuse. One boy from Kos's "club" could not join the suit—he had committed suicide after leaving the circle. (The parents, unaware of his role in the tragedy, asked Kos to be the celebrant at their son's funeral.) The jury, angry at the church's long neglect of every sign of abuse, awarded the plaintiffs a record $110 million dollars in damages in the civil suit for neglect. (Kos was later convicted in a criminal suit and sent to prison.)

It had come out in the trial that Kos had, as a teenager, abused his own younger brothers. An early marriage was annulled when his wife told the priest of the marriage tribunal that "he had a problem with boys." After one unsuccessful application to enter the diocesan seminary in Irving, Texas, Kos was admitted by the vocation director, over the misgivings of the man who had first rejected him. Since his record of abuse was continuous before entering and immediately after leaving the seminary, it is presumed that he was active there, too, yet he was ordained.

The jury was especially offended by the conduct on the stand of Bishop Grahmann and Monsignor Rehkemper. Jurors asked the judge's permission to write these priests a letter of rebuke to go along with their verdict. Rehkemper said that no parishioner had ever complained to him about Father Kos, though one woman testified that she had done just that. One of the psychiatrists to whom Kos was sent said under oath that Rehkemper had withheld information about the patient the monsignor remanded to him. Rehkemper admitted to having read the twelve-page letter sent to the bishop by Kos's assistant pastor, but when the plaintiffs' lawyer referred him to the section that said the assistant had seen Kos under the covers in bed with a boy, Rehkemper said that he did not remember that passage. Did he ever directly ask Kos if he had molested boys? "I didn't see any reason to."[7] The judge warned Rehkemper that she would hold him in contempt if he kept treating the questions with arrogant defiance.

Though Monsignor Rehkemper found no reason to question the priest—despite warnings from a pastor in one place, an assistant in another one, from lay people, from the social worker who told him Kos was a classic pedophile—he claimed after the trial that the parents should have seen the signs he had failed to discern. In a tape-recorded interview, he fumed that the suit never should have been brought, that the jury made the wrong decision, that the parents were the negligent ones.[8]

No one ever says anything about what the role of the parents was in all this. They more properly should have known because they're close to the kids. Parents have the prime responsibility to look after their kids. I don't want to judge them one way or the other, but it doesn't appear they were very concerned about their kids.

On the one hand, Kos did not do much that was wrong, because the kids were damaged goods anyway:

> I'm sure some kids were damaged, but I think the damage might have happened even without Father Kos, you see. They had problems even before they knew Father Kos, many of them.

On the other hand, these damaged kids should have been perfectly responsible by the age of seven, more so than the adult who was seducing them from a vantage point of power and moral authority:

> They [the victims] knew what was right and what was wrong. Anybody who reaches the age of reason shares responsibility for what they do. So that makes us all responsible after we reach the age of six or seven.

In the course of the same interview, Rehkemper said that the boys' staying overnight was not suspicious, as seen from the diocesan point of view:

> Not when the priests have these Nintendo games and that kind of thing. Kids are drawn to that kind of stuff. This is not new in churches. Kids hang around a lot of times. It keeps them off the street, you see. That doesn't mean any kind of molestation is going on.

But he simultaneously said it *was* a suspicious circumstance, or should have been, from the parents' point of view:

> Why let boys go and stay an unlimited amount of time in a church rectory with priests? I just don't understand it.

Calling the award of money "outlandish" and "very, very unjust," he comforted himself with the thought that it might actually hurt the recipients:

> It just seems like an awful lot of money to me for what happened to them. I don't think it's even possible for the diocese to pay out

all that money. You know people who win the lottery usually end
up bankrupt. Whether the money comes from a court judgment or
a lottery, they still have to know how to use the money and not be
swindled out of it and so forth.

When a diocesan spokesman, Father John Bell, was asked on the "Larry
King Live" show if he could justify Rehkemper's outburst, he answered,
mysteriously, that his words reflected "a time when things could easily be
explained in Aristotelian logic." Rehkemper had told the interviewer
taping him that he was proud of his testimony at the trial, and he had no
intention of resigning from his current post, as pastor of All Saints, the
parish that had three child molesters in residence during the preceding
decade. But the firestorm that greeted his comments made Bishop Grahmann decide he had to pay for his "Aristotelian logic" with his job.

Though Grahmann made a public apology *if* there had been hurt to
the children—lawyers warned that insurance companies would not pay
damages if the church admitted neglect—his own attitude came out in
minutes of a private meeting held with his advisers (the minutes were
leaked to one of the plaintiffs' lawyers, Sylvia Demarest). A priest "com-
mented that he feels very abused by the legal system; he has a great deal
of resentment." Bishop Grahmann said, "We are a church of the abused
and of the abuser." He seemed to agree with the editor of the diocesan
newspaper that the church was the victim in this case. The men were
called together to plan "the next step." They wanted to get the judge
dismissed from hearing their post-trial motions. Action to disqualify her
would be successful, it was hoped, since it would come before a Catholic
judge who had assured a lawyer present at the meeting that he would assign the case to himself. But he had to recuse himself after the minutes
of the meeting were published in the newspaper. He said he had not realized that the lawyer had a connection with the diocese (though how
else could he have known the diocese's as yet unannounced strategy?).[9]

What is dispiriting about the Kos case is the way all its main features
recur in the other (and frequent) examples of sexual molestation by
priests—the long ignoring of blatant signs that it was occurring, the
compulsive repetition of the crime despite warnings and counseling,
the reassignment of the priests to new posts without alerting anyone at

the posts that the priests have a record of assault or seduction, the delay and defiance and noncooperation on the part of church authorities when victims come forward. All these elements were present in the first case given full public reporting, a decade before Kos's trial—the nest of seven priest molesters around LaFayette, Louisiana, written up by Jason Berry in his book, *Lead Us Not into Temptation*. This case began with the discovery of multiple abuses by a Father Gilbert Gauthe. A canon lawyer in the Washington diplomatic office of the Vatican, the Dominican priest Thomas Doyle, tried to create a policy for dealing honestly with such cases. With the help of a priest-doctor and a lawyer for Father Gauthe, he drew up a set of guidelines to present to the 1985 meeting of the American bishops. It contained findings that would have precluded recycling of the priests in Dallas from one church to another, without supervision, into the next decade:

> We are dealing with compulsive habits which the priest may temporarily suspend in the face of legal or canonical pressure, but not in all instances. There are many examples wherein sexual abuse took place very soon after the confrontation between the priest and his Ordinary [bishop] had taken place. The priest must clearly be seen as one suffering from a psychiatric disorder that is beyond his ability to control.[10]

The bishops secretly discussed the report, then tabled it. Some did not want to reveal that the problem was a common one by having to adopt an official policy on it. Others had an old priestly contempt for psychiatry (confession is supposed to cure the soul). Still others claimed that Doyle and his companions were just trying to create a power center of their own. Each diocese is jealous of outside control. The control exercised from Rome they cannot exclude. That from anywhere else, whether Washington or other dioceses, they resent. It was hoped that the rash of reported cases was an aberration. It would go away. Doyle continues to be resented by some bishops. He was called in by plaintiffs at the Kos trial to testify on the patterns of molestations around the country—information the bishops do not want to receive, and which they especially do not want to see disseminated in newspapers or on TV. In "the good old days," church scandals were discreetly handled in private. The bishops could not bring themselves to recognize that such an era is gone, that modern media are too pervasive to be defied or manipulated into silence. Some bishops still refuse to face that fact. Doyle argued for honesty as the best policy. It is a recommendation the bishops were by training unable to accept.

In cases of priest molestation, church officials have tried to restrict coverage of the facts. Prominent Catholics call newspapers to suppress stories. As we saw, the minutes of the meeting with Bishop Grahmann revealed a resentment of the media, as if they had created the problems they reported. The local paper covering the LaSalle County priests was boycotted and in danger of bankruptcy from a loss of advertising revenue.[11] Yet the truth cannot be suppressed. There is a serious problem that has festered for years. A survey showed that, from 1983 to 1987, an average of one case a week was reported—and this, like incest, is a classically underreported crime.[12] No diocese, of the nation's 188, has been without its pedophilia case. In September 1994, sixty priests or brothers were in prison for child abuse—and many more in various recovery programs.[13] Disheartening enough are the individual cases—including the famous one of the Franciscan priest, Bruce Ritter, founder of New York City's Covenant House, a man who had been considered a modern Father Flanagan protecting the young.[14] Even sadder is the uncovering of whole cultures of pedophilia, as in Mount Cashel, the Christian Brothers orphanage in Newfoundland:

> Nine Christian Brothers, two of whom were lovers, sodomized, whipped, punched, fondled, and degraded at least thirty Mount Cashel boys for more than twenty years. Testimony pointed to a ring of overlapping pedophiles and sado-masochistic homosexuals, including five men, living in town, who had grown up in the orphanage and returned to molest boys.[15]

Newfoundland was a kind of pedophile's paradise, where four diocesan priests were convicted of the crime (out of seven charged).[16] This is an international problem for the church. Christian Brothers schools in Australia showed patterns of abuse like that in their Newfoundland orphanage.[17] In Ireland, the Prime Minister was forced to resign in 1994 for inadequate prosecution of sexual abuse in the clergy.[18]

Though religious superiors' first instinct is to allege that reported abuses are single lapses, in fact almost every priest caught has been a multiple offender, extending his abuse over years. This is a crime of deep compulsion. It also tends to repeat itself over generations. Many child abusers were themselves abused as children. In Australian prisons, 93 percent of the men serving time for child molestation said they had been abused as children, *half of them by priests or brothers*.[19] A study of "regressive pedophiles" estimates that such a man "will have sexual encounters with an average of 265 youngsters in a lifetime" if he is not caught and controlled.[20] But how is he to be controlled? John Money, the Johns Hopkins University specialist in sex studies, says: "If you put a pedophile in jail, there's not a chance he'll grow up and learn to love a woman of his own age . . . Because when they get out they'll do it again. Every pedophile I know in jail says the fantasies drive them wild."[21]

When "Larry King Live" devoted a show to the Dallas case, in August 1997, a lawyer for the diocese said that Father Kos's crime had nothing to do with priestly celibacy. He pointed out that noncelibate people in professions that care for the young have their own cases of pedophilia—youth counselors, teachers, Scout masters, and so on. That is true of the "helping professions" in general. A 1989 survey showed that 5.5 percent of male psychologists had sexual relations with their patients. Ten percent admitted to "erotic practices" short of intercourse.[22] But most of those patients were adults. And the priest pedophile differs from others in three important ways, all of them connected with celibacy.

First, the Scout master is not one who has publicly claimed membership in a group vowed to lifelong abstention from sex of any kind, with any partner, male or female, young or old. The priest was especially trusted because he is someone who has undertaken a heroic act of self-control. The professed celibate was thought of as the athlete of sexual mastery. For him to deal with the young is, in the official ideology, a meeting of the innocent with the innocent. After all, Pope Paul VI said that this is the advantage of celibacy—that it gives one a special aura of the otherworldly, that it is an "eschatalogical sign" of human transcendence. According to *Sacerdotalis Caelibatus*, the priestly life gives us a foreglimpse of the way "in the resurrection they neither marry nor are given in marriage, but are like angels in heaven."[23] What this meant, in practical terms, for many of the parents of the molested, was that they trusted their children to a priest almost as if to God—and certainly more than to any other teacher or counselor. Since that was the trust that was betrayed, the consequent bitterness, or disillusion, or loss of faith was proportionately great. It is not an ordinary experience to be betrayed by God.

The second way that celibacy affects priests' pedophilia is that the reverence due to heroic abstention has made civil officials chary of investigating, reporting, or prosecuting celibates' offenses. As we saw, the military police turned Mike Miglini over to another priest, honoring the status of the celibate as a class even when forced to arrest an individual from that class. The military police complied when Mike's parents asked them not to prosecute Father Peebles, since they wanted to avoid scandal in the church. For years, priests caught drunk were not arrested by the police. During the investigation in LaFayette, Louisiana, a prosecutor told Father Gauthe's lawyer: "I want you to carry a message to the bishop. The other night vice squad officers apprehended Father Tom Bathay [pseudonym] for soliciting sex in the men's room of a truck stop outside town. He was not charged. That's the second time this has happened with him. You tell the bishop that if it happens again Bathay's ass is going to jail."[24] Even a warning shows an extended (but not infinitely extendable) deference. One reason the press's new-found aggressiveness is so resented by the clergy is that they were used to having their wishes accommodated. Catholics felt protective, and non-Catholics did not want to offend religious sensibilities. The cops were nice to priests in the way that the movies were. The image of the priest that people wanted to maintain was that of Bing Crosby or Spencer Tracy in Roman collars. Nothing is more damaging to that image than pedophilia. The stakes are much higher, in every way, when a sex criminal is a priest.

They are highest of all, of course, for priests themselves—which is the third and most important thing that makes clerical pedophilia different. For a priest to be a pedophile raises the question whether the celibate discipline for a whole class of men (not just for the spiritually gifted individual) is a false, because unrealizable, ideal. If a man cannot control even the most corrupting kind of sexual predation in himself, can we really believe that the masses of them control more normal and pervasive instincts? Priests themselves widely doubt it, and some of them have begun to say that they do. Even the respected Cardinal Seper told the 1971 synod of bishops in Rome, "I am not at all optimistic that celibacy is being observed."[25]

Those in the best position to know agree that it is not. The most-respected work in this area is that of Richard Sipe, a monk himself for twenty years and then psychiatric specialist in the study of clerical sexual habits. From years of interviews, counseling, surveys, and discussion with other experts, he made a conservative estimate in 1990 that about 20 percent of priests are sexually active with women at any one time, with an added 8 to 10 percent still exploring some kind of intimate ties with women. He found 20 percent of priests homosexually oriented, with 10 percent of them sexually active (4 percent of them with children). And he concludes that about 80 percent of priests masturbate, at least occasionally.[26] Others have reached figures at least as high in all these categories. The Jesuit sociologist Joseph H. Ficher, S.J., credited an account of over 30 percent of German priests having affairs with women.[27] Andrew Greeley says that 25 percent of priests under thirty-five are gay, half of them sexually active.[28] Jason Berry reports seminarians telling him Greeley's numbers should be doubled.[29] Dr. William Masters found that ninety-eight out of the hundred priests he surveyed were masturbating.[30] Sipe would revise some of his figures upward with new evidence for a book he published five years after his first one (see Chapter 13).

Whatever one thinks of the morality of any of these acts, such figures are obviously related to the thesis of this book, that the life of church authorities is lived within structures of multiple deceit. It is not surprising that priests are unwilling to impose moral claims on others, in areas like contraception and the role of women, when they daily live in contravention of what the Pope claims about sex and their own celibacy. Masturbation and homosexuality are not, in themselves and always, the "objective disorder" that papal teaching continues to make of them. But that *is* the teaching. And priests must hide from lay people and superiors and each other (and, sometimes, themselves) the "witness of their lives," as Paul VI called it.

This goes a long way toward explaining the sad actions described at the beginning of this chapter. How, we ask at first, could the priests and superiors and bishops look the other way while children were being abused? Looking the other way is a deeply ingrained habit and necessity, a tactic of survival, for men whose lives are honeycombed with furtive acts. One's own life, or that of one's friends, or of people one must depend on, will not admit any very severe scrutiny. It would be dangerous—in terms of scandal and lay disappointment, for those being observant themselves—to let light flood the shadowy underworld of secrecy and evasion and misrepresentation that is the priestly way of life. It may be understandable that homosexual priests would be hesitant to report, or even to know about, the abuse of little boys—why expose their own situation by stirring up trouble about another's? This is the perfect occasion for maintaining an *ignorantia affectata*. But why would heterosexual priests protect homosexual offenders? According to Sipe, some of them have victims of their own on their consciences, not quite as helpless as children, but nonetheless dazzled by the aura of the priesthood and usually abandoned when the priest's "experiment" with his own sexuality ends. The forgiving community of priests that welcomes back heterosexual offenders usually blames the "temptress" that lured him from his duty, reviving the old view of women as carnal lures.[31] Some women (Sipe knows a support group of fifty of them) have been told they must get an abortion so as not to reveal the priest's affair.[32]

My point here is not to judge the priests but to return to the dissonance between papal claims and lived reality. The gap between the two widens every day as the Pope ignores the reality and reasserts the claims in a bluster of authority. Take the matter of masturbation. Until very recently, young boys were taught that every act of masturbation was a mortal sin, one that drained the soul of grace and sent it to hell if one died before repenting and confessing it. They were even given weighty arguments in theology. In matters of the Sixth Commandment (in the Catholic numbering), there is "no parvity of matter"—every sexual act but that between marital partners not practicing contraception is "grave" (i.e., every such sin is a mortal sin). This made young teenagers hardened sinners, who were blackening their souls time after time, all through adolescence. Yet they were often confessing to men who, without the excuse of adolescence, were masturbating themselves.

But surely things have changed now? No priest still teaches that stuff about parvity of matter? Things have not changed at the official level—how could they? The church, at that level, claims never to change its teaching. In 1994, after long years of preparation, John Paul II wrote a commendatory letter for the new catechism approved by Cardinal Ratzinger, which has this to say:

> By masturbation is to be understood the deliberate stimulation of the genital organs in order to derive sexual pleasure. Both *the Magisterium* of the Church, in the course of *a constant tradition*, and the moral sense of the faithful have been in *no doubt* and have *firmly maintained* that masturbation is an intrinsically and *gravely* disordered action. [Emphasis added.][33]

There is still no parvity of matter, just "gravely disordered action." So has nothing changed? Well, there is a "pastoral" note appended, saying that moral immaturity—like that of Joseph Kennedy, invalidating his marriage—may temper judgment:

> To form an equitable judgment about the subject's moral responsibility and to guide pastoral action, one must take into account the affective immaturity, force of acquired habit, conditions of anxiety, or other psychological or social factors that lessen or even extenuate moral culpability.

There is more at work here than just the face-saving claim that the teaching itself has never changed. To yield on that point would endanger the condemnation of other "unnatural" acts. All sex but the sex act itself in licit circumstances is *against nature,* which ties every sexual pleasure, of necessity, to procreation. You cannot get a baby by masturbating. What is more, you cannot use masturbation *even in order to get a baby.* Cardinal Ratzinger's Congregation, with the approval of John Paul II, issued a controversial document in 1987 called *Donum Vitae (The Gift of Life),* which said:

> Artificial insemination as a substitute for the conjugal act is prohibited by reason of the voluntarily achieved dissociation of the two

meanings of the conjugal act [procreation and expression of love]. Masturbation, through which the sperm is normally obtained, is another sign of this dissociation: *even when it is done for the purpose of procreation,* the act remains deprived of its unitive meaning. [Emphasis added.][34]

At the Second Vatican Council, it was hailed as a great advance when the magisterium finally admitted the expression of love as a valid element in the marriage act (so long as it is not dissociated from procreation). Now that "advance" is used to say that a husband, expressing his love for his wife by giving her a child she cannot otherwise conceive, must do this only by the direct sexual congress of their bodies. Love cannot be conveyed through an "unnatural" act that involves masturbation.

The "changeless doctrine" keeps coming back in many absurd ways. For instance, the danger of AIDS cannot be averted by using condoms, certainly not in homosexual intercourse (which is unnatural, anyway) but even by a married couple when one has AIDS. Monsignor Carlo Caffara, dean of the Vatican's Institute on Marriage and Family Studies, pronounced that such a couple has one of two choices—to abstain from sex with each other, or to risk infection by doing the "natural" thing without unnatural interference by a condom.[35] Most people thought that New York Cardinal O'Connor's opposition to the distribution of condoms for AIDS prevention was aimed at homosexuals. It turns out it is meant to threaten the life of married people as well. The condom is more evil than death by AIDS.

Is it any wonder, given such "doctrine" on sex, that priests themselves do not take it seriously? The papal teaching has trivialized itself. By clinging to the "no parvity of matter" view on unnatural acts, it has reduced the discussion to a level where there is no seriousness of matter. Condoms and masturbation are opposed as much as adultery or child abuse. Bernard Häring has lamented the fact that people lost their concern about abortion because the church authorities made so much of contraception as another form of "baby killing." If some found it impossible to agree on contraception, they could have no confidence in arguments from the same source on other matters.[36] Priests know that the Pope's insistence that women cannot be priests is scriptural and logical nonsense. Then why should they not suspect the same thing about priestly celibacy or homosexuality? It is hard for them to make distinctions when superiors forbid open disagreement on any point along a line from the trivial to the tragic.

The distinctions, then, have to be made in private, without the healthy correction of open debate. Priests are not allowed publicly to sort the sound from the silly, to condemn abortion but condone contraception, to condemn child abuse but condone homosexuality. Everything comes under the same ban. Disagreements grow in secret. The freedom that celibacy was supposed to give for selfless action is snuffed out at the most basic level when freedom of discussion is outlawed. A conspiracy of silence covers many kindnesses—departures from the official line that serve the pastoral needs of perplexed Catholics. The priests must do even good things furtively. The conspiracy also covers many shameful and vicious things, including hundreds and hundreds of children abused and women abandoned by priests.

The result is ironically self-canceling. The Pope has made the number of priests dwindle sharply by insisting on celibacy, and he has ended up not only with a smaller number of priests but with a diminished band that is *less celibate*. Almost all the priests who left in the massive hemorrhage of the 1970s and 1980s left to marry. The homosexual priests stayed, which meant that their proportion of the whole went up even when their absolute numbers stayed the same. And now even that absolute number is rising. Many observers suspect that John Paul's real legacy to his church is a gay priesthood.

---

[1]Bette L. Bottoms, Philip R. Shaver, Gail S. Goodman, and Jianjian Qin, "In the Name of God: A Profile of Religion-Related Child Abuse," *Journal of Social Issues* 51 (1995), p. 95.

[2]For the Miglini family's story, I rely on my own interviews with Tony Miglini and with his lawyer, Sylvia Demarest, on an article by Dan Michalski, "Innocence Lost," in the September 1995 issue of *D* (pp. 98–103, 139, 141, 143), and on the *Dallas Morning News* coverage of the Kos trial.

[3]Ed Housewright, "Another priest's records enter Kos case," *Dallas Morning News*, June 18, 1997.

[4]Ibid.

[5]The *Dallas Morning News* printed a useful chronology of the diocesan record on Kos, based on news coverage of the trial, "Rudolph Kos and the Catholic diocese of Dallas," on July 25, 1997.

[6]Ed Housewright, "Victim says Kos phoned from center," *Dallas Morning News,* May 29, 1997.

[7]Ed Housewright, "Ex-official says he never questioned Kos," *Dallas Morning News,* June 6, 1997.

[8]Ed Housewright, "Parents of abused boys share blame in Kos case, ex-diocese official says," *Dallas Morning News,* August 8, 1997.

[9]Brooks Egerton, "Catholic judge steps down from Dallas diocese case," *Dallas Morning News,* August 23, 1997.

[10]Jason Berry, *Lead Us Not into Temptation: Catholic Priests and the Sexual Abuse of Children* (Doubleday, 1992), p. 100.

[11]Ibid., p. 165.

[12]A. W. Richard Sipe, *A Secret World: Sexuality and the Search for Celibacy* (Brunner/Mazel Publishers, 1990), p. 162.

[13]A. W. Richard Sipe, *Sex, Priests, and Power: Anatomy of a Crisis* (Brunner/Mazel Publishers, 1995), p. 26.

[14]Berry, op. cit., pp. 316–17.

[15]Ibid., p. 302.

[16]Ibid., pp. 314–16.

[17]Jack Taylor, "Child molesters blame Catholic church for cycle of abuse, study shows," *Agence France Presse,* January 6, 1995.

[18]Sipe, *Sex, Priests, and Power,* p. 26.

[19]Taylor, op. cit. The survey was done by Professors Freda Briggs and Russell Hawkins of the University of Adelaide.

[20]Berry, op. cit., p. 159.

[21]Ibid., p. 75.

[22]Sipe, *Sex, Priests, and Power,* p. 129.

[23]Paul VI, *Sacerdotalis Caelibatus,* Vatican translation, paragraph 34.

[24]Berry, op. cit., p. 51.

[25]Edward Schillebeeckx, *The Church With a Human Face,* translated by John Bowden (Crossroad, 1985), p. 228.

[26]Sipe, *A Secret World,* pp. 74, 133–34, 139.

[27]Sipe, *Sex, Priests, and Power,* p. 115.

[28]Thomas C. Fox, *Sexuality and Catholicism* (George Braziller, 1995), p. 176.

[29]Berry, op. cit., pp. 259–73.

[30]Sipe, *A Secret World,* p. 139.

[31]Ibid., pp. 122–30.

[32]Ibid., p. 124.

[33]*Catechism of the Catholic Church* (Liguori Publications, 1994), p. 564.

[34]*Respect for Human Life (Donum Vitae),* Vatican translation (Pauline Press, 1987), Part II, Section 6, p. 32.

[35]Fox, op. cit., p. 297.

[36]Bernard Häring, "A Theological Evaluation," in John T. Noonan, Jr. (editor), *The Morality of Abortion: Legal and Historical Perspectives* (Harvard University Press, 1970), p. 134, on "an urgent need for more careful and sharper distinctions between actions as totally different as abortion and contraception."

13.

A Gay Priesthood

The figures quoted from Richard Sipe showed that the sexual activity of gay and straight priests was roughly the same—20 percent inclined to sexual affairs, and half of those engaging in them. That balance is far from the proportion in society at large. The figures for gay priests may exceed those for gays in general, but the figures for heterosexual activity are far lower than the general ones. Half of those with a homosexual preference are (or were) acting on it, but only an eighth of those with a heterosexual inclination were doing so. No wonder the mass of those who left the priesthood did so in order to marry. That, as Willie Sutton would have said, is where the women are.

It is not surprising that proportionally more gays would be active in the world of the seminary and rectory. It is an all-male environment. Temptations and opportunities will be more frequent there than for heterosexuals, whose contacts with women are less frequent, and isolated, and are looked at with more suspicion. That is true for any exclusively male situation—in the army, the non-coed school, the Boy Scouts. Such an environment tends to attract some gays in the first place. The study of the priesthood that the bishops first commissioned, in the 1980s, and then canceled when they saw where it was going, found these traits in seminarians (as summarized by Sipe):

1. Dependency—a tendency to depend on others rather than on oneself.
2. Low sexual interest in the complementary sex.

3. Heightened aesthetic interest as opposed to athletic or mechanical pursuits.

4. Mother dominance, or a prevalence of a dominant unconscious mother image (an idealized view of women).[1]

That does not describe every gay man, but it does indicate that some gay men would, other things being equal, find such company congenial. As Sipe puts it, "Is this finding a reflection of a larger homosexual component among the celibate clergy than in the general population? The answer is yes." The "helping professions," as they were earlier called, have somewhat more gays than other callings, in large part because gays are good at them.

Though this was always true, recent developments have accelerated tendencies already present. For one thing, massive resignations of heterosexual priests altered the overall makeup of the priestly community. Even the heterosexuals who stayed have shown in polls that they approve of a married clergy, and this seems to have lowered their own resistance to sex with women. This in turn was bound to affect the attitude of gays toward the licitness of sex in the priesthood, especially since the surrounding society—including that of straight priests—has become far more tolerant of homosexuality, less certain that it is "an objective disorder," more wary of being called or considered "homophobic." This is a time, after all, when the New York City police force is openly recruiting gays in order to have a more accommodating relation with parts of the community.

Concomitantly, the tacit gay support system, the kind that all endangered groups have to form for their own self-esteem or self-protection, has become more open and confident, more defiant of the discredited homophobia. Beyond that, the number of priests being treated for AIDS, or dying of it, broke some of the taboo of discussing priests' homosexuality. An extensive survey made by the *Kansas City Star* showed that there are at least 400 known deaths of priests from AIDS, and probably twice that number—ranging from four times to eight times the rate in the general population.[2]

For a conjunction of such reasons, most observers find that seminaries have become more gay than they used to be. Sipe has noticed this change in statistics over his years of observation. As Thomas Fox, the editor of *The National Catholic Reporter*, concluded from his own interviews and his paper's coverage of the Catholic culture, "In some cases there have been reports of predominantly gay seminaries and homosexual climates within them that became so pronounced that heterosexual seminarians felt uneasy and ultimately left."[3] Gays themselves register the change. In a survey of 101 gay priests, those ordained before 1960 remember their seminary as having been 51 percent gay. Those ordained after 1981 say their seminaries were 70 percent gay.[4]

The existence of such surveys is itself a sign of the altered condition of gays in the priesthood. Greater tolerance has made it possible to learn more about the existence and attitudes of gay priests, whose internal network was almost invisible to outsiders until recent decades. Of course, the respondents may be inflating their numbers, deliberately or subconsciously, to proclaim themselves the norm. Those willing to respond to such a survey, even anonymously, are not a representative sample. They may also be counting as gay anyone they feel is "really" gay in orientation, even if the person has not recognized his own tendencies. But what is important here is the proportion, not the absolute numbers. The gays who are younger have a sense that their ranks are growing. So do most observers.

Why, one might ask, would gays respond to such a survey? The results show that the respondents feel frustrated at not being able to join the gay liberation movement more openly. They welcomed this opportunity— provided by their quiet self-support system—to say what they would like to be telling people, if they could do it without being ousted from the priesthood, which they love. Actually, there have been two polls. There is general conformity in the findings of the two, which might provide some confirmation of their results but for the fact that, since the respondents were allowed anonymity, we do not know how much overlap there was of the two groups—presumably a fair amount, since the average age was roughly the same in the two (men in their mid-thirties).[5] The surveys' separate importance comes not from polling entirely different groups but from the distinct forum each gave the respondents by a different range and method of questioning. The first one was undertaken by a priest, Richard Wagner, for his 1980 dissertation at the Institute for Advanced

Study of Human Sexuality in San Francisco.[6] Though Wagner could find only fifty respondents, he was able to interview them himself in sessions lasting an average of an hour and a half. The other project, which had a sample of 101 priests, allowed long written answers and essays, some of which are published with the poll, edited by James G. Wolf.[7]

The majority in both polls consider themselves happy, their priesthood fulfilling, and their future fairly certain. Those in the Wolf poll regret the limited range of their search for lovers, but the Wagner respondents averaged 226 partners in sex, a number reached only because 22 percent of them had over 500.[8] Half of the Wagner sample, but three quarters of the Wolf one, knew they were gay before ordination.[9] Those who knew by then that they were gay had experienced sex in the seminary, and some of their superiors knew it. They were allowed to proceed to ordination, perhaps (this is not clear) by complying with the judgment that this was "just a phase" or a lapse. (Catholic authorities have traditionally held that sin was under the will's control—which is why so few sought early help in handling alcoholism.) About a third of the priests' superiors know they are gay—the same number whose parents know.[10]

The higher salience of gays in seminaries has led some homophobic men to avoid entering the seminaries or to withdraw from them. In fact, the admission of married men and women to the priesthood—which is bound to come anyway—may well come for the wrong reason, not because women and the community deserve this, but because of panic at the perception that the priesthood is becoming predominantly gay.

How do gays currently in the priesthood, when there is supposed to be a law of celibacy, reconcile their vow of celibacy and their active sex life? Some think the command to abstain from sex is absurd, a formality. Others think it means an inner dedication to the gospel. A significant number (35 percent in Wolf, 22 percent in Wagner) think that celibacy means not being married to a woman—a definition that would make all single gay men, even the most promiscuous, celibate.[11] On the more basic issue of the morality of homosexuality itself, gays would seem to have some theological problems. After all, scripture has nothing to say about abortion or contraception or a married priesthood. But there are several clear condemnations of at least some kind of homosexuality in both the Jewish Bible and the New Testament. Most of the Wagner sample (88

percent) had read a challenge to the biblical injunctions against homosexuality—John McNeill, S.J.'s *The Church and the Homosexual*—and most
of them (95 percent) had found it reassuring.[12] When McNeill's book appeared in 1976, it had the support of his Jesuit superiors and their license
(*imprimi potest*) to publish. But within a year the Vatican had ordered the
Jesuits to rescind the license and order McNeill not to speak or publish
on the subject of homosexuality. He observed the ban until Cardinal
Ratzinger issued a new statement, in 1986, condemning all forms of homosexual sex. McNeill then broke his silence, denounced the letter, and
was dismissed by the Jesuits.

McNeill was able to draw on the one significant book that preceded
his—*Homosexuality and the Western Christian Tradition*, by the Anglican,
Derrick Sherwin Bailey (1955)—and on the research of John Boswell, a
gay Catholic scholar whose own book, *Christianity, Social Tolerance, and
Homosexuality*, would appear to great acclaim in 1980. The major claim
by Bailey, Boswell, and McNeill was that Saint Paul's condemnations of
homosexuality were not directed at the homosexual orientation itself, an
"inversion" not yet discovered, but against heterosexuals committing the
"perversion" of homosexual acts. Biblical scholars remain unconvinced
on this point.[13] But the work of the three men led to later and better
analyses of the relevant passages in scripture, especially the levelheaded
book by Robin Scroggs, *The New Testament and Homosexuality* (1983).

Scroggs points out that the subject of homosexuality is not a major
concern in scripture. It is allegedly referred to just four times in the Jewish Bible and three in the Pauline corpus of the New Testament. Each
passage has its problems. To take the Jewish scripture first:

1. Sodomy gets its modern meaning from the story of Lot in Genesis
19. When avenging angels disguised as men visit Lot in the city of
Sodom, evil neighbors demand that Lot send them out "so we may know
them" (19:8). He offers his virgin daughters instead, but the villains insist
on the men. Since the story of Onan "spilling seed" in Genesis had been
misunderstood as a sexual crime, rather than an offense against the family code, Bailey and McNeill try to find something parallel here—that the
attempted crime is not homosexuality but an offense against the code of
hospitality.[14] But Boswell, followed by Scroggs, makes a better case that
attempted *rape* is the crime, regardless of the sex of the person assaulted.[15]

This is confirmed by parallels with another rape story, that of the Levite visiting Gibeah, the second place where homosexuality is supposed to be condemned.

2. Again men gather and demand that the stranger be sent out "that we may know him" (Judges 19:22). He sends out instead his concubine, who is raped and killed—the crime (rape) is the same as that in Sodom, regardless of the sex of the victim. Two of the four passages in the Jewish scripture are not, then, really about homosexuality at all.

3. The third and fourth passages do refer to homosexuality. In Leviticus (18:22) it is forbidden to "lie with a man as with a woman." That is an "abomination."

4. This ban is repeated at Leviticus 20:13–14, with the penalty of death attached to it. These laws are part of the Holiness Code, declaring many things unclean. Mary Douglas has analyzed the rationalizing of apparently arbitrary things in this Code in her book on ritual impurities, which says that proper pairing (or mismatching) is the norm.[16] William Countryman used the Douglas norms to discuss the Leviticus law on homosexuality, noting that "a confusion of kinds" creates the impurity:

> It is equally polluting if things which do not belong together are mixed with each other . . . [so] different species of domestic animals must not be allowed to mate (e.g., to produce mules), or a field to contain two different kinds of seed, or a fabric to be woven of two kinds of fibers . . . this is the reason for the condemnation of homosexual acts, as the phrasing of the rules makes clear: the offense is described literally, as man lying with a male "the lyings of a woman." The male who fulfills the "female" role is a combination of kinds and therefore unclean, like a cloth composed of both linen and wool; and the act that renders him unclean is the joint responsibility of both partners. The same point is made in the prohibition of cross-dressing (Deut 22:5).[17]

Ritual purity is not, for most modern people, a moral category.

What, then, has the New Testament to say of homosexuality? There is nothing in the gospels, but there are two passages in Paul and one in the pastoral letters:

1. The earliest passage (I Cor 6:9) is part of a list of evil doings, in which two terms are linked together, "softies" (*malakoi*) and "man-bedders" (*arsenokoitai*). The first term is translated "the effeminate" in the King James Bible and with the German equivalent of "sissies" by Luther and the German version of the Jerusalem Bible. But an effete manner seems hardly a matter of choice, and everything in this list is cause for exclusion from God's kingdom—rather severe for a lack of macho. That is why the term has been taken as a euphemism for homosexual in general—for which, interestingly, there was no Greek word. But then what is the other term to mean? The first edition of the Revised Standard Version underlined the problem by translating both words the same way—"homosexuals and homosexuals" will be excluded!

Scroggs follows others (including Bailey) who see here the passive and active partners in that pederasty which was the characteristic Greek form of homosexuality. Since Paul was writing to a Greek town known for its sexual license, this makes sense—better sense than to think he was talking of "temple prostitutes." The Hellenistic Jew Philo, a contemporary of Paul, was especially fierce in denouncing pederasty:

> When Philo discusses these laws [Lev 18:22 and 20:13], he introduces the topic with the following sentence: "Much graver than the above [marriages with barren women] is another evil, which has ramped its way into the cities, namely pederasty." The entire discussion which follows centers on pederasty and what Philo considers disgraceful about it. Thus it is clear that when Philo reads the general laws in his Bible against male homosexuality he is thinking entirely about the cultural manifestation in his own environment [pederasty].[18]

The same can be said of Paul.

2. The pastoral epistle to Timothy (1:10) also puts "man-bedders" in a list of criminals, this time linked with "male prostitutes" (*pornoi*) before it and "kidnappers" after it. Since kidnapping was usually a tactic for collecting slaves, and male prostitutes were often slaves, Scroggs argues that pederasty, once again, explains this conjunction of terms.[19]

3. The harshest words are in Paul's letter to the Romans, where the list of things deserving death includes this (1:26–27):

God therefore surrendered them [the pagans] to their own passions which bring disgrace. The women gave up their normal practice for one not normal. In a parallel way the men left off their normal practice with women and were inflamed with desire for each other, male with male accomplishing indecency and receiving the deserved return for going astray.

I translate as "not normal" what is usually given as "unnatural" (*para physin*). That translation has led Catholic moralists to treat this passage in terms of a theoretical natural law. But Paul had no such theory of natural law. *Physis* for him means the normal way of things. Sometimes it is good to depart from the ordinary. In this very letter to the Romans, Paul says (11:24) that Gentiles are grafted onto the salvation that comes from the Jews like branches taken, against the normal course—*para physin*, the very phrase used in our passage—from their own tree and transferred to another. Sometimes *physis* is a social custom worth observing, as when he says that "Normal usage (*physis*) ordains that it is a disgrace (*atimia*, the very word used of the men and women in the Romans text) if a man's hair is worn long" (I Cor 11:14).

Natural law is not at issue, then. What is? Scroggs argues that Paul is still talking of pederasty here, as in his letter to the Corinthians (and as Philo did). The real surprise is the mention of lesbianism—the only such reference in the Jewish or the Christian scriptures. Scroggs says that since Paul is describing the corruption of the entire pagan world (these are not sins in general but the *proofs* he offers of *Gentile* shame), he had to find some way to show that women were included in the general shame. Because Paul says that the women's case is on a parallel (*homoiōs*) with men's, they too must be imagined as molesting little girls. Philo spoke of female pederasty in his *Contemplative Life* (59–62).[20] Scroggs is justified in concluding that Paul is like Philo in his contempt for pederasty—which is not a condemnation of homosexuality in general.

Even if one does not agree with Scroggs, it has become evident that the biblical condemnation of homosexuality as "unnatural" can no longer be assumed. Not that this will change the minds of those who are fixed in their opposition to gays. They will react as theological conservatives did when the Onan story was taken away from them as a basis for condemning birth control. They will draw on other sources than the Bible—fear and contempt for sex itself, the belief that "natural law" demands procreation from every sexual act, and so on. Humane modern laws respecting the dignity of gays and lesbians will not erase prejudices of long standing. They will just infuriate some. That is why I feel that only their resentment of gays will change their minds on other things—like the admission of women and married heterosexuals to the priesthood. Even those will be less abominated than a gay priesthood.

What is wrong about gays and lesbians as priests or ministers? Nothing is—as other denominations are realizing when they ordain them. But that does not make the presence of gay "celibates" in the current Catholic priesthood a healthy thing. They may claim that they are "celibate" by their own private definition of that word. But they took a public vow of celibacy, and the aim of any oath is communicative, is a *contractual* commitment. Both sides of the contract must agree on its terms. Gay priests are living a lie. It may be imposed on them by a senseless rule. Yet they uphold the resulting structure of deceit. People are fooled by them. One reason pedophiles have been given access to children is that Catholic parents were under the misunderstanding that priests refrain from all sex. In the surveys made of them, the gay priests say they must be careful to keep others from learning their secret. Every move they make is gradated to keep some people at least in the dark.

In the surveys taken of them, the most outspoken or risk-taking priests seem to have been willing to talk. But two thirds even of these men have contrived to keep the truth from their superiors, and even from their parents—those Catholic parents so proud of their sons' status and selflessness. Living in fear of the truth is not a good way to exemplify the truth that shall make you free. One of the respondents to the Wolf survey said, after listing the ways he had achieved peace with himself:

> Some fears still remain. If the parishioners found out, for example, that I am a homosexual, what would they do? This fear saddens

me. I sense a possible alienation from the very people "whom I so love and long for, who are my joy, my crown, my dear ones" as Saint Paul writes (Phil 4:1). People love me, but they don't know me completely. I cannot let myself be known for who I truly am and be loved for who I truly am. So much of what is going on inside me I cannot share with people. There is such richness now in how I experience life and how I view the world, and I have to hold that back. To disclose my homosexual orientation to my parishioners would, to the best of my discernment, cause the following: polarization of the people for and against me; suspicion or accusation of immoral activities, especially with teens and children; a request for my removal; a need for the Ordinary [bishop] to make some statement or take some action about me; a witch-hunt for other closeted priests; and continued fear in the young who are becoming aware of being gay. The risk seems far too great.[21]

Fear of what this priest calls a witch-hunt for closeted priests enlists many gays in that conspiracy of silence that shelters the pederasts. Gays will certainly be as reluctant to have pederasty discovered as was a *non-gay* priest who told Richard Sipe:

A priest I know from [my] diocese was one of three who got into trouble for molesting boys over the summer. I was assigned with him when I was first ordained and I felt for him. I cannot imagine the pain that he is going through. The other two I do not know. The priest I know fondled an eighteen-year-old at a party—a party held in the rectory for his being named a monsignor. Actually, it didn't surprise me. What did surprise me was that the kid ran off to the police that night, at two in the morning. The priest was drunk, and you would have thought that the kid would have let it go. It was all over the media.[22]

As Sipe notes, this man was very compassionate in trying to imagine what the priest was going through, but he did not care at all for what happened to "the kid." And the speaker, Sipe assures us, is a "conscientious and actively celibate priest." The system causes a blind instinct for preserving the priestly aura, at whatever cost to the abused. "Personal exposure is not even the greatest danger; psychological revelation—how the system works, how it all falls into place—poses a higher degree of threat to institutionalized power and is thus assiduously resisted."[23] Under the license of "preserving the church from scandal," a corrupt bargain is struck: "The system is a brotherhood of guaranteed employment, respectability, prestige, and power. The price is the appearance of celibacy; for all of the benefits accrue automatically as long as the semblance of celibacy is publicly or officially espoused."[24]

Gays can say that they are not doing anything that heterosexually active priests are not doing. True. The latter, too, are living a lie, gaining emotional access to women under a pretence of virtue, using and abandoning them because they cannot make a true and open commitment to a woman, or conscripting them into a life of deception if they prolong a furtive affair. They, too, must observe a discipline of deceit lest their secret slip out. They are in their own prison of falsehoods. Nothing could be further than this from the gospel ideal of "open speech" (*parrhēsia*) that will be discussed later (Chapter 21). Pederasts are not the only priests who prey on others.

---

[1]A. W. Richard Sipe, *A Secret World: Sexuality and the Search for Celibacy* (Brunner/Mazel Publishers, 1990), p. 71.

[2]*Kansas City Star*, series by Judy L. Thomas, January 2000. In a poll answered by 800 priests, two thirds said they knew at least one priest who had died of AIDS, and one third knew at least one priest living with it.

[3]Thomas Fox, *Sexuality and Catholicism* (George Braziller, 1995), p. 177.

[4]James G. Wolf (editor), *Gay Priests* (Harper & Row, 1989), p. 60.

[5]Ibid., p. 20. Richard Wagner, O.M.I., "Gay Catholic Priests: A Study of Cognitive and Affective Dissonance," p. 17.

[6]Wagner, op. cit. The lawyer Sylvia Demarest kindly supplied me with a Xerox of the dissertation.

[7]Wolf, op. cit., p. 26.

[8]Wagner, op. cit., p. 26.

[9]Wolf, op. cit., p. 34.

[10]Wagner, p. 93, Wolf, p. 52.

[11]Wagner, p. 56, Wolf, p. 38.

[12]Wagner, p. 64. John McNeill, S.J., *The Church and the Homosexual* (Sheed, Andrews & McNeill, 1976).

[13]See, for instance, Joseph A. Fitzmyer, S.J., *Romans* (AB, 1993), pp. 286–88, which convicts Boswell of tendentious translation of Paul's "against nature" (*para physin*) as "beyond nature." For a devastating treatment of Boswell's tendentious translations in his later book, *Same-sex*

Unions in Premodern Europe, see Daniel Mendelsohn, "The Man Behind the Curtain," *Arion,* Fall 1995, pp. 204–73.

[14]D. S. Bailey, *Homosexuality and the Western Christian Tradition* (Longmans, Green and Co., 1955), pp. 1–28. John McNeill, S.J., *The Church and the Homosexual* (Sheed, Andrews & Mc-Neill, 1976), pp. 42–50.

[15]John Boswell, *Christianity, Social Tolerance, and Homosexuality* (University of Chicago Press, 1980), pp. 92–99. Robin Scroggs, *The New Testament and Homosexuality* (Fortress Press, 1983), pp. 73–75.

[16]Mary Douglas, *Purity and Danger: An Analysis of Concepts of Pollution and Taboo* (Routledge & Kegan Paul, 1966), Chapter 3, "The Abominations of Leviticus," pp. 41–57.

[17]L. William Countryman, *Dirt, Greed, and Sex: Sexual Ethics in the New Testament and Their Implications for Today* (Fortress Press, 1988), pp. 26–27.

[18]Scroggs, op. cit., p. 88.

[19]Scroggs, ibid., pp. 118–21.

[20]Ibid., p. 115.

[21]Wolf, op. cit., p. 151.

[22]Sipe, *Sex, Priests, and Power*, p. 64.

[23]Ibid., p. 85.

[24]Ibid., p. 85.

14.

Marian Politics

One support of the celibate system has not been considered yet—the Virgin Mary. Modern Popes tell priests to think of themselves as virgins consecrated to the Virgin. The study of the priesthood mentioned earlier—the one American bishops commissioned, and then canceled when they saw where it was going—found this trait in seminarians: "Mother dominance, or a prevalence of a dominant unconscious mother image (an idealized view of women)." It is often said that Mary enhances the dignity of women. But for misogynists an idealized mother is both safe in herself and an alternative to lesser women. The Virgin is repeatedly used to prevent the ordination of women—if Mary was not a priest, how can they be? John Paul II even told women that they do not need to be priests since they raise and dedicate the boys who will become priests, and they are in the thoughts of the priests as they stand at the altar and consecrate the host.[1] We saw in an earlier chapter how Vatican dispatches on the subject of Mary's humility were used to torpedo the American bishops' attempts at a statement on the role of women in the modern world. No wonder the Catholic novelist Mary Gordon could write:

In my day, Mary was a stick to beat smart girls with. Her example was held up constantly; an example of silence, of subordination, of the pleasure of taking the back seat . . . For women like me, it was necessary to reject that image of Mary in order to hold onto the fragile hope of intellectual achievement, independence of identity, sexual fulfillment. Yet we were offered no alternative to this Marian

image; hence, we were denied a potent female image whose application was universal.[2]

Precisely because the Marian image held women back, it contributed
to male immaturity as well as male power in the church (the two often
go together). Sipe finds that a feeling of being "children of Mary" can in-
fantilize spiritual life: "Both the idealization of women as virgin/mother
and their demotion to a role less than equal to man stultify emotional
growth and actually retard celibate development."[3] The past development
of a childish piety in minor seminaries helps explain the simplistic sermons that priests produced later on, and the endless concentration on
Marian feasts and devotions all through the year. Intellectual adventure
and depth in sermons was not for the "little people" who imitate the Virgin's submissiveness.

Although there has been a falling off of devotions like novenas and
rosaries in much of the laity, the hierarchy is more Marianized than ever,
and private apparitions to women and children result in waves of emotional weeping.[4] Thus on two fronts, as it were, in the center and at the
periphery, Marian devotion is kept white hot. The conservative minority
at Vatican II kept lamenting that Mary was not getting enough attention,
that *she* should have been the subject of the treatise on the church, that
her role in redemption and in the distribution of graces should have been
reaffirmed and emphasized. The only two formal exercises of papal infallibility in modern times have been definitions of Marian dogmas—of her
Immaculate Conception by Pius IX and of her Assumption into Heaven
by Pius XII.

The popularity of Mary makes infallible statements about her hard to
oppose. Her feast days fill the calendar, and there is constant pressure to
add more. The dates of her various appearances are celebrated—John
Paul II is sure that Our Lady of Fatima saved him from an assassin because the attempt made on his life occurred on the anniversary of Mary's
first appearance to the children at Fatima in Portugal. He undertook a
pilgrimage there to thank her for her intervention, and the bullet from
Mehmet Ali Agca's gun is now mounted in the crown on the Virgin's
statue in the Fatima shrine.[5]

I quoted in an earlier chapter the Dominican Yves Congar's lament

that the role of the Holy Spirit in the church has been neglected. There
I referred to his claim that the cult of the Pope has in some measure become a substitute for the Spirit's active guidance of the church. He added
another substitution that has occurred—of Mary for the Spirit. Actually,
the two reinforce each other. As an example of the erroneous treatment
of Mary, Congar cites an 1894 papal encyclical that endorses these words
of Saint Bernardino of Siena: "All grace that is communicated to this
world comes to us by a threefold movement. [Three should suggest the
action of the Trinity, right? But no:] It is dispensed according to a very
perfect order from God in Christ, from Christ in the Virgin, and from the
Virgin in us."[6] Congar quotes a more recent (1965) theologian: "When I
began the Catholic study of theology, every place I expected to find an
exposition of the doctrine of the Holy Spirit, I found Mary."[7] This state
of things was reflected in the apology of a priest I referred to earlier for
having to refer to anything so abstract as the Trinity on the feast of the
Trinity. Mary is not abstract. No one apologizes for preaching about her.

Catholics might be surprised to learn how late was this proliferation
of Marian titles and feasts. There were no church celebrations of her, at
least in the West, till well past the fifth century. In all the hundreds of Augustine's sermons, there is not one preached about her. In fact, he says far
more about two other Marys in the gospels—Mary of Bethany (a symbol of contemplation) and Mary of Magdala (a symbol of love). When
the mother of Jesus does come up in the gospel passages Augustine ex-
pounds, he does not find the deep importance of her role that modern
preachers do. In the gospel of John, for instance, Jesus looks down from
the cross at Mary and Saint John, telling them, "Mother, this is your son,"
and "Son, this is your mother" (19:27). I have heard many Lenten sermons that claim we are all, along with John, given into Mary's care as our
protectress, making her a symbol of the church. But Augustine looks at
the gospel's next words, "From that moment John took her to his own,"
and makes the obvious conclusion that she is committed to John's care.
Augustine even says that Jesus is reminding his disciples of their duty to
care for the old and widowed. Mary is not protecting, but in need of protection—hardly the role John would give to the church personified.[8]

Since John gives symbolic meaning to everything about the crucifixion, it is probable that what is being symbolized here, as an ecumenical

board of scholars decided, is that Mary is being adopted into Jesus' eschatological family, the new family formed of his disciples—a family she was regularly excluded from, along with other mere blood relatives, during his ministry (compare Jn 7:1–10 with Mk 3:31–35, Mt 12:46–50, and Lk 8:19–20).[9] Rather than being the church, Mary is finally admitted into the church.

Another passage in John's gospel is important because it is the only text in the New Testament that John Paul II can find for his claim that Mary is the mediatrix of all graces. This is the treatment of a wedding at Cana. When Mary tells Jesus that the party has run out of wine, he responds, "What claim have you on me? My hour has not yet arrived" (2:4). Nonetheless, Mary tells the servants to do whatever Jesus tells them, and he changes water to wine. The Pope, in his exposition of this story in the encyclical *Redemptoris Mater*, says that the apparent harshness of Jesus and her serene reaction just goes to show "what deep understanding existed between Jesus and his mother."[10] He argues that Mary actually "contributes to that beginning of the signs which reveal the messianic power of her Son"—i.e., the miracle is worked because of her intercession, despite the fact that Jesus says his hour had not come. She can actually bend the will of the Father, who has set the hour of her son:

> There is thus a mediation. Mary places herself between her Son and mankind in the reality of their wants, needs, and sufferings. She puts herself "in the middle"—that is to say, she acts as a mediatrix, not as an outsider but in her position as mother. She knows that as such she can point out to her Son the needs of mankind, and in fact she "has the right" to do so. Her mediation is thus in the nature of intercession.[11]

Augustine's reading of the passage is quite different. He notes that some try to soften the harshness of Jesus' words to her. But he does not.[12] He says that the words are meant to point up a mystery:

> Because she was not the mother of his divinity, and the miracle she was asking for had to be worked through his divinity, he answered her in this way: "What claim have you on me? But lest you think I

do not recognize you as mother, I add that my hour has not yet arrived. Then I shall recognize you when the weakness you bore has begun its hour hanging on the cross." [That is when] he gives the mother into his disciple's care. Dying ahead of the mother, to rise before the mother, he, as a human, gives to another human the care of that human from whom he drew his humanity.[13]

Mary is the mother of Jesus' weakness, not his strength. He makes it clear that he will do the miracle but *not* because of her—his divinity has its own aims, connected with the hour of death to which he steers under the Father's guidance. She is not privy to that higher mission. His mortal debt to her as a fellow weak human he will pay when he provides for her care after his death.

The striking thing about this sermon of Augustine is the way it anticipates on all major points the best modern exegesis of the Cana story. Raymond Brown points out that the Father controls Jesus' hour, and Jesus is obedient to Him. That is what must be emphasized:

Before he does perform this sign, Jesus must make clear his refusal of Mary's intervention; she cannot have any role in his ministry; his signs must reflect his Father's sovereignty, and not any human or family agency.[14]

John Paul II, eager to foist his view of the mediatrix on the revealed word, has got it exactly backward. How did we get from Augustine's view of the Virgin to John Paul's? Part of the story can be traced in Jaroslav Pelikan's five-volume history of Christian doctrine, though he emphasizes that liturgical and private devotions were often as important as doctrinal debate. It was not till the Middle Ages that a separate Mariology began to arise. All through late antiquity, Mary had been the subject of speculation only as an offshoot of Christology. Early in the second century, Ignatius of Antioch, whose theology (as we saw earlier) was Spirit-drenched, stressed that Jesus was "born of Mary" to oppose "docetist" views that Jesus was not a real man.[15] The term "God-bearer" (*Theotokos*) was used to fight the opposite error, that Jesus was not true God. Bishop Alexander seems to be the first to use the term.[16] After the early heresies

had been defeated, there was a lull in doctrinal activity, filled in by popular piety. In the Eastern church, court ceremony and deferential title-
giving fashioned Mary as an empress, revered in miracle-working icons
and celebrated by poets in the tradition of Romanos the Melodist (sixth
century).[17] In the West, feudal legalisms made Mary an advocate with the
overlord. As Ildefonsus of Toledo (seventh century) put it, "We cannot
find anyone more powerful in merits than thou art for placating the
wrath of the Judge."[18] In the New Testament, it is the Spirit who gives
people the confidence to address the Father as adopted sons and daughters. Now they are hedged off from that inner life of the Trinity, like
manor slaves not allowed up to the great house. Mary must run errands
for the lowly.

The Middle Ages became obsessed with the physical facts of Mary's virginity. Modern commentators often use the term "virgin birth" for the
idea of virginal conception (the Spirit's descent at the Annunciation) or
immaculate conception (Mary's own exemption from original sin). But the
Middle Ages meant, literally, the virgin *birth* when they used those words—
that Christ was somehow delivered without breaking Mary's hymen:

> Yet it was neither the way in which Mary was conceived nor the
> mode in which she was assumed into heaven but the manner in
> which she gave birth to Christ that became an issue between Rad-
> bertus and his [ninth-century] monastic confrere, Ratramnus. On
> this issue the patristic tradition was ambiguous, for "it is clear that
> the fathers paid attention to the virginal conception, not to the
> miraculous birth" of Christ; but the details of the parturition had to
> be part of the doctrine of Mary's perpetual virginity. Any alterna-
> tive to the perpetual virginity was unthinkable. The formula, "vir-
> gin before giving birth, virgin while giving birth, virgin after birth"
> was universally accepted. Ratramnus took this to mean that "her in-
> violate virginity conceived as a woman and gave birth as a mother."
> The miracle consisted in the preservation of the virginity in con-
> ception and in birth.[19]

The whole birth was so miraculous that one church claimed as a relic
some of her mother's milk.[20]

By the middle of the thirteenth century, Mary had acquired a detailed biography memorialized in *The Golden Legend* by James of Verazze (Jacobus de Voragine), a biography with close parallels to that of her son. Her birth, too, involved an annunciation (to her father), a visitation (to her mother), a nativity with miracles, a presentation in the temple, and a sorting out of suitors that was a kind of massacre of the innocents.[21] These scenes from the *Legend* would be painted over and over—notably by Giotto in the Arena Chapel in Padua. A kind of competitive chivalry, as in courtly love, made men pay Mary escalating compliments. She was not only the highest of humans, according to Peter Damien (eleventh century), she was greater than the angels—taking her even further out of reach as a model for other women.[22]

Not even that praise was high enough. Words used of each person of the Trinity were applied to her. The text of John 3:16 was recast, with her substituted for the Father: "Mary so loved the world, that is, sinners, that she gave her only Son for the salvation of the world."[23] Her son's claim was usurped when it was said that "the world was redeemed through her."[24] The Spirit's titles were given to her when she was called "comforter and teacher."[25] This inflation of titles was rationalized by Duns Scotus (fourteenth century) with his maximalist principle of Marian dignities: any privilege her son *could* give her, he *would* give her. (Wouldn't any good son?) What was possible with her was plausible; and if it was plausible it was performed. *Potuit, decuit, fecit.*[26]

There were some voices of caution. Bernard of Clairvaux (twelfth century), an eloquent celebrator of Mary in general, denied that she could have been immaculately conceived. A legend grew up just after his death that God placed a black mark on his soul for writing against his mother.[27] Thomas Aquinas (thirteenth century), undeterred by the threat of a black mark, argued forcefully against the immaculate conception of Mary. All humans descended from Adam, he maintained, inherit the blight of original sin. To exempt Mary from this human condition would mean that Jesus was not born a man in the line of David, taking on himself the human condition of sin he meant to defeat. Besides, if Mary had no need of redemption, like the rest of Adam's children, "this would deny Christ the honor by which he is the savior of *all* people" (ST 27 2r).

The early doctrines of Marian glory clarified the character of the Incarnation and were centered on Mary's son. This doctrine would muddy and confuse the nature of the Incarnation. Exemption from the historical human condition would make Mary superhuman. It would also make it hard to explain why she suffered the effects of original sin (pain, fatigue, death) without having contracted original sin. Jesus could suffer in his human nature because he also had a divine nature. A parallel with Mary would give her a divine nature. Some argued that she did not, in fact, die. It was even said that God set aside a portion of "prime matter" at the creation of the world, which was kept separate from the sinful course of the universe to be used when he made Mary.[28] Her very flesh was a cosmic marvel, like kryptonite, unable to die.

When Henry Adams visited the French cathedrals of Notre Dame from the high Middle Ages, he found in her shrines a separate deity, with values different from the other God's. The male God was all severity and justice, the female one all mercy and forgiveness. He could hardly compete with her. It was better not to enter the churches by His door, the main one with a forbidding last judgment over it, but to slip in the side door, under the scene of her coronation sculpted above it. The devotion that built Mary's cathedrals, Adams claimed, "expressed an intensity of conviction never again reached by any passion, whether of religion, of loyalty, of patriotism, or of wealth."[29]

When the Reformation came, this idol-goddess was razed from her side doors by iconoclasts, which made Catholics more loyal to her and defensive of her. She suffered again the indignities of the eighteenth- and nineteenth-century revolutions, so that—at a time of growing secularism—Alphonsus Liguori (eighteenth century) revived Scotus's standard that one must favor any "opinion when it tends in any way to honor the Most Blessed Virgin." He argued this position in *The Glories of Mary*, which Pelikan calls "one of the most influential books ever written about Mary."[30] Mary is the one, Alphonsus claimed, who will deliver us from death.[31] The nineteenth century launched what Pelikan calls the age of major apparitions—to Catherine Labouré (1830), to the children at La Salette (1846), to Bernadette at Lourdes (1858).

No one showed more devotion to these appearances than Pope Pius IX, whom we met earlier as the kidnapper of Edgardo Mortara. His Marian piety, like John Paul's, was formed in childhood. A sickly boy, subject to fits that may have been epileptic, he had only spotty formal schooling. But he was intensely devout to the Virgin. His mother took him to pray for health at the Holy House of Loreto (Mary's home in Palestine miraculously transferred to Italy). John Paul, as the young Karol Wojtyla, was taken to the shrine of the Black Madonna of Czestochowa by his father—Karol's mother had died in his childhood, and he considered himself the Virgin's entirely as he grew up (*Totus Tuus* as his episcopal motto put it). When Pius IX, as Pope, survived the collapse of a convent he was visiting, he attributed his rescue to the Virgin of Loreto and made a pilgrimage to her shrine—exactly as John Paul would go to thank Our Lady of Fatima for saving him from an assassin.[32]

Pius felt that the Virgin was closely associated with his papacy. She appeared at La Salette during his first year in office. Her earlier apparition to Catherine Labouré was popularly taken as a call for the definition of her immaculate conception as infallible dogma. After Pius defined that dogma in 1854, the Virgin announced to Bernadette at Lourdes (in 1857) that "I am the Immaculate Conception," proving to Pius that he had done the right thing. He tried to associate major actions and statements with the feast day of the Immaculate Conception, December 8. Not only did he proclaim the dogma on that feast in 1854. He issued his major denunciation of the modern world, his *Syllabus of Errors*, on that date in 1864, and opened the Vatican Council that would declare his infallibility on it in 1869.

The dogma of the Immaculate Conception was closely linked with two other things dear to Pius's heart, resistance to the modern world (whose democratic ways he would condemn in the *Syllabus*) and the power of his own office. The connections between these three things are clearly brought out in the second volume of Giacomo Martina's magisterial three-volume history of Pius's reign. When Pius felt panic over the Risorgimento, the movement that was uniting Italy by driving out foreign powers and seizing the Pope's domains, he took comfort in the thought that Mary would protect him if he only fought harder for her. The means for doing so were suggested to him by the action of a synod of Umbrian bishops meeting in Spoleto in 1849, the year after the publication of Marx's *Communist Manifesto* and the socialist revolutions in Europe. In response to this threat from the left, the bishops published a list of the errors of the modern world. Pius was very taken with this document, and would develop his own longer list when he published his *Syllabus of Errors* in 1864.[33]

But first he would have to take care of the Virgin's business, which he saw as integral to the struggle with modernity. Here he drew on a book that appeared in 1851, Count Emiliano Avogardro della Motta's *An Essay Considering Socialism and the Socialist Teaching and Tendencies*, which said that focusing on Mary's sinlessness would make people realize the sinfulness of the communist/socialist assault on the church.[34] Another fan of the book, either from Pius's prompting or on his own, was the Jesuit editor of *La Civiltà Cattolica*, where the book was reviewed at length and used as the premise for his article, "The Social Aptness of a Dogmatic Definition of the Immaculate Conception of the Blessed Virgin Mary."

When Pius was temporarily run out of Rome by the Risorgimento's advance, he stayed in the southern Italian town of Gaeta until French troops could conduct him back. He returned with a determination to summon the Virgin to the fray by declaring her immaculately conceived. As Father Martina puts it:

> The special circumstances of this period—the exile to Gaeta, the impending proclamation of the Roman Republic—were bound to drive the Pope down his chosen path, which, as was characteristic of his attitude, seemed not simply a matter of theology, but also a powerful cure to effect the recovery of the church, of its leader, and of the world, from the evils that put it in such peril.[35]

Since this was his way of conceiving the definition of the dogma, Pius was eager to follow the suggestion of della Motta and the *Civiltà* editor that he combine an attack on modern errors (what would later become the separate *Syllabus*) with the definition of the Marian dogma. He dumbfounded Dom Guéranger, the respected abbot of the Monastery of Solesmes, who had been called to Rome to write a draft of the definition, when he said that a denunciation of political liberalism would be a necessary part of the document. Guéranger tried to resist, but the Pope was inflexible.[36] When the draft was turned in, Guéranger's attack on modernity was not strong enough for Pius, so he turned the job over to a panel that spent so much time trying to find scriptural and patristic support for the doctrine that it never got around to the modern part.

The theologians were coping with objections that had long been raised to the definition—not only Thomas Aquinas's resistance to it as lowering Christ's dignity, but the objections that had made Pius's predecessor, Gregory XVI, reject petitions from Marian enthusiasts calling for the proclamation. Pope Gregory felt that the definition of doctrines without the need to combat some contrary error was not traditional, and that the use of papal authority to fix dogma without the support of a council would be too brusque an affront to modern attitudes.[37] But it was just this chance to flex his own authority that appealed to Pius. He went through a motion of consulting the bishops by sending them a letter to ask if the Catholics in their dioceses favored the dogma. Of 603 replies, 546 were in the affirmative.[38] This popular support for the dogma itself did not meet theologians' objections to the opportuneness and venue of its definition, but Pius did not want those attitudes aired. He was counting on the popularity of Mary with Catholics to ride over such niggling restraints.

After driving the project of a proclamation through endless rewritings of its text, composed by differing committees, the Pope became eager to define the dogma in 1854 on the relevant feast day, December 8. (He would show a similar headlong need to get the result he wanted at the Council, after theologians had been arguing too long over infallibility.) He summoned bishops to Rome for that feast, but not to consult them. He met with them in a secret consistory on December 1, more to inform them than to ask their advice. On December 4 he met with four cardinals to go over the final (seventh) draft of the defining document. The Pope, wanting to put his stamp on it, told them to reverse the order of subjects in the text and compress various items. This was an affront to the theologians' work, but he said later on that "this was necessary, to prevent its being said that the whole thing was the work of Jesuits."[39] It was his work, and no one else's, and he wanted that made clear.

Because of the last-minute changes he called for, the whole document could not be readied for the proclamation day, so Pius—in a four-hour ceremony—read just the formal part of the definition. It took him eight minutes to read two pages, so overcome was he, repeatedly breaking down, sobbing and streaming tears on the pages, awed by the fealty he was paying to Mary, and by the power he was using to do it.[40] Mary was being exalted. But so was the papacy:

> To the honor of the Holy and Undivided Trinity, and to the grace and dignity of the Virgin Mother of God, to the exaltation of the Catholic faith and the advance of the Christian religion, by the authority of our Lord Jesus Christ and of the blessed apostles Peter and Paul, *and by our own authority*, we declare, pronounce, and define . . . [Emphasis added.]

As church historian Owen Chadwick says, "No previous Pope in eighteen centuries had made a definition of doctrine quite like this."[41] Fifteen years on, when some at the Vatican Council argued that the Pope was not infallible, he responded with the assurance that he had already proved he was, in the formula by which he defined the Immaculate Conception. Mary was his Trojan horse for sneaking the dogma of his own power into the citadel by her special side door. When his own Secretary of State told him that he was alienating the world with this drive for a formal declaration of infallibility, he answered, "I have the Blessed Virgin on my side."[42]

The political use of Mary to fight communism, which began with della Motta's 1851 book and continued through Pius IX's reign, was renewed in this century through the call of Our Lady of Fatima to pray for the conversion of Russia, which led to the formation of a worldwide "Blue Army" in her service.[43] Pius XII reported in 1951 that he had a vision replicating that at Fatima in 1917.[44] Pope John Paul's devotion to Our Lady of Fatima is connected with his resistance to communism in his native Poland. But he has larger and grander visions of his service to her, comparable to that of his hero, Pius IX. In 1997 he established a special commission of twenty-three scholars to consider defining Mary as Co-Redemptrix of the human race.[45] This goes beyond the usurpation of the Spirit's activity represented in calling her the Mediatrix of All Graces. Now she is to be made the joint agent of a divine work. Once more the Spirit's intimate action in the body of Christ is removed off to a distance only she can traverse for our sake. Nothing could be more alien from the treatment of Mary in the gospels.

There is only one place (but an important one) where Mary is given

a leading role in the gospels—the nativity narrative of Luke (in the nativity passages in Matthew, the leading role is Joseph's). Luke takes the
prayers and hymns of the church on the coming of Jesus into its life and
presents them as the prelude to his story of Christ's earthly ministry. In
this most Hellenic of the gospels, four canticles of Jewish form provide a
framework for the narrative—Mary's Magnificat (1:46–55), Zechariah's
Benedictus (1:67–79), the angels' Gloria in Excelsis (2:13–14), and
Simeon's Nunc Dimittis (2:28–32).[46] In the narrative Luke constructs on
these pillars, Mary is not praised for being unique, for the privilege of
physical motherhood (which Jesus rejects when he proposes the alternate, the eschatological family). She is incorporated into the body of believers by her answer to the message brought her from God: "You see a
servant of the Lord—let your word for me be done" (1:36). By giving
her this response, Luke is asserting that Mary meets the criterion for be-
longing to the new (as opposed to the natural) family, as Jesus defines the
new later in this gospel: "My mother and my brothers are ones who hear
the word of God and do it" (8:21).

Luke reemphasizes the point when he has Elizabeth say to Mary,
"Blessed are you among women, blessed what your womb bears . . .
Happy is she who believed the Lord's word to her would be done" (1:42,
45). This is paired with Luke's description of the woman who cries out
to Jesus, "Happy the womb that bore you, happy breasts that nursed," to
which Jesus replies: "Happy, rather, are those who hear the word of God
and do it" (11:28). Mary is not being set above other Christians, but included among them, by the church's remembrance of her as a fellow
disciple. Here Luke resembles John when he admits Mary to the eschatological family from the cross. This express assurance that Mary belongs
with the disciples may reflect the resistance of other relatives of Jesus that
is apparent in the gospels.

That Mary, in fact, has a special place among the disciples is affirmed
when Luke puts the church's own hymn on her lips, the Magnificat:

> My soul expands to the Lord,   47
>   my spirit has found joy in God who saves me,
> who looked from on high to his low servant,   48
>   that I should be called happy down the generations,

for Power itself has expanded me   49
  according to his name's holiness.

His mercy runs from each to the following generation 50
  for those who hold him in awe.
He has flexed his right arm's power   51
  and swept off pride's mad dreamers,
he has brought down the lofty from their thrones   52
  and lifted up those under them,
filling abundantly whoever hungers,   53
  sending the rich off destitute.

He has taken up his servant Israel's cause   54
  in memory of mercies past,
according to the word he gave our fathers,   55
  to Abraham and all his large descent.

The preexisting hymn seems to begin at verse 50. Luke introduces this by applying to Mary (speaking in the first person) the general praise of God's acts in the hymn. Thus verse 47 (spirit has found joy) anticipates the sense of verse 53 (filling abundantly). Verse 48 (to his low servant) anticipates the sense of verse 52b (lifting up those under). Verse 48b (down the generations) that of verse 50a (each to the following generation). Verse 49 (according to his name) that of verse 55 (according to the word). The fulfilled messianic triumph of the hymn applies with special appropriateness to Mary, the model recipient of the grace that animates the whole Christian body.

Luke teaches us, then, how to pray to Mary—or, rather, with her. Not as to a queen or empress (the last thing suggested anywhere in the gospels), but as with our sister in the Spirit, a witness to God's power, not the wielder of it. Hers is a profound dignity, far from the hollow and bombastic titles heaped on her so that she might preside over papal structures of deceit. The Magnificat celebrates *God's* action, which deposes throned powers and sends the rich off destitute. That is the authentic voice of Mary, the disciple who joins the Christian company instead of ruling it— a voice that has been muffled and distorted by the papal uses made of her.

This use of Mary for papal purposes can be seen as early as the end of the fifteenth century. In Florence's Uffizi Gallery, Botticelli's painting of "The Coronation of the Virgin" shows God wearing a papal tiara as he crowns Mary in heaven—offering a pattern for the Pope's glorification of her on earth, and a simultaneous comparison of the Pope to God. The replacement of the Spirit by Mary, which Yves Congar lamented, can be seen elsewhere in Florence. In the Accademia Gallery, Orcagna's "Pentecost" (c. 1365) shows the Apostles, while the Spirit is descending on them in tongues of fire, kneeling in adoration *not* of the Spirit that inspires them all but of the Virgin placed in their midst. Even the angels turn away from the Dove, symbolizing the Spirit, in order to worship Mary. Elsewhere in the Accademia, Sogliani's "Dispute Concerning the Immaculate Conception" (c. 1550) presents the Virgin hovering in the sky above the dead body of Adam, not drawn from his flesh like Eve but begotten in heaven (again with angels to worship her), in effect beginning the new creation before the second Adam she will beget.

One reason the Virgin is semideified in this way is that "feminine" functions of God—formation and nurturing of the church—are not assigned to the Father and Son, whose relationship is symbolically male. Some feminist theologians oppose this monopoly of male analogues by suggesting that Father and son be replaced by mother and daughter, which retains a gender monopoly by simply reversing it. The historical circumstances of New Testament revelation make that an arbitrary revisionism. The better course is to welcome a female analogy for God, but assign it to the third person of the Trinity. The usage even of theologians and Bible translators is misleading when the Spirit is referred to as It—"It breathes where it will." The personhood of God makes such objectification degrading. The pronoun for the Spirit should be She, which will make clear that many of the functions assigned to Mary (as a symbol of the church, or its protector) truly belong to the Trinity in its female analogue. One should pray to Her as well as to Him. Congar argues that the Spirit frames and fosters the new creation of the church just as the Spirit hovered over chaotic waters to form the world in Genesis. This is a motherly vision of the Spirit that Gerard Manley Hopkins expressed in his sonnet "God's Grandeur":

> Because the Holy Ghost over the bent
>   World broods with warm breast and with ah! bright wings.

¹John Paul II, Letter of March 25, 1995, paragraphs 1 and 3 (*Donne e Prete*, Pauline Editoriale Libri), pp. 74, 77.

²Mary Gordon, "Coming to Terms With Mary," *Commonweal*, January 15, 1982, p. 11.

³A. W. Richard Sipe, *Sex, Priests, and Power: Anatomy of a Crisis* (Brunner/Mazel, 1995), p. 102.

⁴There is good coverage of the kinds of Marian apparitions that make people weep for the world as Mary takes pity on it in Michael W. Cuneo, *The Smoke of Satan: Conservative and Traditionalist Dissent in Contemporary American Catholicism* (Oxford University Press, 1997), Chapter 5, "Mystical Marianism and Apocalypticism," pp. 121–77.

⁵Eamon Duffy, *Saints and Sinners: A History of the Popes* (Yale University Press, 1997), pp. 286–89.

⁶Yves Congar, O.P., *I Believe in the Holy Spirit*, translated by David Smith (Crossroad, 1997), Vol. 1, p. 163.

⁷Ibid.

⁸Augustine, *Explaining John's Gospel* 119. 1–3. Augustine rightly says that "one's own" (*sua*, Greek *idia*) must mean John's care (*officia*), not possessions (*propria*).

⁹Raymond E. Brown, Karl P. Donfried, Joseph A. Fitzmyer, and John Reumann, *Mary in the New Testament* (Fortress Press, 1978), pp. 194, 213.

¹⁰John Paul II, *Mother of the Redeemer (Redemptoris Mater)*, Vatican translation (Pauline Books, 1987), p. 30.

¹¹Ibid., p. 31.

¹²"What claim have you on me" is, literally, "What is to you and to me." The same words describe a *rejection* in the Greek of the Septuagint at II Kings 3:13 (Elisha says kings have no right to ask him to prophesy) and at Hosea 14:8 (Ephraim has no right to idols).

¹³Augustine, *Explaining John's Gospel* 8.9.

¹⁴Raymond E. Brown, S.S., *The Gospel According to John* (AB, 1966), Vol. 1, p. 109.

¹⁵Ignatius of Antioch to the Ephesians 19:1. See William R. Schoedel, *Ignatius of Antioch* (Fortress Press, 1985), pp. 89–91.

¹⁶Jaroslav Pelikan, *The Christian Tradition*, Vol. 1, *The Emergence of the Catholic Tradition (100–600)* (University of Chicago Press, 1971), p. 241.

¹⁷Jaroslav Pelikan, *The Christian Tradition*, Vol. 2, *The Spirit of Eastern Christendom (600–1700)* (University of Chicago Press, 1974), pp. 139–41.

¹⁸Jaroslav Pelikan, *The Christian Tradition*, Vol. 3, *The Growth of Medieval Theology (600–1300)* (University of Chicago Press, 1978), pp. 69–70.

¹⁹Ibid., pp. 72–73.

²⁰Ibid., p. 170.

²¹Jacobus de Voragine, *The Golden Legend*, translated by William Granger Ryan (Princeton University Press, 1993), pp. 149–58.

²²Pelikan, *Growth*, p. 161.

²³Jaroslav Pelikan, *The Christian Tradition*, Vol. 4, *Reformation of Church and Dogma (1300–1700)* (University of Chicago Press, 1984), p. 40.

²⁴Pelikan, *Growth*, p. 71.

²⁵Pelikan, *Reformation*, p. 40.

²⁶Ibid., pp. 49–50.

²⁷Ibid., p. 46.

²⁸Ibid., pp. 49–50.

²⁹Henry Adams, *Mont Saint Michel and Chartres* (Library of America, 1983), p. 428.

³⁰Jaroslav Pelikan, *The Christian Tradition*, Vol. 5, *Christian Doctrine and Modern Culture (since 1700)* (University of Chicago Press, 1989), p. 144.

[31]Théodule Rey-Mermet, *Moral Choices: The Moral Theology of Saint Alphonsus Liguori*, translated by Paul Laverdure (Liguori Press, 1998), p. 19.

[32]Frank J. Coppa, *The Modern Papacy Since 1789* (Longman, 1998), pp. 102–04.

[33]Giacomo Martina, S.J., *Pio Nono (1851–1866)* (Editrice Pontificia Universita Gregoriana, 1986), pp. 289–90.

[34]Ibid., pp. 266–67.

[35]Ibid., pp. 263–64.

[36]Ibid., p. 268.

[37]Owen Chadwick, *A History of the Popes, 1830–1914* (Oxford University Press, 1998), p. 120.

[38]Martina, op. cit., pp. 263–65.

[39]Ibid., p. 274.

[40]Ibid., p. 274.

[41]Chadwick, op. cit., p. 121.

[42]Frank J. Coppa, "Cardinal Antonelli, the Papal States, and the Counter-Risorgimento," *Journal of Church and State* 16 (1974), p. 469.

[43]Cuneo, op. cit., pp. 135–52.

[44]John Cornwell, *Hitler's Pope: The Secret History of Pius XII* (Viking, 1999), pp. 242–43.

[45]Kenneth L. Woodward, "Hail Mary," *Newsweek*, August 25, 1997.

[46]For these canticles as hymns of the Jewish Christian community, expressing the significance of Jesus's earthly descent, see Raymond E. Brown, S.S., *The Birth of the Messiah: A Commentary on the Infancy Narratives in Matthew and Luke* (Doubleday, 1977), pp. 346–55. Their difference from the Hellenic opening verses of the gospel is brought out by Loveday Alexander, *The Preface to Luke's Gospel: Literary Convention and Social Context in Luke 1:1–4 and Acts 1:1* (Cambridge University Press, 1993).

15.

The Gift of Life

The Vatican has some of the same problems with abortion that it has with contraception. Neither is mentioned in either Jewish scripture or the New Testament—you would think it might have been condemned if it held such a high place on the list of crimes as modern religious leaders give it. Since there is no revealed teaching on the matter, the argument against abortion must be made from natural reason, and that brings it within the Vatican conception of natural law that has been discredited with regard to contraception. (For some people, having an abortion is not a choice that would arise if the Vatican were not always and everywhere opposed to condoms and other birth control devices.)

With abortion as with contraception, a natural morality argument should be within the capacity of normally intelligent and good-willed people. Then why do so many persons, not perverse in their other judgments, fail to see the force of that argument? Women's right to an abortion has been upheld by the American Law Institute, the American Medical Association, and the American Public Health Association. As John Noonan writes:

> The Deans of all the medical schools in California, the American Civil Liberties Union of Southern California, and some fourscore professors of law, teachers of gynecology, and practitioners of obstetrics drawn from all parts of the nation have asked the Supreme Court of California to assert the constitutional right of a woman to have an abortion when she seeks it and the constitutional right of a physician to perform an abortion if he finds it medically appropriate.[1]

Admittedly, many societies have condemned abortion, but some of these bans resemble those looked at earlier in the case of contraception—they were felt to be evil because magic was used to prevent the birth, or the woman was condemned for depriving a man of heirs (the rights of the child mattering less than the prerogatives of the patriarch). Few of these societies treated the crime as murder. Even the modern crusaders against abortion do not really treat it as murder. Though they would prevent or penalize the doctor performing an abortion, they rarely call for punishment of the mother. But if the crime is murder, then hers is clearly the greatest guilt. She kills her own child, which has, from at least the time of Medea, been considered a particularly heinous act.

What is even more significant, Catholic authorities do not treat the fetus as a person by baptizing it. If, as the Vatican teaches, every fertilized human ovum contains a human soul, and each soul (but that of the immaculately conceived Mary) inherits original sin, and baptism is needed for a soul freed from original sin to enter heaven, then each fetus from the fertilized egg stage should require baptism. But not even nuns in Catholic hospitals baptize each miscarriage (presuming it is a late enough miscarriage for them to find the fetus in flushed material). Even the anti-abortion protestors who inveigh against "baby killers" have not mounted a quiet campaign to baptize all the fetuses, though they have made a few spectacular fetus baptisms for the press. Thomas Aquinas actually opposed the baptizing of fetuses.[2]

Others who oppose abortion make exceptions for the case of incest or rape, which proves they do not consider the fetus a person. Whatever the male did, the fetus is innocent of it, and if it is an innocent *person*, it should not be killed for its father's sin. Some casuists have made the case that the fetus can be killed in those cases as an assailant is licitly slain for treating one's body with force. But the fetus does not normally threaten the mother's life—and only the fear for one's life allows one to take the life of an assailant. And the fetus is not itself the assailant—the man has departed by the time an abortion is performed. The only even partial parallel would be seeking out an invader whose attack has been survived, and killing him in cold-blooded retribution—but even that is not a true parallel, since the father is not killed, only the fetus he left behind. What scenario can we construct that would be approximate? Let us say that an assailant breaks into your house, threatens your life, and inadvertently leaves his infant in the corner. When he leaves, you do not consider it fortunate that you can save the innocent child from such an oppressive parent. No, you kill the baby out of anger at its father. That comes closest to what happens in rape if you truly believe the fetus is a person.

Many people, many even of those who would not condone abortion in the case of incest or rape, would allow the fetus to be killed if its continued life threatens the mother's. But that, too, shows that the fetus is not being thought of as a person. If the fetus and the mother have equal status as persons, the natural and not the inflicted death should be preferred. If two people are starving, one should not kill the other, even for the last bit of food. The unwilled death of the mother would be, as the insurance companies put it, an "act of God." The willed death of the fetus would— always keeping in mind that the fetus is now thought of as a person—be an act of murder.

Furthermore, few of those who say they believe that the fetus is a person with all a person's rights advocate the policing and punishing of aggressive acts against that person by pregnant women who assault their fetus's bodily integrity and mental development by smoking, drinking, drug use, or poor health practices. They shy from such acts, which would pit the fetus against its own bearer—and then they have trouble drawing a line between a woman's doing all these other things to a fetus but not being the one who decides whether to abort it.

All these occurrences suggest how difficult it is even for the people most opposed to abortion to think honestly and consistently of the fetus as a human person, on a par with the persons we all admit have rights to life, liberty, and the pursuit of happiness. On the other hand, it is impossible to treat the fetus as some merely disposable appendage to the pregnant woman. It has its own teleology, determining it to become itself even at the cost of the woman, and it is always *potentially* a person. The only honest starting point for reflection on the fetus is a respectful agnosticism about it, which is what we shall find Augustine adopting.

What makes it hard to take Vatican teaching on the subject with respect is its rejection of the uncertainty most people, even those well disposed to consider moral problems, betray by their words and actions. The members of the Congregation for the Doctrine of the Faith are blithe in

their certitude that the soul is present in the fertilized egg. Only that certitude can explain a passage like this, condemning *in vitro* fertilization:

> A number of ova are withdrawn, fertilized, and then cultivated *in
> vitro* for some days. Usually not all are transferred into the genital
> tracts of the woman; some embryos, generally called "spare," are de-
> stroyed or frozen. On occasion, some of the implanted embryos are
> sacrificed for various eugenic, economic, or psychological reasons.
> Such deliberate destruction of human beings or their utilization for
> different purposes to the detriment of their integrity and life is con-
> trary to the doctrine on procured abortion already recalled. The
> connection between *in vitro* fertilization and voluntary destruction
> of human embryos occurs too often. This is significant: through
> these procedures, with apparently contrary purposes, life and death
> are subjected to the decision of man, who thus sets himself up as the
> giver of life and death by decree. This dynamic of violence and
> domination may remain unnoticed by those very individuals who,
> in wishing to utilize this procedure, become subject to it them-
> selves.[3]

It does not help that we get the same rhetoric against demonic science
here as in the anticontraceptive *Humanae Vitae* (indeed the same anti-
scientism as in the Holocaust document *We Remember*). Those who want
to have a child by *in vitro* methods are called the victims of a "dynamic
of violence and domination," though they are just seeking the freedom
to have children which defects in their physiques make impossible in the
normal way. Nature, the Vatican repeats, can never be corrected in its fundamental mechanics where sex occurs, even though we correct defects in
multiple ways every day, from using glasses to altering insulin deficien-
cies. The document I quote from is the same one that said *in vitro* fertilization is immoral because it involves masturbation for collecting the
male semen, and that prenatal scans of the womb should not be done by
doctors if they suspect the parents might abort a fetus found to be seriously deformed or fatally diseased.[4]

Restricting ourselves just to the passage I cite above, we are told that
the loss of fertilized eggs, even before they are implanted in the womb

(nidation), is the destruction of human souls. But nature itself, in order to insure procreation, "loses" many fertilized eggs—probably more than are counted "spare" in the *in vitro* process:

> Experiments with animals have shown that the prenatal loss from the time of fertilization averages about 40 to 50 percent. In view of the higher organization of man, the losses may be even greater. At least one-fifth or even one-fourth of the fertilized eggs may perish before implantation in the uterus or during this process.[5]

Those who talk about abortion as a "holocaust" of unborn babies should consider the "holocaust" of all those fertilized ova perishing in the natural process. What happens to those souls? No one can baptize them, even if they wanted to. Is God himself sending them by the millions to Limbo, never to enjoy the beatific vision?

Bernard Häring, the respected moral theologian, raises other problems with thinking of the fertilized egg as instantly ensouled. For one thing, after fertilization takes place, the ovum can develop in further ways, including differentiating itself into twins. If it had one soul at fertilization, did one soul beget another soul later on?[6] He suggests that the fetus may develop toward being a human person, just as animals developed toward being humans in the long evolution process. Though there is a potency to become human persons in both cases, an ape is not a human person, and perhaps an early fetus is not either.

This idea of a development *toward* the human actually fits with Thomas Aquinas's view of the fetus, which was derived from Aristotle. Aristotle thought that the embryo developed from a nutritive soul (the form of life in all plants) that was potentially in the mother, through the addition of a potentially sentient soul (common to all animals) and a rational soul provided by the man. These potentialities developed in three stages, not clearly marked, though they are all present by the time of birth.[7] Aquinas adopted this scheme, insisting only that there was only one soul in a human, the rational one infused by God at the end of the generation process, which subsumes the nutritive and animal life previously provided by the coupling of man and woman (ST 1 q 118, 2 ad 2). Thus the soul was not present at the conception of the human body—

which is one of the reasons Thomas resisted the concept of Mary's immaculate conception. There was no soul there to be immaculate.[8]

Augustine entertained several hypotheses about the fetus, without deciding on its status, since "I have not been able to discover in the accepted books of Scripture anything at all certain about the origin of the soul" (ep. 190.5).[9] He called the removal of fetuses in an early stage "killing them before they live" (i.e., before they have souls).[10] He felt it possible that miscarried fetuses might just perish, since they were without sensation and therefore without soul, or they might be given their intended bodies in the afterlife.[11] Though he opined that the fetus might be ensouled on the forty-sixth day, after the analogy of the Temple being built in forty-six years, his most complete passage on the morality of abortion does not consider the fetus's fate but the intentions of married people who abort the fetus to defeat the aim of marriage. Their act is not a marital act in this case. They are not called murderers but married adulterers.[12]

Then when and how does the soul contract original sin? Augustine did not know. All he knew was that Adam's children live in some kind of spiritual community with him. Adam was *in potentia* the whole human race at the outset, and we still live in him, as John M. Rist has seen in a fine analysis of later Augustinian texts, which gives humankind a double life, a shadow life, a dark underlife of weakness. To which is added, when we are baptized into Christ's body, a bright overlife of strength. And we *are* this combination in a uniquely personal way—a vision that helps explain Augustine's ability to find depths and layers in his own psychological makeup.

> The human complex, including the body, is both in Adam and in Christ more mysterious, and more uniquely individualized, than its *common* humanity or even its *common* likeness to God. Augustine's "double-life" theory, though developed, as we have seen, for predominantly theological reasons, might well have seemed attractive for reasons more philosophical. It seems to go some way toward doing justice both to the metaphysical claims of Plotinus about human identity with one another, and to the historical claims of

Christianity about the importance of human individuality and uniqueness.[13]

Though Augustine was not sure when the soul appeared, it was an interpersonal soul from the outset, in communication with mankind's history in Adam. The person, as Augustine reflected on that concept in *The Trinity*, must exist in an interactive relationship with other persons. Thomas Aquinas said something related to that when he opposed baptizing a fetus because "As long as it exists in the womb of the mother, it cannot be subject to the operation of the ministers of the Church, as it is not known to men."[14] It is not in communication with church authority. It is not even in communication with natural authority (which Thomas took to be the parents—especially, in his culture, the father). When Thomas addressed a query about baptizing infants, who might seem out of communication too, since they cannot yet speak or decide, he answered:

Man is structured toward God through reason, which is capable of knowing God. So a child, before the exercise of its own reason, is structured by nature's own structure toward God through the parents' reason, so it must perform its religious duty to God at the parents' direction. (ST 3 q 68, 10 ad 3.)

Even an infant, then, has a duty and can take direction. It exists in a reciprocal relationship at birth, and not before—which involves Thomas in the logical consequence that the soul is infused at birth.

The infant's communication with other persons is signaled by Virgil when he says that a newborn can "recognize your mother with a smile" (*Eclogue* 4.60). We saw in an earlier chapter how Edith Stein claimed that an empathic interplay with others—an "intersubjectivity"—is necessary to the formation of a self. Here it could be objected that we recognize rights in other people who are incapable of reciprocating duties—the mad, the senile, those in a coma. But they have all entered at some time into communication with others, been part of the human interchange system, formed selves that are recognizable in our traffic with them. The same cannot be said of the fetus.

One thing that hampered Augustine and Thomas in their discussion of this subject was their assumption that the soul is infused by God, complete and entire, in a single act performed at some time after conception. They did not allow for the development of personality as a *process*, of the sort Bernard Häring looked to when he compared it with hominization in the species. But modern science is far more at home with developmental systems. The person is not a given, a product delivered whole and complete.

Some fear that, if abortion is licit, then euthanasia will not be far behind—though I have distinguished between the formed but diminished personhood of people who have joined the interpersonal exchange and the fetus in a preconversation stage. But an interesting comparison has been made between the right-to-life issue and the right-to-die movement by the ethicist Paul Ramsey (himself an opponent of abortion). He notes that even Catholic moralists have accepted that extraordinary means do not have to be employed to prolong life. But modern science is continually adding extraordinary means for beginning life, and most opponents of abortion deplore the omission of any of these.

> Some percentage of genetic defectiveness would, in the ordinary course of "nature's deliberations concerning the man," be eliminated by miscarriages. If more and more of these lives are brought to birth, and then to child-bearing age, and then to ability to engender or bear children of their own by the steady advance of the practice of scientific medicine, the result will be a steadily increasing number of seriously defective individuals among the population in all future generations. Fetology seems apt to accelerate this tendency. These considerations open serious medical and moral questions. The principled question is whether it is not morally responsible, or at least morally tolerable, to negate some of the negative consequences of the practice of saving life. Should not this practice be eliminated by the sort of respect that esteems life enough to allow it to die on occasion even if it technically could be saved?[15]

Ramsey's concern with "defectiveness" will make some accuse him of a eugenic impulse; but he is not talking about deliberately planning an

ideal type of life, just of not using extraordinary means to thwart a natural process of elimination. What he and other measured opponents to
abortion come up against, in the pro-life movement, is the Vatican attitude that opposes any control over life by science, and speaks of a "culture of death" as if any and every addition of life were wanted and needed
by God. The more sentimental even talk of babies wanting to be conceived and being denied that "right," as if their souls preexisted conception as well as birth. (Actually, if conceiving as many new souls as possible
were a goal in itself, the Pope should order all celibates to marry.)

But even though abortion is not murder, it is not a thing that can be
proposed as an ideal. It should be avoided, principally by all safe measures
of birth control—the one effective anti-abortion measure the Vatican will
not allow. Though the fetus may not be a person, it is human life, it has
the potential to become a person. It is something that should not be
lightly done away with or deprived of all respect. Women have the legal
right to decide whether to have an abortion, but they should not take
that as a dispensation from a moral decision-making task that goes deeper
than the law. I cannot be certain when personhood begins, any more than
Augustine was certain when the soul was infused. But against all those
who tell us, with absolute assurance, when human life begins, we should
entertain some of his knowledge of our limits. On the whole subject of
the origins of life, he said, "When a thing obscure in itself defeats our capacity, and nothing in Scripture comes to our aid, it is not safe for humans to presume they can pronounce on it" (ep. 190.5).

---

[1] John T. Noonan (editor), *The Morality of Abortion* (Harvard University Press, 1970), pp. ix–x.

[2] Thomas Aquinas, *On the Sentences of Peter Lombard* 4.6. See Noonan, op. cit., p. 54.

[3] Congregation for the Doctrine of the Faith, *Instruction on Respect for Human Life in Its Origin and on the Dignity of Procreation (Donum Vitae)*, in Edmund D. Pellegrino, John Collins Harvey, and John P. Langan (editors), *Gift of Life: Catholic Scholars Respond to the Vatican Instruction*, (Georgetown University Press, 1990), pp. 19–20.

[4] Ibid., pp. 13–14.

[5] Bernard Häring, "A Theological Evaluation," in John T. Noonan (editor), *The Morality of Abortion: Legal and Historical Perspectives* (Harvard University Press, 1970), p. 130.

[6] Ibid.

[7] Aristotle, *Animal Generation* 736b–737a.

[8] Thomas Aquinas, *Commentary on the Four Books of the Sentences* 3.1.1. See Noonan, op. cit., p. 23.

[9]Otto Wermelinger, "Abortus," (Cornelius Mayer et al., editors), *Augustinus-Lexikon* (Basel: Schwabe, 1986–), coll. 6–10.

[10]Augustine, *On Marriage and Concupiscence* 1.15.

[11]Augustine, *Encheiridion* 85, *The Trinity* 22.13.

[12]Augustine, *On Marriage and Concupiscence* 1.15–17.

[13]John M. Rist, *Augustine: Ancient Thought Baptized* (Cambridge University Press, 1994), p. 129.

[14]See Note 2 above.

[15]Paul Ramsey, "Points in Deciding About Abortion," in Noonan, op. cit., p. 99.

III.

THE HONESTY ISSUE

S̲ince the role of the priest is primarily that of a credible witness, it is of the utmost importance that all Church structures, all basic relationships within the Church, and the whole of moral formation promote and encourage absolute sincerity and transparency.

— BERNARD HÄRING

16.

The Age of Truth

In 1896, when Lord Acton was drawing up the plan for his great project, the Cambridge Modern History, he said that an objective account of the past was now possible, since its sources were at last free to be scrutinized:

> There has been not only progress but subversion and renewal, since manuscripts have come into use almost without limit, since crowds of scholars are on the watch for them, and the supply of documents exceeds the supply of histories. The policy of concealment, abandoned in so many places—as neither Italy nor Prussia was interested in keeping the secrets of fallen governments, whose records were in their hands—has broken down altogether, and at last the Vatican discloses the guarded treasures of Galileo's tower [site of the secret archives].[1]

The earthquake of the French Revolution and the Napoleonic wars tumbled out archives from their hidden recesses, from regal and state and aristocratic libraries, and the aftershocks of that seismic event laid bare new rifts of documents—the French and Prussian revolutions of 1848, the Austrian recapture of Venice that same year, the Italian capture of the papal libraries in 1848 and 1870. Acton himself benefited from most of these exposures of old documents to the light, and he was just one of those who greeted them as if they were new lodes struck in a scholarly gold rush.

Napoleon had set the pace when he took the Vatican archives (3,230 large chests of them) by wagonloads back to Paris.[2] People had long wanted to confirm their worst suspicions about the Galileo trial, the Inquisition, the Borgia papacy, the Council of Trent, and other dark secrets of the papacy. Napoleon himself asked to see the Galileo records, and when, at his downfall, the rifled papers were sent back to Rome, those records had disappeared, to be returned only partially and years later.[3] General curiosity, along with the scholars' focused zeal, had been titillated. The paper chase was on.

Of course there had been political unrest before that made archives vulnerable—during the sack of Rome by Charles V's army in 1527 papal documents had been scattered about and used as stable bedding.[4] The difference now was that historians knew the value of these stored treasures. A new attitude toward history had arisen, usually symbolized by Leopold von Ranke's famous ideal of recovering "simply what at any point happened" (*wie es eigentlich gewesen*). The Renaissance historian Anthony Grafton points out that Ranke had not really discovered any new research techniques, or even lived up to his own famous slogan, but that he added two essential things to the historian's craft—a cultist's enthusiasm for the original document, and the formal graduate seminar which turned history into a professional discipline.[5]

Acton, born in 1834, drew on both these new things from their Germanic source. As a Catholic nobleman, he had not been able to attend Oxford or Cambridge at a time when that still entailed professing the established (Anglican) religion. He undertook, instead, intense studies in Munich, from age sixteen to twenty-four, with a Bavarian priest, Ignatz von Döllinger, who was one of the pioneer archival historians of the age. The two traveled together to newly opened archives in Venice, Rome, and elsewhere, intoxicated with the vistas opening out into the past.[6] Acton, young as he was, could help the famous Döllinger because of his own vast network of highly placed relatives in the European aristocracy. He had grown up speaking four languages at the family table, reflecting these connections. Acton's and Döllinger's travels were explorations into a brave new world for both of them. Inspired by them, Acton conceived the historian's high calling as a new kind of priesthood of the truth. For him, the nineteenth century had become the age of truth, and archive after archive was going off like a bomb explosion to bring down the mythical structures of old institutions—all but the Catholic church, which he considered (at this time) the great beneficiary of these developments. After all, how could the repository of God's truth be opposed to the truth?

Acton has been accused, with some justice, of a naive epistemology about the ability to get at the bare truth. But he did have a deep awareness of what was original in the researches of his era. He knew that its quest for truth was of a different kind from that which informed the histories of the past. Classical history, in its best practitioners (like Thucydides), had pioneered elements of scientific inquiry, but these were held within a framework of rhetoric, whose working norm was probability (*to eikos*).[7] The reasons for action were framed in terms of speeches put in the mouths of history's principal agents. The New Testament gospels, in so far as they were history at all (and that was not their main genre), had been history of this sort, as the exchanges between Jesus and Pilate demonstrate.

Greek history was future-oriented, drawing lessons from research (*historia*) into what had happened before, whereas Jewish history was past-oriented, recalling at every turn the contractual relations of the nation with its God.[8] Medieval history was made to bear witness to the claims of holiness, healing, or miracle.[9] This concentration on the power of holiness was all too easily read backward as the holiness of power when whole nations were converted through their leaders. The founding document of medieval history was, significantly, Eusebius's church history, with a celebration of the Emperor Constantine's conversion as its driving event.[10] Much of later history would depend on the vindication of that claim to power—even to the point of favoring the fraudulent "donation" by which Constantine gave the church its earthly realm.

Renaissance and Reformation history would sift these issues in more refined ways, often by returning from power to probability as the classical revival brought back Thucydides as the model rather than Eusebius. Lorenzo Valla, for instance, disproved the authenticity of the Donation of Constantine, in 1440, not by the philological or archaeological instruments that the nineteenth century would use, but by subjecting apparent anachronisms to the *eikos* test. Enlightenment history—that of Montesquieu, Hume, and Gibbon—was "philosophical" because it made probability more explicitly a "conjecture" about what happened in the past.[11] Gibbon's famous offering of alternative answers to question after question, with the implied query "Which is more likely?" made this procedure transparent.

The nineteenth century's forward leap in historical self-consciousness could not have occurred without parallel and reinforcing developments in other disciplines. Archaeology made the earth itself an archive surrendering its secrets of lost civilizations. The geological theories of Charles Lyell and others shattered the world chronology that had been derived from the Bible; and biblical philology was breaking the framework that held those old-time schemes together. Vast new stretches of time were opened up, providing an arena for the long biological developments that Darwin and others were shaping into evolutionary schemata. Science was emboldened by such convergent discoveries to challenge miracle and superstition in official accounts of the past. The keepers of official myths were thrown on the defensive, presented with a narrow range of choices—they could either accommodate the new trends or defy them, in varying degrees of flexibility or rigidity. If they accommodated, they were accused of surrendering to the spirit of a godless age. If they resisted, they were called obscurantist, the feckless defenders of a dead past.

The collapse of old archival bastions also meant the loss of patronage by them, which had made their custodians' use of the documents tendentious. Support for research had to be found in new places. Britain's nineteenth-century scientists, for instance, did not come from the classically oriented universities (Oxford and Cambridge): "With a few exceptions they had not been educated in the English universities but in their Scottish counterparts or in London medical schools, the civil service, the military, or in provincial dissenting communities."[12] In certain new areas, private resources seemed needed to push forward the new work—as when Heinrich Schliemann put up his own fortune to explore Mycenaean sites. In history, access to archives often required the money and connections of gentleman researchers, producing the paradox that a professional discipline was first being explored by amateurs (who were ahead of their university contemporaries in their conceptions and techniques). Acton was the very embodiment of this type (and he would set the professional standards when he founded the Cambridge Modern History), but there were others with his aim—though few with his rigorous intelligence. In England, for instance, there were George Grote, James Mill, Thomas Carlyle, Thomas Macaulay and his nephew George Trevelyan, W. E. H. Lecky, and J. A. Froude. Similar types could be observed in America—William H. Prescott, Francis Parkman, George Bancroft, Henry Cabot Lodge, Theodore Roosevelt, and Henry Adams. These men were, in effect, their own patrons, subsidizing their own research, declaring that history was no longer the province of institutions impervious to outside scrutiny or committed to official versions of the past.

Given his high ideal of the historian's independence from institutional bias, Acton's first effort on his return to England from Munich, in 1858, may seem contradictory. He subsidized and edited Catholic quarterlies to express his own deep loyalty to the church of his birth. But he saw no contradiction, at this stage, between scientific history and gospel truthfulness. Admittedly, the church had been tarnished in the past by dishonest history and forged claims to power; but only because it lacked the tools it was now being given to find and deploy natural truths in support of its supernatural openness to reality of every sort. He had come back to England with Germany's scholarship to offer at the altar. In this way he could disprove what he felt was a canard:

> I know, for I have experienced the thing, that the great prejudice against the Church among educated Englishmen is not a religious one against the dogmas, but an ethical and political one; they think that no Catholic can be truthful, honest or free, and that if he tries to be he is subject to persecution.[13]

Acton had, at first, some reason for the hopes that would soon be disappointed. His mentor, Döllinger, was an honest and searching historian who was also a priest in good standing with his church. He was known, so far in his career, as a defender of the papacy who had discovered documents embarrassing to Lutherans. He had been welcomed at all the Catholic centers of study that he visited with his bright young student Acton in the early 1850s. In Rome, Augustin Theiner, another scholarly German historian and priest, had helped Döllinger work in the Vatican archives of which he was the superintendent. Theiner was given greater freedom than his predecessors by a Pope who began his reign as the darling of Italian nationalists. On his election in 1846, Pius IX was young for a Pope (fifty-four), four years younger than John Paul II would be when he was welcomed as a young Pope in 1978. Pius seemed to be open to new ideas—just as John Paul would appear in his first years at the Vatican. Acton later described the false dawn of Pius IX's papacy this way: "He had striven to be a liberal and patriotic Pope; he had seemed to Metternich almost a revolutionary, and to [Father Gioacchino] Ventura almost a rationalist, and his views touching the salvation of Protestants have been quoted with admiration by Lutheran divines."[14] Acton had audiences with the snuff-consuming Pope in the 1850s, both with Döllinger and on his own (Pius knew some of Acton's many noble relatives), and found him neither very interesting nor very dangerous. The only threat he seemed to offer was his evident ignorance, which would lower the standards of those around him: "Now nobody feels that the Pope will think less of him because he knows nothing at all."[15] Little did these two men realize that they would end up considering each other almost the embodiment of evil.

So Acton took over the Catholic quarterly, the *Rambler*, with all confidence that he could raise the intellectual level of English Catholicism with long reports on continental scholarship and fresh inquiries into the church's past. The cardinal in England's recently restored hierarchy, Nicholas Wiseman, was a conservative, but Acton had attended Wiseman's Catholic boys school (Oscott), and he anticipated no trouble from his old schoolmaster, who knew he was loyal to the church. But the influence of zealous Catholic converts was rising in England—Wiseman's successor would be a papolatrous convert, Henry Edward Manning—and these converts would hear nothing critical of their church. They put pressure on Cardinal Wiseman to discipline the freespeaking *Rambler*, and the cardinal wrote a letter reproving Acton for printing a dispatch from Döllinger claiming that Augustine was the father of the Jansenist heresy. Acton consulted with the distinguished convert from Anglicanism, John Henry Newman, whom he had met in a visit from Munich with Döllinger, and Newman—to his lasting regret—agreed to take over the editorship of the *Rambler*, in a move meant to reassure the converts that an older and wiser head was now in charge. (Newman was in his fifties, Acton still in his twenties.)[16]

As it turned out, Newman's own writings angered the zealots even more than had Acton's. In the July number for 1859 Newman published a long article, "On Consulting the Faithful in Matters of Doctrine," which argued that infallibility belongs only and always to the church as a whole, not only and always to the teaching part of it: "the *Ecclesia docens* is not at every time the active instrument of the Church's infallibility."[17] His proof is that, in the Arian period of the fourth century (which had been a subject of special study with him while he was moving toward conversion to Catholicism), the laity had been more orthodox than the hierarchy. This article so disturbed the Pope's partisans in England (who were sure that only the Pope is infallible) that it was sent to Rome for censure, and Newman had to explain himself. About this time, Monsignor George Talbot, Pius IX's closest English adviser in Rome, conceived a fear of Newman as "the most dangerous man in England." The days of the *Rambler* were clearly numbered.

Acton meanwhile had moved on to found another journal, the *Home and Foreign Review,* which he hoped to keep clear of Catholic controversy. But in 1864 he felt obliged to fold the project in solidarity with Döllinger, who had been reprimanded by Pius IX for a speech in Munich (summarized and praised by Acton in his quarterly) that claimed theologians should free themselves from a tired scholasticism and adopt the methods of modern research.[18] This was so clearly the program of Acton's own journal that he felt he could no longer put it out under the implicit ban of the Pope. His attempt to put the age of truth at the service of his church had failed.

Acton got out of the field of Catholic journalism just in time. Shortly after his quarterly ceased publication, Pius IX issued his response to the age of truth—a flat rejection of all its tenets. He published a list of condemned positions which comprehended the whole liberal agenda of a man like Acton. Eighty propositions were condemned, including these:

15. Every man is free to embrace and profess that religion which, guided by the light of reason, he shall consider true.

55. The Church ought not to be separated from the State, and the State from the Church.

63. It is lawful to refuse obedience to legitimate princes, and even to rebel against them. [Pius was thinking first of himself as the prince of his temporal estates, as we see from the next thesis.]

76. The abolition of the temporal power of which the Apostolic See is possessed would contribute in the greatest degree to the liberty and prosperity of the Church.

77. In the present day it is no longer expedient that the Catholic religion should be held as the only religion of the State, to the exclusion of all other forms of worship.

78. Hence it has been wisely decided by law, in some Catholic countries, that persons coming to reside therein shall enjoy the public exercise of their own peculiar worship.

80. The Roman Pontiff can, and ought, to reconcile himself, and come to terms with progress, liberalism and modern civilization.

How did a nineteenth-century person come to hold these ideas in horror? Newman would try to explain this list away by noting that the Pope himself had not signed it, only the papal Secretary of State, and that lesser types in the Curia were always trying to be more papal than the Pope. As he put it, "the Rock of St. Peter on its summit enjoys a pure and serene atmosphere, but there is a great deal of Roman *malaria* at the foot of it."[19] He may have believed this, since there was a fair amount of maneuvering by lesser clerics in the composition of the *Syllabus*. But in fact the driving force behind it was Pius, both in its general conception and in all its details.

We saw in an earlier chapter how Pius tried to include a condemnation of modern errors in his definition of the Immaculate Conception. When the drafters of that proclamation could not elaborate their theological arguments for the dogma *and* formulate an attack on modernity, Pius kept them at work after his ceremony defining the Marian doctrine. Dom Guéranger and others came up with a document trying to lay a broad theological basis for criticizing the nineteenth century's secular goals, but that was too abstract for Pius. He wanted a concrete list of all those bad things he saw out there. He offered them as a model the list drawn up by an opportunistic ex-liberal, Philippe Gerbet, who had scrambled to the right after the Pope's condemnation of his earlier hero, Félicité de Lammenais. Gerbet, a bishop who was not respected by other members of the French hierarchy, liked to address grandiose pastoral letters to his diocese; it was one of these, issued in the summer of 1860, that fatally caught the eye of Pius IX. It contained a list of 85 theses to be condemned by Catholic authority.

Pius told his drafting committee that this was the kind of thing he wanted. Giacomo Martina, in his account of Pius's reign, sees this as the root of many early blunders leading to the disaster of the *Syllabus*:

> One might ask what motives drove the Pontiff to set aside the first draft [of January 1864], so much better than Gerbet's, and give his preference to a list so vulnerable in different ways. The choice, which had little to do with the personalities of his Roman consultants, hinged essentially on the character and outlook of Pius IX, a man incapable of deeply conceiving an argument as a whole, one more drawn to look at single instances than to large syntheses or the deep examination of principles.[20]

From now on, through a long series of redraftings by different committees, Pius would cling to his notion that the best way to attack the modern world was by cataloguing its enormities. These were such obvious affronts to him that he thought the mere naming of them would make others shudder. He did not realize that the striking concreteness of such a list would be as vivid for those opposing his views as it was for him. He was putting his case in a manner that was easy to caricature, that was almost a caricature to begin with.

The list format had the added advantage, in his eyes, that while it was taking shape he could pop into it any new annoyances that arose. Thus, when Charles de Montalembert called, at an 1863 ecclesiastical conference in Malines, for "a free church in a free state," Pius could slip five new items into his list, condemning Montalembert's views.[21] It was by drafting a refutation of Montalembert that a newcomer to Rome, Luigi Bilio, came to Pius's attention. The Pope put Father Bilio in charge of ongoing reformulations of the list, rejecting the advice of more seasoned counselors:

> As often happens in the history of the church, a collaboration took place between the Pope, the Roman Curia with its various tendencies, and certain members of the hierarchy. Nonetheless, throughout the course of this labor, which Pius IX followed quite closely (as is proved by various documents in the archives), the Pontiff gave it his personal drift, one not only strengthening the drift of the hardliners [*intransigenti*] but showing a certain free association [*eclecticismo*] of his own, little concerned with the need for a robust internally-coherent synthesis, one that would not lose itself in details, would not fail to emphasize the essential. Finally, the contributions of mature theologians like Abbot Guéranger, Monsignor Pie (the bishop of Poitiers), Monsignor de Ram (the rector of the University of Louvain), had little effect, while the basic initiatives came from an obscure French bishop, Monsignor Gerbet of Perpignano, and a Barnabite theologian still relatively young, Father Luigi Bilio, who would win the complete confidence of the Pope and later, promoted to cardinal, would participate intimately, especially during the Vatican Council, in the most important decisions made by Pius IX.[22]

For years Pius kept Bilio working on his dream list, which bounced around from 70 theses to 62, then down to 55, or to 22, before going back up to 84 before reaching the final number of 80.

Meanwhile the Pope tried to create a correspondence of support from the bishops, as he had with the Marian definition. When they assembled in Rome in 1860 for the canonization of sixteenth-century martyrs in Japan, he asked them to write separate opinions to him on the question whether modern liberalism's errors should be condemned. Of course, they were not given a specific list of the errors Pius had in mind. (How could they have been, when it was in a state of continual flux?) Of the 255 bishops canvassed, 96 did not reply. Among those who did, a third opposed the idea of such a list, saying that since constant papal admonitions had already been issued, including an apocalyptic address the Pope just gave at the Japanese canonizations, there was no need to be unnecessarily provocative with formal condemnations.[23] The Pope was undeterred.

Among those trying to deflect the Pope from a rush down this dangerous path was his board of Cardinal Inquisitors, who said that the stream of statements already on the record made such formal condemnations otiose. This attempt to make things better made them worse, since Bilio, trying to placate the cardinals, hunted up a prior statement of Pius to quote in each thesis. By wrenching short citations from context, he made the theses look either more vague or more specific than he intended. The most famous case was thesis 80, which condemned the idea that the Pope can be reconciled with modern progress. The actual citation was aimed at modern states that were overtly trying to break concordats with the church or suppress religion, but its use suggested that the Pope must oppose all modern states.[24] The need to frame the theses in terms of exact quotations from different papal documents also helped give the list its odd form of condemning the positive statements of error. This led, in the case of thesis number 79, to a weirdly phrased double negative, saying that what was condemned was a *false* statement that civil liberty does *not* corrupt morals.

As usually happened with momentous projects undertaken by Pius, he stretched out the process by his obsession with it, then got bored with it and wanted a quick termination. In the rush to conclude the matter, Bilio took it on himself to strike out two theses (condemning constitutional regimes and the Italian Risorgimento). The Pope did not notice; and when there was a furor over the document on its release, he referred all questions about it to Bilio. "It was more than odd that the man truly responsible for the document showed no ability at the moment to explain the exact meaning of positions it took."[25] His mind had already moved on to the next phase of his war with modernity. Two days before signing the *Syllabus*, the Pope announced to those around him that he intended to call a general council. While the rest of the world was saying that he had gone too far, he felt that he had not (yet) gone far enough. More was needed: "The definition of the Immaculate Conception, the *Syllabus*, and Vatican I, though separate items, were closely linked in a single campaign—the three stages of a papal strategy."[26]

Though the Pope thought of each stage in this campaign as dealing out punishment to the diabolical schemes of modernity, the *Syllabus* was nearly a knockout blow delivered to himself. He was lucky that some took it as a joke, since those who took it seriously were almost hysterical. Here was a nineteenth-century leader denying any validity to freedom of conscience, of speech, or of government. Laboring to control the damage, the urbane Bishop Dupanloup in France defended the *Syllabus* by gutting it of salvageable meanings. He showed that the papal citations were taken out of context (by the authors of the list themselves); he argued that the list could not mean what it seemed to, since that would make it internally contradictory; and he distinguished between an ideal "hypothesis" (it would be nice for everyone to have such clear apprehension of the truth that error would not be countenanced) from a real "thesis" (the world is messier than that). As Owen Chadwick says, "By the time Dupanloup had finished with the *Syllabus* it was almost as though it had never been."[27]

The Pope, so far as he understood Dupanloup's subtle distinctions (which were not Pius's strong point), thought he disagreed with them, but the papal Secretary of State, Filippo Antonelli, no theologian (and no priest), was realist enough to see that this was the best means available of containing the damage Pius had done with the *Syllabus*, and he coaxed from the Pontiff a letter endorsing the Dupanloup interpretation. This papal declaration of the fecklessness of his own fulminations made it possible for Newman to argue in good conscience that someone must have put something over on the Pope in issuing the *Syllabus*. But Pius, so far from regretting what he had said in the *Syllabus,* was planning to reaffirm it all with a new forcefulness, that of infallibility. By summoning an ecumenical council for that purpose, he called Acton back into action. Acton was determined to prevent anything that would give the *Syllabus* the stamp of eternal truth. For him, it was eternal falsehood, the locking of his church into a fundamental and self-destructive dishonesty.

---

[1]Acton 3.677.

[2]Owen Chadwick, *Catholicism and History: The Opening of the Vatican Archives* (Cambridge University Press, 1978), p. 17.

[3]Ibid., pp. 20–21.

[4]Ibid., p. 5.

[5]Anthony Grafton, *The Footnote: A Curious History* (Harvard University Press, 1997), pp. 223–26.

[6]See Acton's own account of his archival adventures reprinted in Damian McElrath, *Lord Acton: The Decisive Decade, 1864–1874, Essays and Documents* (Publications universitaires de Louvain, 1970), pp. 1127–40.

[7]Gordon S. Shrimpton, *History and Memory in Ancient Greece* (McGill-Queen's University Press, 1997), pp. 21–48, 114–15.

[8]Arnoldo Momigliano, *The Classical Foundations of Modern Historiography* (University of California Press, 1990), pp. 18–21.

[9]Peter Brown, "Arbiters of the Holy," in *Authority and the Sacred* (Cambridge, 1995), pp. 55–78.

[10]Arnoldo Momigliano (op. cit., pp. 137–41) notes that Eusebius grounded his work to a new extent on *documents*. But these were deployed to prove doctrinal consistency in scriptural, conciliar, and patristic texts. See also Momigliano, *Essays in Ancient and Modern Historiography* (Wesleyan University Press, 1977), pp. 115–19.

[11]For this conjectural history, see J. G. A. Pocock, *Barbarism and Religion* (Cambridge University Press, 1999),Vol. 1, p. 156,Vol. 2, p. 310.

[12]Frank M. Turner, *Contesting Cultural Authority: Essays in Victorian Intellectual Life* (Cambridge, 1993), p. 181.

[13]Francis A. Gasquet (editor), *Lord Acton and His Circle* (London, 1906), p. xlvii.

[14]Acton 3.390: "Review of Friedrich's Geschichte des vatikanish Konzils" (1877).

[15]Acton, Cambridge Manuscripts Add. MSS. 5751.

[16]Ian Ker, *John Henry Newman* (Oxford University Press, 1988), pp. 472–77.

[17]John Henry Newman, *On Consulting the Faithful in Matters of Doctrine,* edited by John Coulson (Sheed & Ward, 1961), p. 86.

[18]For Acton's treatment of Döllinger's Munich speech, see "The Munich Congress" (Acton 3.215–23).

[19]John Henry Newman, *A Letter Addressed to His Grace the Duke of Norfolk* (1875), in Alvan Ryan (editor), *Newman and Gladstone on the Vatican Decrees* (University of Notre Dame Press, 1962), p. 166.

[20]Giacomo Martina, *Pio Nono (1851–1866)* (Editrice Ponteficia Universita Gregoriana, 1986), p. 301.

[21]Ibid., p. 338.

[22]Ibid., p. 288.

[23]Ibid., pp. 310–14.

[24]Ibid., pp. 343–44.

[25]Ibid., p. 349.

[26]Ibid., p. 147.

[27]Owen Chadwick, *A History of the Popes, 1830–1914* (Oxford University Press, 1998), p. 178.

17.

Acton's Reckless Truth

Pius IX was an unlikely figure to take on the whole modern world and sweep the papacy up to its dizziest heights of spiritual power. A soft man, lachrymose, he charmed people with his infectious emotions and quietly lilting voice. He could almost be said to have wept himself into power. The more he lamented the loss of his temporal domain, the more Catholics clustered to him in sympathy and showered other gifts on him. As Acton put it, "the promoters of infallibility were able to coin resources of the enmity which was shown the church."[1] To criticize him became a way of joining his persecutors, who drove him from Rome in 1858 and sealed him within the Vatican in 1870. He could have used this sympathy to redefine the church's mission for a new era. But instead he looked back to what was lost and sent up a keening demand that it be restored. Roger Aubert, the best French student of Pius's Vatican Council, described Pius with a shrewdness that calls for extensive quotation:

Pius IX labored under a threefold handicap. He was affected in his youth by an illness resembling epilepsy, which left him with a bias toward emotional excess tempting him at times to violent fits of temper or to ill-considered words, which were quickly inflated by those who did not have his interests at heart. This volatility explains as well his frequent reversals of policy in accord with the last advice he had received—which is not to say that, when he felt his prerogatives were at stake, he could not show himself strong-willed and face his troubles with courage.

In the second place, like most Italian clerics of his time, he had to settle for a sketchy education, with scarcely any idea of modern scholarly methods, especially in the field of history. And even in the field of theology and canon law, he was only superficially informed and did not always take into account the complexity of some questions or the uncertainty of some positions—not that he was altogether without interest in spiritual things, or lacked an Italian instinct that, without a great deal of learning, can grasp the fundamentals and size up concrete situations with common sense, at least when they are represented to him with accuracy.

Unfortunately—and this was his third handicap—he had a weak staff around him. His confidential advisers were for the most part pious and full of devotion, but excitable as well, viewing things with hard-line presuppositions out of touch with contemporary thought. It is not surprising, in these circumstances, that Pius IX could not bring the church into accord with the deep changes that were gradually transforming every other social body, or with the shifts in perspective that the progress of natural science and history required from some traditional theological claims.[2]

How did a man with these weaknesses and handicaps force from the church an exaltation of the papacy? He had one source of strength, which stiffened his spine and tempered his disappointments. He did not believe in himself, but he did believe—simply, passionately, indeflectibly—in his office, which he considered God's singular point of entry into the world. Others encouraged this belief with an almost idolatrous attitude toward them. At a time when other symbols of authority were losing their potency—kings, aristocrats, even the Bible itself—some of the yearning for a point of stability and certitude drained into this last receptacle of autonomy. Theologians from the past were marshaled in its defense—like one who defended indulgences by saying, "We have not the authority of Scripture [for this] but we have the higher authority of the Roman Pontiffs."[3] Or like that of a bishop who said "that in matters of faith he would believe a single Pope rather than a thousand Fathers, saints and doctors [of the church]."[4]

When Pius sent bishops the formal summons to an ecumenical council, it was announced that this was for the reform of the church and the consideration of modern errors. Nothing was said about using the Council to declare the Pope infallible, but the liberals in the church thought that was the real goal of the summons, and they were right. Father Martina, in his authoritative history of Pius's reign, notes:

> The head of the Church knew well the trick of governing, and knew that it was better not to impose a plan from above but to inspire a popular movement and then to reinforce and guide it after it arose. His policy in these years looked precisely to supporting the hardliners (*intransigenti*), encouraging their desire for a definition of the doctrine. The papal diplomacy, *La Civiltà Cattolica*, the Pope's own frequent audiences—these were the devices used for this purpose.[5]

Newman, who thought change in the church should come from the interaction of all its members in open and shared reaction to the Spirit, later condemned this way of sneaking a doctrine into the body of beliefs (see Chapter 21 on *parrhēsia*). He noted that Cardinal Manning had told the British ambassador that infallibility "has long been intended [at the Council]. Long intended, and yet kept secret! Is this the way the faithful ever were treated before? Is this in any sort of sense going by Tradition?"[6]

At one point, as preparations for the Council were going forward, Pius tired of more subtle methods of encouraging the pro-infallible forces and planted a story in the Vatican newspaper, *La Civiltà Cattolica*, that caused a shocked reaction from outsiders. The newspaper printed a letter from France calling for the Council's declaration of the Pope's infallibility by acclamation, with no debate or vote. That was what Pius really wanted, but it was foolish to give such a blatant signal that he did.

The Pope's defenders accused the paper's Jesuit editor, Pietro Picirillo, of indiscretion and claimed Pius could not have known about the publication beforehand. But Picirillo was an ally of the Pope who was in constant communication with him (he would concert strategy with him almost daily during the Council), and Martina is justified in concluding that he would not have done this without the Pope's involvement:

Pius IX, cut off from all vital connection with reality, surrounded by hardline counselors with little or no feel for the requirements and expectations of middle-class intellectuals, did not reckon on the negative consequences this move could provoke—but which were instantly confirmed: amazement, irritation on the part of many, along with argument, heightened emotions that made the atmosphere on the eve of the Council very tense.[7]

The cause of such anxiety was not simply a suspicion that the Pope was angling toward infallibility, but an uncertainty about the scope he would give to that prerogative. Would he include the *Syllabus of Errors* among his infallible statements? Every encyclical? All his political statements? These questions can seem alarmist in retrospect, but Martina and others have found in the records material that justifies the anxiety. Cardinal Manning of England did work, together with other bishops at the Council, to make the definition of papal infallibility "broad enough to protect from any gallican or liberal dismissal the ordinary doctrinal statements of the Pope, even when he was not declaring positions formally heretical or orthodox—that is, his encyclicals, the *Syllabus*, the proscribing of positions as rash, etc."[8] For the reactionaries who were closest in spirit to Pius, this is what they principally wanted from the definition in the first place, and he encouraged this attitude. He expressed to Picirillo his bitterness at those trying to limit the definition so as to end up with an empty infallibility, one that would let them continue being liberals despite the *Syllabus*. "In the Pope's eyes, the *Syllabus* was substantially a defense of the supernatural order, and that was what was dearest to his heart."[9] He made his own desires obvious. A delegation of German bishops had sent a carefully prepared and respectfully phrased confidential letter to him, not challenging his infallibility as such but urging that this was the wrong time for making it formal. When they were received in audience after their arrival in Rome, the Pope did not offer his hand to be kissed but stuck out his foot to them (a favorite move of Pius toward Catholics who displeased him), and they had to kiss it, one by one.[10]

Since it was clear what the Pope was aiming at with his Council, Acton conceived the audacious plan of concerting a strategy with liberal bishops to defeat the Pope. After he had folded his own journal, the *Home*

and Foreign Review, he had written long articles in quarterlies run by
Catholic friends, the *Chronicle* and *North British Review.* He kept up his
own study of church history and stayed in contact with Döllinger, his disciples and supporters. He was in continual consultation with Bishop Dupanloup, the man who had done his best to pull the fangs of the *Syllabus.*
In the extraordinary international education Acton had received, he spent
time at Dupanloup's school for boys on the outskirts of Paris (before
moving on to Wiseman's Oscott and Döllinger's Munich). Dupanloup
was a friend of Acton's family, and the adult Acton moved up from student to friend himself. Dupanloup, on his way to attend the Council,
stopped off at one of Acton's ancestral homes, Herrnsheim in the Rhine
Valley, to confer with Acton and with fellow bishops who would lead the
effort against the declaration of infallibility at the Council—Hefele of
Rottenberg and Ketteler of Mainz.[11] They compared their knowledge of
historical arguments against infallibility and evaluated other bishops as
possible allies. It is astounding that these seasoned, even famous, leaders
of the church would accept the leadership of Acton, a layman still in his
early thirties. But Acton and his family were intimates of the hierarchy in
many countries (one of his uncles was a cardinal), and with government
officials throughout Europe. Most important, Acton was a close friend
and adviser of the British Prime Minister, William Ewart Gladstone.
Acton's deep book learning and wide worldly acquaintance made people ready, even in his youth, to accept his counsel.[12] Besides, the bishops
caucusing at Herrnsheim in 1869 realized that Acton, as a layman, could
have a freedom of movement and advocacy at the Council that would be
denied them under the discipline they expected Pius to impose on bishops.

   Their fear and suspicions were confirmed from the outset of the
Council. Since what the Pope wanted was so clear to his Curia, it set up
the rules of debate and voting, and drew up the questions for discussion,
in such a way as to rig the outcome. When it became clear that there
would be some sizable dissent, it was decreed that any discussion could
be cut off by mere motion on the part of ten bishops, and that any decrees of the Council could pass by a mere majority, though other Councils had aimed at consensus.[13] Even the sixteenth-century Council of
Trent, which was considered an authoritarian and Pope-ridden Council,

had demanded passage of decrees by an overwhelming majority. It also allowed considerably more freedom of debate in preparing decrees. The Pope did not want such precedents as these to be brought up, and he commanded his archival librarian Augustin Theiner, who had for years been preparing the records of Trent for publication, not to let any bishop consult them. Church history was sealed against the bishops of the church itself. Though they were assembled to continue the work of previous Councils, they were denied the means of studying them. When some bishops nonetheless cited, from other sources, what had occurred at the Council of Trent, Theiner was erroneously accused of leaking the records in his care:

> Pius IX suddenly summoned Theiner to his presence. He was excited and angry. He said that Theiner was reported to have taken Lord Acton into the Secret Archives and given him documents for his use. Theiner denied it with decision, and his denial seemed to make the Pope more excited. Theiner then offered to take a solemn oath that it was untrue. The Pope quietened. But he started blaming Acton—"he is not one of us"—and [Johann] Friedrich [another Döllinger student] and Döllinger—and then all the German bishops.[14]

Even acoustics were pressed into service for controlling the bishops. There were efforts to hold the general sessions in some other Roman church than the cavernous Saint Peter's, where, in that era before microphones and loudspeakers, it was hard if not impossible to conduct any real discussion. (As it turned out, the results of votes taken had to be shouted in relays around the crowd of bishops, showing how little ordinary speeches could be heard.) The Pope would not hear of any sessions being held elsewhere. He wanted the proceedings to be on his own turf, under his own scrutiny—in the transept of Saint Peter's closest to his palace. He even forbade the bishops to meet informally away from Saint Peter's. He thought of the rest of Rome as somewhat alien territory, since unrest there was being inhibited by occupying French troops friendly to him. As for the power of hearing people in Saint Peter's, he said "the speakers will have to shout more or the audience chatter less."[15] Adding to the difficulty of communication at the Council was the requirement that all business be conducted in Latin. Even the minority of those bishops who knew Latin well had trouble understanding the Italian pronunciation, which was the hallmark of the active Curia members as they steered events.

Acton was the best weapon bishops opposed to the papal domination of the Council could find. He knew Rome and its machinery from working in the past with Theiner at the archives. He transcended the language barriers between those bishops resisting the Curia's manipulation, bringing Americans together with the French, British with the Germans. He organized networks of communication inside the Council, and set up a propaganda operation to the outside world. He and his fellow Döllinger student Johann Friedrich sent surprisingly well-informed reports on what was happening inside the Council to Döllinger in Munich, to be published in the journal *Allgemeine Zeitung* under the pseudonym "Quirinus." The rest of the world soon learned that Quirinus was the best source to be consulted for news of the Council.

Since Rome was still under the secular rule of the Vatican state, freedom of speech was denied even to laymen not in the Council, and the public mails were subject to interception, so Acton had to rely on his Bavarian family and political connections to send his dispatches out in diplomatic pouches—Cardinal Hohenlohe, his ally in the resistance within the Council, was the Bavarian Prime Minister's brother. There was a thorough police search for "Quirinus," who would have been expelled from Rome if he were found. Acton was suspected, and spies shadowed him. They had reason to. After it became clear to Acton that the Vatican was going to silence the opponents to infallibility, he began to agitate for interference from the secular rulers of Europe to prevent this. This may seem outrageous to modern readers, but we have to remember that state participation in councils had been a fact of life since Constantine's presiding role at the fourth-century Council of Nicaea. Even at Trent, the first council called since the breakaway of Protestant states, Catholic powers had been invited, though not Protestant ones. Pius IX had in fact been torn by the question whether state representatives must be invited to the Council, in accord with ancient tradition. He evaded decision on the issue by saying that secular rulers (of whom Pius was still one, after all) were allowed to come, though not formally invited.[16] This made

Acton's appeal less far-fetched than we might at first think. This was especially true since France—a Catholic state under Napoleon III—was upholding Pius's shrunken realm with occupying forces in Rome. The Council would be broken off when war against Austria made France withdraw its troops, so that an independent Italy's warriors came flooding up to the very gates of the Vatican city.

There was also a good case for England's intervention, even though that was a Protestant state. Acton had worked closely with Gladstone for the cause of Catholic emancipation in Ireland, in which they had to fight off accusations that Catholics could not be good British citizens since their real allegiance lay with the Vatican. If papal infallibility made Catholics accept the *Syllabus* as binding, with its condemnation of British freedoms, then Parliament could revoke the rights granted to the Pope's subjects in Ireland. This argument convinced Gladstone, when Acton made it, and the Prime Minister proposed that England should send a formal protest to the Vatican; but he was overruled by Parliament. Some English politicians agreed with the British ambassador in Rome, Odo Russell, that it would be good for England and Protestantism if the Pope weakened Catholic claims in the modern world by declaring himself infallible.[17]

The only success Acton had with "the powers" (as he put it) was with Bismarck's Prussia. Acton had cultivated the Prussian ambassador, Count von Arnim, and he inspired dispatches to Bismarck saying that the Council's attacks on Protestants were an international affront. The preface to one schema was so hostile to the Reformation that Cardinal Strossmayer caused a sensation in the Council by denouncing it during the March debates—he was cut off by the presiding officer and not allowed to continue, a ruling that demonstrated the lack of free speech at the Council.[18] Bismarck threatened to withdraw his government's ambassador from Rome, but the schema's preface was softened and his protest faded.[19] Acton's great effort to block infallibility can look feckless in retrospect, but it frightened Pius and his Curia. Odo Russell, the ambassador who (as was just mentioned) hoped Pius would make a fool of himself by succeeding, had to admire Acton's work against the outcome he favored:

Both Dupanloup and Strossmayer [the Bavarian leader of bishops against infallibility] admitted that the opposition could not have been organized without Lord Acton whose marvelous knowledge, honesty of purpose, clearness of mind and powers of organization have rendered possible what appeared at first impossible. The party he has so powerfully helped to create is filled with respect and admiration for him. On the other hand the infallibilists think him the devil![20]

Pius himself conceived such an intense dislike for Acton, whom he saw behind all the opposition to his favored dogma, that he refused to give a blessing to his children at an audience.[21]

As the months dragged by at the Council, the Pope became angry at the organized resistance that was kept up despite all his efforts at control. (For one thing, after the reductions in his own income on losing much of his temporal kingdom, he chafed at having to support 300 bishops who lacked sufficient funds to pay for their own lodgings during such an extended stay.)[22] At one point, he shocked even his close ally, Father Picirillo, when he said, "I am so determined to push on that if the Council maintains its silence on the matter I will dismiss it and proclaim the dogma on my own authority."[23] He was especially angry at the respected Dominican Filippo Maria Guidi, the archbishop of Bologna, who made a carefully prepared speech on June 16 presenting the argument that the Pope can never be infallible when acting on his own, apart from the church. This speech, whose preparation was known, was greeted with rapturous applause from the minority of resisters, and bitter silence from the majority supporting Pius. Guidi was given a hero's reception in the corridors and at his lodgings, where a hundred bishops went to congratulate him. An Italian prelate punned on his name, "Guidi was misguided (*Guidi sguidato*) today, but he spoke true."[24]

The Pope summoned Guidi to a private interview where Guidi defended his position by citations from the whole tradition of the church, only to have the angry Pope shout at him, "*I* am tradition, *I* am the church." A stunned Guidi told intimates about the exchange when he left the audience, and reports of it spread through the city. The Pope sent word that Guidi was to deny hearing any such thing—i.e., he was asked to lie for the good of the church. Guidi, a man of honor, would not lie, but he agreed to keep silent, neither confirming nor denying.[25]

After it became clear that some form of infallibility was going to pass, opponents and moderates collaborated to temper the definition. Bilio, the author of the *Syllabus*, now Cardinal Bilio, was one of these, and his moderation caused a break with the Pope he had served so obsequiously theretofore. Pius was at length persuaded that he could not claim what he wanted—that infallibility was his personal prerogative, not something to be exercised in and with the church.[26] But he still managed to get the concluding phrase into the final document:

> The Roman Pontiff when he speaks <u>ex cathedra</u>—that is, when in discharge of the office of the Shepherd and Teacher of all Christians, in accordance with his supreme apostolic authority, he defines a doctrine regarding faith or morals which must be held by the whole Church,—by the divine assistance promised him in blessed Peter, is possessed of that infallibility with which the divine Redeemer willed that his Church should be endowed in defining doctrine regarding faith and morals; and that therefore such definitions of the Roman Pontiff are irreformable of themselves, <u>and not from the consent of the Church.</u> [Emphasis added.]

When the preliminary vote on this text was taken, 88 bishops voted against it, and 62 others voted for it in part (*juxta modum*—their objection was probably to the addition underlined above), and between 80 and 90 abstained from voting. This tally cannot register possible objections from another 80 to 90 who had drifted back to their dioceses in the course of the long Council and could not vote at the end.[27] Dissidents met to decide what they should do. Acton had wanted all dissidents to remain in Rome and vote no, to show the scale of the opposition, but Bishop Dupanloup said that the insult to the Holy Father was not something they were ready to deliver in person, so he urged the dissidents to leave for home before the ceremonial definition. Only two negative votes were cast at that session. Even if all the bishops who first assembled for the Council had remained for the final vote, they would

not have been representative of the entire church, since the Pope had
named many more bishops from Italy and Spain than from more distant
and less docile lands. Gertrude Himmelfarb summarizes the arguments
Acton had made in the "Quirinus" letters:

> The 700,000 inhabitants of the Roman States were represented by
> sixty-two bishops constituting half to two-thirds of every [concil-
> iar] commission, while the 1,700,000 Polish Catholics were repre-
> sented by the Bishop of Breslau, who was not chosen for a single
> commission; four (out of sixty-two) Neapolitan and Sicilian bishops
> could, and did, out-vote the archbishops of Cologne, Cambray and
> Paris, representing a total of 4,700,000 Catholics. In ecclesiastical
> statistics, it appeared that twenty learned Germans counted for less
> than one untutored Italian. "The predilection for the Infallibilist
> theory," Quirinus deduced, "is in precise proportion to the igno-
> rance of its advocates."[28]

There was something hollow about this victory, which prevented even
the hardliners from showing true ebullience.[29] Many of the most respected bishops had remained in opposition to the end, along with the
most learned (mainly German) theologians. In England, John Henry
Newman refused for long to recognize the validity of the decree on infallibility, saying that "so tyrannical an act as the vote of the majority"
could not count as the moral unanimity needed to reveal the mind of the
church.[30] He said he would not feel bound by it unless and until the minority bishops expressly affirmed it.[31] Acton went to work to prevent the
minority from such a capitulation. Though he felt that most of them had
shown cowardice by their behavior at the end of the Council, he did not
see how some of the men he admired could act against their consciences
by accepting what they had themselves branded as false. He published an
open letter in the German press calling on them to remain true to their
convictions. The Council had not been dissolved, merely adjourned
(temporarily, it was hoped), because of the disorder impending when
France withdrew its peacekeeping troops from Rome. A reassembled
Council could temper or refine the decree. To keep that option open was
the moral duty of the anti-infallibilist minority.[32]

The British hierarchy did not know what to do with Acton. It would be hard to discipline an admired aristocrat who was the friend of the Prime Minister. The letter he published in Germany could be ignored. It was harder to overlook an angry essay on the Council that Acton published just three months after its suspension, an essay in which Acton castigated the minority for its yielding to tyranny:

> They approved what they were called on to reform, and solemnly blessed with their lips what their hearts knew to be accursed. The Court of Rome became thenceforth reckless in its scorn of the opposition, and proceeded in the belief that there was no protest they would not forget, no principle they would not betray, rather than defy the Pope in his wrath.[33]

When a translation of this long essay appeared in Germany, the Vatican put it on the Index of Forbidden Books.[34] It seemed, at one point, that Acton would spare Cardinal Manning the difficulty of excommunicating him by withdrawal from the church on his own. In May 1871, ten months after the decree had passed, a body of German opponents of it, including Döllinger, declared the formation of a resisting church, and Acton's name appeared on the declaration. But he said it was put there by mistake, and matters rested there until 1874, when Gladstone, now out of office, showed that he had been convinced by Acton that members of a church professing infallibility could not express the freedom necessary to good British citizenship. He published a pamphlet, *The Vatican Decrees in Their Bearing on Civil Allegiance*, which became wildly popular, selling 145,000 copies in its first two months.[35]

Newman, who had kept a cautious silence on infallibility with most people, felt obliged to come to the defense of his fellow Catholics with a pamphlet of his own, *A Letter Addressed to His Grace the Duke of Norfolk*. But Acton fired off a quicker response in the *Times* of London. He had known that Gladstone was preparing the pamphlet, and he had urged him to abandon the project. When he failed at that, he readied his own answer for dispatch to the *Times* the minute Gladstone's pamphlet appeared. It was a missive that puzzled non-Catholics and infuriated many Catholics. It said that the church's leaders had always taught outlandish things, which had not prevented honest Catholics from following their consciences and ignoring the immoral directives from above. After all, throughout the period of the church's life as a secular kingdom, it had followed the Machiavellian practice of other kingdoms, condoning torture and assassination. What was the Vatican decree in comparison with the Inquisition or the Saint Bartholomew's Day Massacre? This exoneration by incrimination seemed a foolish tactic to some. What kind of defense is it to say that the church is even worse than Gladstone thinks, but that doesn't matter? But Acton was just displaying his customary dedication to the truth. He had long believed in all these sins of the church, and it had not shaken his devotion to the gospels, so why should he take a different view of the church now that it had perpetrated another enormity? It is true that he had hoped for a different response of the Vatican to the age of truth, but it had failed that test and reverted to the bad old days. Acton would prove just how bad they were. As he wrote later to Döllinger, "it is impossible honestly to apply a moral standard to history without discrediting the Church in her collective action."[36]

The *Times* letter was too much for Manning, who now formally asked Acton whether he submitted to the Vatican decree. His answer was evasive: "I have not felt it my duty as a layman to pursue the comments of divines, still less to attempt to supersede them by private judgments of my own. I am content to rest in absolute reliance on God's providence in His government of the Church."[37] That was a truthful report on the kind of faith he had. Though Döllinger left the church, Acton remained a devout participant in its sacramental and prayer life. In fact, Acton was less willing to forgive the church its sins than was Döllinger, who—in Acton's eyes—was too lenient in his judgment of the prelates and potentates of the past. This difference was so fundamental for Acton that he broke off further discussion with Döllinger, and had to confess that his first mentor was a compromiser with the truth.

As a historian, Acton came to be considered a hanging judge, applying the highest moral standards to all past actions, not allowing for the cultural blindnesses of specific eras. This reflected his own code of integrity. He placed such a high evaluation on honesty that he refused a part of his family fortune—that derived from his grandfather, who was the Prime Minister of Naples—because it was gained by corrupt practices.[38] But the criticism of dishonesty in high places came mainly from his experience as a critic of the church's historical record. He was so acutely aware of the way churchmen used a good cause to justify evil means of promoting it that he acquired laser vision for seeing through the multiple excuses always available for condoning dishonorable action. This most offended him in the church because it should be the friend of truth, not its enemy. It was the great sadness of his life to discover that this was not the case.

[1] Acton 3.305, "The Vatican Council" (1870).

[2] Roger Aubert, *Vatican I* (Editions de l'orante, 1964), pp. 35–36.

[3] Acton 3.308, "The Vatican Council" (1870).

[4] Ibid.

[5] Giacomo Martina, *Pio Nono (1867–1878)* (Editrice Pontificia Università Gregoriana, 1990), p. 172.

[6] Stephen Dessain et al., *The Letters and Diaries of John Henry Newman* (Oxford 1978–) 25.82.

[7] Ibid., p. 157.

[8] Ibid., p. 198.

[9] Ibid., p. 17.

[10] Ibid., p. 163.

[11] Damian McElrath, *Lord Acton: The Decisive Decade, 1864–1874* (Publications universitaires de Louvain, 1970), pp. 22–23.

[12] See the fine chapter, "With Gladstone," in Owen Chadwick, *Acton and History* (Cambridge University Press, 1998), pp. 139–85.

[13] Ibid., p. 182.

[14] Owen Chadwick, *Catholicism and History: The Opening of the Vatican Archives* (Cambridge University Press, 1978), pp. 63–66.

[15] Martina, op. cit., p. 164.

[16] Ibid., pp. 146–47.

[17] Chadwick, *Acton and History*, p. 82.

[18] Acton 3.330–32.

[19] Ibid., pp. 84–85.

[20] Ibid., p. 82.

[21] Gertrude Himmelfarb, *Lord Acton: A Study in Conscience and Politics* (University of Chicago Press, 1962), p. 106.

[22] Martina, op. cit., p. 167.

[23] Ibid., p. 175.

[24] Ibid., p. 206.

[25] Ibid., pp. 207–8.

[26] Ibid., p. 210.

[27] Himmelfarb, op. cit., p. 106.

[28] Ibid., p. 102.

[29] Martina, op. cit., pp. 215–16.

[30] Dessain, op. cit., 25.132.

[31] Ibid., 25.185.

[32]Himmelfarb, op. cit., pp. 110–11.

[33]Acton 3.333.

[34]Himmelfarb, op. cit., p. 113.

[35]Ibid., p. 117.

[36]Acton 3.666.

[37]Ibid., pp. 122–23.

[38]Robert L. Schuettinger, *Lord Acton, Historian of Liberty* (Open Court, 1976), pp. 140–41.

18.

Newman's Cautious Truth

The age of truth made more people than Acton suspect that the Catholic church instilled a discipline of lying, of Jesuitical equivocation and mental reserve. In England, these suspicions focused for a long time on John Henry Newman, whose personality seemed to elude men behind his great hawk beak of a nose, his effeminate manner, his softly seducing voice. This distrust crystallized at two special points, whose demands on him are reflected in two pamphlets, *What, Then, Does Dr. Newman Mean?* (1864) and *What Will Dr. Newman Do?* (1870). The first arose from a casual insult delivered by a famous man, Charles Kingsley, the second from uncertainty about Newman's acceptance of infallibility, an uncertainty voiced by an obscure man, Edward Husband.

It is often said that Newman overreacted to Kingsley's insult, that he responded to a pop gun with a rhetorical artillery barrage. This is a perception that comes in part from a sense that Kingsley was a puny adversary, but that was not how he was seen at the time. Kingsley was not only a popular novelist but a religious leader (Canon of Chester) and Regius Professor of Modern History at Cambridge. Besides, Newman rightly sensed a larger historical suspicion of him behind Kingsley's poorly crafted arguments. Though Kingsley publicly claimed that he had no resentment of Newman prior to his passing insult in a review published in 1864, he confessed in private, "I have a score of more than twenty years to pay, and this is an installment of it."[1] This "score" came from Kingsley's resentment, in the early 1840s, at the fact that his fiancée was much drawn to the authors of the Tracts being published then by Anglican priests of the Oxford Movement, of which Newman was a principal leader. Kingsley warned her against these men's wiles: "Whether willful or self-deceived, these men are Jesuits, taking the oath to the Articles with moral reservations, which allow them to explain them away in senses utterly different from those of their authors. All the worst *doctrinal* features of Popery Mr. Newman professes to believe in."[2]

That was a widespread apprehension about the Oxford Movement— that it was an attempt to smuggle Catholicism into the Anglican church. The leaders of the movement were opposed to modernity, on grounds Pius IX could have endorsed. Newman called liberalism an antidogmatic principle, and therefore an antireligious assault. He wrote to his mother in 1833: "The majority of the laity who think run into infidelity. The priests have lost influence exceedingly since the peace [struck at the Congress of Vienna, 1815]. The French Revolution and Empire seem to have generated a plague which is slowly working its way everywhere."[3] He struck the same note in some of his Tracts, arguing, for instance, that religion should not be subjected to rational criticism in Tract No. 73 (1835).

The Oxford Movement began with laments that the established religion was yielding on points like Catholic emancipation and ordination of priests not strictly orthodox. This made it very confusing when the same authors began to stretch the norms of orthodoxy to say that the Anglican articles of belief could admit Catholic interpretations. This was a signal that some of the Oxfordians were giving up on the established church of England, as too liberal itself, and moving toward Rome. When Newman himself broke with his past to become a Catholic in 1845, taking a number of followers with him, it was said that he had schemed all along to Catholicize the English church, that he was leaving only because he had failed at his subversive project. The "honest" Tractarians, like Edward Pusey, were the ones who stayed faithful to their own church.

Newman's copious writings gave ammunition to his foes, since he had moved with agonizing steps, each precisely marked, from one church to another, each stage in effect canceling what was said before, so that his words could be pitted against each other in apparent contradiction. While he was still trying to stay in the English church, he criticized papalism to show that he was not the Catholic he was taken to be. Some of what he wrote in this phase sounds like what Kingsley would say against him. In the *British Critic* of 1840, for instance, he wrote:

We Englishmen like manliness, openness, consistency, truth. Rome
will never gain on us, till she learns these virtues, and uses them; and
then she *may* gain us; but it will be by ceasing to be what we now
mean by Rome, by having a right, not to "have dominion over our
faith," but to gain and possess our affections in the bonds of the
gospel.[4]

Nor were Newman's problems with seeming inconsistency ended by
his conversion. His mind was still in motion, since he had been forced to
work out a theory of doctrinal development in order to justify his own
move to Rome. This meant that the man who had begun as a conservative Anglican defender of the British hierarchy became a liberal Catholic
denier that the papal hierarchy had a monopoly on truth. He was greeted
with great distrust, therefore, by his new coreligionists, and he had to
elaborate ever newer formulas to explain himself. In all this motion of his
developing mind, he gave some readers a sense of blur or evasion, as if always sliding off from a point as soon as he made it. It was this conception of Newman, fueled by the old resentment of his influence over his
wife, that led Kingsley to say, in an aside while reviewing a history of
England: "Truth, for its own sake, had never been a virtue with the
Roman clergy. Father Newman informs us that it need not, and on the
whole ought not to be." When Newman asked for the basis of this accusation, Kingsley cited a sermon delivered when Newman was not one
of the "Roman clergy," and said he would take Newman's word that he
did not mean what he said on that specific occasion. But he did not retract the general accusation. Newman naturally wondered aloud why a
man would take the word of someone he had called a liar on general
principle. Letters flew back and forth, Kingsley unable to retract his general accusation, Newman not settling for evasions from a man who had
accused him of evading the truth.

When an exasperated Newman published the correspondence, Kingsley's wife, who knew the high-strung condition of her husband's nerves,
advised him to drop the matter; but he undertook what he was sure would
be a final, obliterative blow. He ransacked Newman's works for examples
of duplicity, and arrayed them in his pamphlet *What, Then, Does Dr. Newman Mean?* Newman's reply to this was a series of pamphlets, one pub-

lished every Thursday for seven weeks in a row, which were then printed
together as the *Apologia Pro Vita Sua*. Rather than keep going round and
round on the specific points Kingsley was trying to make, Newman traced
the whole course of his religious thinking, stage by stage, to show that he
was making an honest statement of what he truly felt at each point.

One of Kingsley's most plausible accusations was that Newman shaved
or shaded or hid the truth for polemical or apologetic purposes. He
would embarrass Newman with a term he had repeatedly used—an
"economy" of truth—suggesting that he could be stingy with the truth,
dealing it out in minimal amounts, holding parts of it back, denying it
entirely to some audiences. Newman had acquired the term in his reading of the Greek fathers of the fourth century, who used the word *oikonomia* to describe the various dispensations that affect the ways truth can be
told or framed or withheld. The assumption on which all this talk was
based is that God is unknowable, that His truth is beyond the reach of
the human mind. As Saint Augustine put it in the Latin church, "Since it
is God we are speaking of, you do not understand it. If you could understand it, it would not be God."[5]

Though all statements made about God are bound to be inadequate,
some are more or less adequate, more or less appropriate for different eras
or persons. The Jewish scriptures, the fathers said, were an *oikonomia*, re-
vealing parts of truth that would receive a fuller manifestation in Jesus.
That same kind of revelation by stages goes on when one speaks to a
child or a beginner in the pursuit of religious truth. To draw an angel
with wings is an economy, meant to suggest some idea of a higher being
to the young mind. It is false, but not a lie.[6] As one advances in knowledge, economy does not become less important, just subtler. Karl Rahner and other modern theologians say that the whole theology of the
Trinity is an economy, since fatherhood and sonhood are no more literal
truths about God than are wings about angels. They are analogous terms
useful (though dangerous, like all namings of God) when talking about
God's revelation of Himself in the economy of salvation.[7] In the same
way, since Newman's form of thinking was always dynamic, a process of
moving from truth to truth, he says that the truth one leaves behind is
not necessarily false but an economy—a less adequate expression of truth
that led to a more adequate one.

This kind of progression is not, he claims, a mere reformulation of logical propositions. The mind does not advance syllogistically in a single dimension of speculation.

> For myself, it was not logic that carried me on; as well might one say that the quicksilver in the barometer changes the weather. It is the concrete being that reasons; pass a number of years, and I find my mind in a new place; how? the whole man moves; paper logic is but the record of it.[8]

He had described the process even as he was undergoing it. This excerpt from an Anglican sermon looks forward to his final concept of "real assent" as opposed to a shallow "notional" truth:

> The mind ranges to and fro, and spreads out and advances forward with a quickness which has become a proverb, and a subtlety and versatility which baffle investigation. It passes on from point to point, gaining one by some indication; another on a probability; then availing itself of an association; then falling back on some received law; next seizing on testimony; then committing itself to some popular impression, or some inward instinct, or some obscure memory; and thus it makes progress not unlike a clamberer on a steep cliff, who, by quick eye, prompt hand, and firm foot, ascends, how, he knows not himself, by personal endowments and by practice, rather than by rule, leaving no track behind him, and unable to teach another. It is not too much to say that the stepping by which great geniuses scale the mountain of truth is as unsafe and precarious to men in general as the ascent of a skilful mountaineer up a literal crag. It is a way which they alone can take; and its justification lies alone in their success. And such mainly is the way in which all men, gifted or not gifted, commonly reason—not by rule, but by an inward faculty. Reasoning, then, or the exercise of reason, is a living spontaneous energy within us, not an art.[9]

Most of us, I wager, recognize in that passage the real way we form our opinions, though we are not so honest as to confess that it is not pure reason that guides us on important or doctrinal matters. Newman, in other words, was accused of dishonesty precisely because he was being so truthful to the lived experience of the formation of real assent to our inmost convictions. It is as a psychological self-observer that he deserves to rank with Augustine. The wonder of the *Apologia* is that he conveys the experience of coming to new depths of knowledge in a concrete and convincing way. Accused of dishonesty, he sets a new standard for what honesty to one's own thinking should be. Much of his later work would be a deepening in analysis of this mental process, which Chesterton put with characteristic rapidity in a kind of symbolic shorthand: "A man may well be less convinced of a philosophy from four books, than from one book, one battle, one landscape, and one old friend. The very fact that the things are of different kinds increases the importance of the fact that they all point to one conclusion."[10]

A Kingsley can object that any defense of partial explications of the truth can serve as a rationale for hiding or softening unpleasant or embarrassing truths. Of course. But you do not need the theology of economy to resort to that. And we must remember that Newman's model is *God's* economic revelations. They are not meant to block the access to truth but to lead on to larger truths. They open up the field of vision rather than close it down. You are not meant to think only and always of God as in a parental relationship with Himself (as father and son). That is just a help to more exalted conceptions, of the sort Augustine explored in his book, *The Trinity*, where the parental relationship is less important than aspects of the mind's inner structure. Human use of economy, if it is modeled on God's, cannot be used to deceive or to steer away from truth but only toward it.

The *Apologia* not only restored Newman's reputation for truthfulness with Protestants but made Catholics see that he was honest in his expression of the need for development within their own fold. But five years after the appearance of the *Apologia,* he had to meet a new test of truthfulness when the Vatican Council convened. Acton was as open in denouncing the idea of the Pope's infallibility as Manning was in supporting it. But Newman seemed to hesitate between the two, bringing back his image as vacillating or equivocating—which led Edward Husband, an Anglican, to challenge Newman when the Vatican decree appeared. In his pamphlet *What Will Dr. Newman Do?* Husband argued that Newman should return to his original church now that the Vatican had gone too far for him to accept its doctrines honestly.

The common way to characterize Newman's view of infallibility is that he always believed in it, in some sense, but thought that Vatican I was the wrong time and way to proclaim it. The mode of its passage offended him—pushed forward by people he regularly called the "violent party" or the "cruel" coercers of men's consciences.[11] This puts him in the fairly large body of "inopportunists," as they were called, who evaded the issue of the doctrine's soundness by saying that it should not be brought to the fore in such a way that it seemed to support the *Syllabus* in defiance of all modern values. But John R. Page, by carefully collecting everything Newman said about infallibility throughout the whole controversy over it, shows that Newman had far deeper objections to the doctrine than the mere timing of its declaration. We should not be surprised by this. He had contended early in his Catholic career that the laity should be consulted on doctrine, since it was sometimes more faithful to the revelation than was the hierarchy (including the Pope). He said that the promise of the Spirit was to the whole church. The church, he thought, was like a triangle that rested now on one side, now another, for its secure basis in truth—sometimes on the lay people, at other times on the theological community (*schola theologorum*), at other times on the hierarchy (never exclusively on the Pope).

Furthermore, in the *Apologia*, he had traced the development of doctrine in the body of believers as analogous to the growth of the individual mind. As "the whole man moves" to come to a deep apprehension of truth, so the whole church moves toward finding sound doctrine:

> Perhaps a local teacher, or a doctor in some local school, hazards a proposition, and a controversy ensues. It smoulders or burns in one place, no one interposing; Rome simply lets it alone. Then it comes before a Bishop; or some priest, or some professor in some other seat of learning takes it up; and then there is a second stage of it. Then it comes before a University, and it may be condemned by the theological faculty. So the controversy proceeds year after year, and Rome is still silent. An appeal perhaps is next made to a seat of au-

thority inferior to Rome; and then at last after a long while it comes before the supreme power. Meanwhile, the question has been ventilated and turned over and over again, and viewed on every side of it, and authority is called upon to pronounce a decision, which has already been arrived at by reason. But even then, perhaps the supreme authority hesitates to do so, and nothing is determined on the point for years; or so generally and vaguely, that the whole controversy has to be gone through again, before it is ultimately determined. It is manifest how a mode of proceeding, such as this, tends not only to the liberty but to the courage, of the individual theologian or controversialist. Many a man has ideas, which he hopes are true, and useful for his day; but he is not confident about them, and wishes to have them discussed. He is willing, or rather would be thankful, to give them up, if they can be proved to be erroneous or dangerous, and by means of controversy he obtains his end. He is answered, and he yields, or on the contrary he finds that he is considered safe. He would not dare to do this, if he knew an authority, which was supreme and final, was watching every word he said, and made signs of assent or dissent to each sentence, as he uttered it. Then indeed he would be fighting, as the Persian soldiers, under the lash, and the freedom of his intellect might truly be said to be beaten out of him.[12]

This model of interaction between members of the body of Christ is very far from the way a tyrannous faction sneaked infallibility into a Council where it was not even announced as on the agenda, where freedom of speech was curtailed, where openness was penalized. As Newman wrote after the decree was announced, "whatever is decided eventually about the definition of the present Council, the scandals which have accompanied it will remain, and the guilt of those who perpetrated them."[13]

He also opposed the definition on the grounds that where there is no need to make doctrines binding, in opposition to some heresy, it is unwise to burden the conscience of believers with extra obligations. "Hitherto nothing has been ever done at Councils but what is *necessary*; what is the necessity of this?"[14] There may even be adventitious motives for using this kind of unnecessary definition. "My memory went back to an old saying, imputed to Monsignor Talbot, that what made the definition of the Immaculate Conception so desirable and important was that it opened the way to the definition of the Pope's Infallibility. Is it wonderful that we should all be shocked?"[15] Newman was voicing the same criticism that Acton had: "People even said that it was the real object of that decree [on the Immaculate Conception] to create a precedent which should make it impossible afterward to deny papal infallibility."[16]

A further reason for Newman's objection to the doctrine was his English sense of what good constitutional government entails. He thought of the college of bishops as the church's legislature and the Pope as its executive officer. Thus "we have a right to judge of what is likely or not by our political experience, and to say that such a union of legislative and executive powers in one person is not like [fitting], as being, as human politics teach us, too great for one man to sustain, and a temptation to abuse."[17] The definition would therefore issue from and indurate corruption: "We have come to a climax of tyranny. It is not good for a Pope to live 20 years. It is anomaly and bears no good fruit; he becomes a god, has no one to contradict him, does not know facts, and does cruel things without meaning it."[18]

Continuing his political analogy, Newman thought the body of church teachers, the *schola theologorum*, resembled the judiciary in a constitutional order: "All these are questions for the theological school—and the theologians will, as time goes on, settle the force of the wording of the dogma, just as the courts of law solve the meaning and bearing of Acts of Parliament."[19] Since Newman thought the whole church should move together in seeing where the Spirit is leading it, he gave a very high role to theologians, who make the internal conversation of the church with itself possible by articulating questions and presenting them to Christians to be tested in their lives and prayers. This attitude made the Vatican Council suspect in his eyes, since so many of the learned theologians were excluded.

All these objections to the definition could, I suppose, be brought within the rubric of inopportunism. But there are other places where Newman just flatly says the idea of the Pope's infallibility is wrong in itself. Even a month after the decree was issued, he wrote: "I do not and cannot *at present* accept the definition for the reason that as far as I can

see the Authority of history and the past *against* it more than counter-
balance the living authority (which, so long as the Minority exists, is deprived of half its weight) in its favor."[20] He dwelt often on the case of
Honorius I, the seventh-century Pontiff who denied that there was a
human will in Christ and was anathematized as a heretic by the sixth ecumenical council (he even encouraged a writer to investigate this case in
a pamphlet that was put on the Index). "How will they deal with Honorius? for *his* letters were on the de fide [basis]."[21] He did not find the
doctrine in his favorite fourth-century Fathers of the church, so he
prayed to them to prevent the definition: "Save the church, O my Fathers, from a danger as great as any that has happened."[22]

He wrote to encourage bishops opposed to the definition, and his letter to his own bishop, William Bernard Ullathorne, caused a scandal
when it became public, since Newman denounced those pushing for the
definition as "an aggressive insolent faction."[23] Newman prayed for some
divine intervention to break up the Council before it could define the
dogma. He hoped the Italian independence forces might seize the Vatican, or that the Pope might die. "We must hope, for one is obliged to
hope, that the Pope will be driven from Rome, and will not continue the
Council, or that there will be another Pope. It is sad that he should force
us to such wishes."[24]

It is impossible to claim, then, that Newman opposed the doctrine just
on the grounds of its inopportuneness. He was so sure that it was wrong
that he repeatedly predicted the Holy Spirit would not let the Council
define it.[25] And when the Council did, he refused to accept the result as
valid until it was clear that the minority bishops were giving up their resistance. Then he accepted the doctrine more because the general church
did than because the Council, which was not a free body, had declared
it. "I should think [it] safer to believe in the '*securus judicat*' [consensus of
the church] than on the Synodal Vote."[26]

Yet after he accepted the dogma, he did tell people that he had always believed in infallibility but had deplored the thuggish tactics of the
people working to define it. It is true that Newman had accepted infallibility, in fact had praised it in the *Apologia*, but he focused then on the
infallibility—sometimes the indefectibility—of the church. At times this
would involve papal infallibility, at other times—as he argued in his ar-

ticle on consulting the laity—it would involve lay infallibility, or the infallibility of the *schola theologorum*. The Spirit would protect the church, but its means would be as mysterious as the divine nature of the protector.

Acton believed that Newman betrayed the truth in accepting the dogma which he (Acton) continued to reject. But truth was always a more complex thing for Newman than for Acton. If the doctrine involved the divine guidance of the church, it was dealing with the unknowable God, and any attempt to restrict Him in narrow bonds of human language had to be examined closely for its real meaning:

> In former times it was by the collision of Catholic intellects with Catholic intellects that the meaning and the limit of dogmatic decrees were determined; but there has been no intellectual scrutiny, no controversies as yet over the Vatican definitions, and their sense will have to be wrought out . . .[27]

The definition could not stand alone. Newman reminded people that the Council was broken off by Italian bayonets, that balancing considerations might still be taken up: "There is a limit to the triumph of the tyrannical. Let us be patient, and let us have faith, and a new Pope, and a reassembled council may trim the boat."[28]

Newman gave prayerful consideration to what the real sense of the definition could be, and finally came up with his reading of it in his answer to Gladstone. First he cleared away Gladstone's objection that the Pope would pronounce some duty inconsistent with British citizenship. Dogmas are about supernatural truths and general propositions, not about concrete acts and temporal arrangements, in which conscience is the supreme guide. That is a fact of nature and "the Pope, who comes of Revelation, has no jurisdiction over Nature."[29] On all such matters, he reassured the former Prime Minister:

> Certainly, if I am obliged to bring religion into after-dinner toasts (which indeed does not seem quite the thing) I shall drink,—to the Pope, if you please,—still to Conscience first, and to the Pope afterwards.[30]

As to the substance of the definition, Newman notes that there is a limit on the Pope's sway within the text itself, which declares that the Pope "is possessed of that infallibility with which the divine Redeemer willed that his Church should be endowed." Admittedly, it goes on to say that his *ex cathedra* statement does not derive "from the consent of the Church." Still, it *is* the power that God gives in the first place to His church. If the Pope ever goes against the church, he is not, *eo ipso*, speaking *ex cathedra*, even if he thinks he is. Pope Clement V, for instance, solemnly declared the defense of usury heretical, but other church bodies allowed it, showing this was not the voice of the whole church.[31] Here the case of Honorius, which had bothered Newman before the definition, becomes a way of showing the limits of the definition. Since a council declared Honorius heretical, he could not have been speaking *ex cathedra*.[32] The Pope's statements, *outside the promise given to the church*, are not infallible:

> Was St. Peter infallible on that occasion at Antioch when St. Paul withstood him? Was St. Victor infallible when he separated from his communion the Asiatic Churches? Or Liberius when in like manner he excommunicated Athanasius? And, to come to late times, was Gregory XIII, when he had a medal struck in honor of the Bartholomew massacre? Or Paul IV in his conduct towards Elizabeth? Or Sixtus V when he blessed the Armada? Or Urban VII when he persecuted Galileo?[33]

Newman came in time to see a providential rescue in the result of the Vatican Council. Not only had Manning and the "tyrannous party" been unable to extend infallibility to cover things like the *Syllabus*. Even Pius IX had been blocked from his real goal. Though he added his own little declaration of independence at the end of the definition, he did not see that its earlier formulas made that phrase nugatory. You cannot exercise the gift of the church apart from the church. Newman still regretted the dogma's declaration, now more as a bar to good relations with other Christians than as an affront to his own ideas, but he knew that any language used about God's power—and that was the thing at issue, not the

Pope's power—must be an economy. The test of an economy is its use to lead on to fuller truths, not serve as an obstacle to truth. That is the only reading Newman would accept of the Vatican definition.

Acton and Newman were far apart in temperament and mode of action, but both were champions of truth within the church—Acton courageously if a little indiscriminately, Newman cautiously but persistently and with a sense of the mystery that is always involved in trying to speak the truth about God. If church authorities begin with disregard for truth in historical and temporal matters, they will have coarsened their ability to handle the greatest truths, which are the most elusive ones.

---

[1]Susan Chitty, *The Beast and the Monk: A Life of Charles Kingsley* (Mason/Charter, 1974), p. 231.

[2]Robert Bernard Martin, *The Dust of Combat: A Life of Charles Kingsley* (Faber and Faber, 1959), p. 47.

[3]Edward Sillem, *The Philosophical Notebook of John Henry Newman* (Humanities Press, 1969), p. 44.

[4]John Henry Newman, *Apologia Pro Vita Sua*, edited by David J. DeLaura (W. W. Norton & Company, 1968), p. 105.

[5]Augustine, Sermon 117.5.

[6]Newman, op. cit., p. 206.

[7]Karl Rahner, *The Trinity*, translated by Joseph Donceel (Herder and Herder, 1970), pp. 21ff.

[8]Newman, op. cit., p. 136.

[9]Ibid., p. 427.

[10]G. K. Chesterton, *Orthodoxy* (Doubleday, 1959), p. 143.

[11]N 96, 132, 133, 137, 142, 148, 155.

[12]N 204–5.

[13]N 128.

[14]N 400.

[15]N 110.

[16]Acton 3.295.

[17]N 30.

[18]N 163.

[19]N 202.

[20]N 137.

[21]N 45, 80. For Newman's continued reflection on this case during the Council's deliberations, see N 62, 66, 153, 211, 227, 229, 235, 312, 313, 326, 383.

[22]N 78.

[23]N 86.

[24]N 154—and see pp. 162–63.

[25]N 80, 84, 89, 90.

[26]N 135.

[27]N 208.

[28]N 187.

[29]John Henry Newman, *A Letter Addressed to His Grace the Duke of Norfolk* (1875), in Alvan S. Ryan, *Newman and Gladstone: The Vatican Decrees* (University of Notre Dame Press, 1962), p. 133.

[30]N 138.

[31]N 195–96.

[32]N 179–81.

[33]N 135.

IV.

THE SPLENDOR OF TRUTH

Christ likes us to prefer truth to him, because, before being Christ, he is truth. If one turns aside from him to go to the truth, one will not go far before falling into his arms.

—SIMONE WEIL

19.

Augustine vs. Jerome

Augustine (354–430) wrote two books against lying—*Deception* in 395 CE, *Against Deception* in 420—and the occasion for each was a coreligionist's attempt to use deception for the promotion of Christianity. The first attempt was made by Augustine's contemporary, Saint Jerome, who thought that two apostles had used edifying lies to instruct people. Relying on prior scriptural commentaries, of which Augustine was ignorant, Jerome argued that Saint Peter and Saint Paul were only *pretending* to differ during a conflict between them at Antioch, a clash described by Paul in his Letter to the Galatians. It is ironic that a pious cover-up should be attempted here, where the words of the New Testament are so frank and unevasive. Paul is pulling no punches in his angry report of what happened in Antioch—though translators tend to mute the sting of his words:

When Stone [Peter] came to Antioch, I stood up to him in open confrontation. His own acts proved him wrong, since he had eaten with the cosmopolitans before James's emissaries came [from Jerusalem], but he retreated after their arrival and cut himself off, cowed by the defenders of circumcision. The other separatists acted with him in bad faith, even Barnabas was caught up in their bad faith. I, by contrast, when I saw that they were not keeping to the straight course of revealed truth, told Stone in everyone's presence, "If even you, a Jew, have lived with the cosmopolitans and not the separatists, why are you now forcing the cosmopolitans to live like the separatists?" (Gal 2:11–14).[1]

Jerome can describe that forthright, even blistering, passage this way: Paul "stealthily and with sidling moves picks his way from covert to covert" (PL 26.310). Jerome cannot allow the blunt words to have their plain meaning, because that would allow Christ's enemies "to brand Peter as erring and Paul as crowing over him, saying that we hold made-up doctrines and our church's founders were at loggerheads" (310–11). Rather than let the two men disagree, Jerome has to imagine a situation in which they are both putting on a false show, each to please one faction in the church until time allows their followers to reach a more advanced view of their relations: "Peter's feigned observance of Jewish law (which was offensive to gentile believers) was countered by Paul's feigned rebuke, so that both camps would be kept safe—those favoring circumcision would follow Peter, and those resisting it would praise the liberty preached by Paul" (339). This is what Jerome calls "profitable dissemblance" (*utilis simulatio*), by which "one dissembles for a time, in order to work out one's own and others' salvation" (340). His solution allows him to maintain that the two apostles could never *really* disagree on anything fundamental.

Before taking up Augustine's attack on this form of holy dissemblance, it is best to look more closely at the situation he and Jerome were considering, the conflict at Antioch (which took place circa 51–52 CE, about two years before Paul's description of the event in his letter to the Galatians). This was one engagement in the major internal war that both divided the early church and helped to spread it. Christianity propagated itself as amoebas do, by bipolar fission. The poles into which it split were described as "Hellenists" and "Hebrews" in Acts of the Apostles (6:1) and as gentiles (*ethne*) and "Judaizers" by Paul (Gal 2:14). Older and simpler readings of these poles *within the Christian community* were either ethnic or linguistic—the Hellenists (or gentiles) were thought to be non-Jewish Christians, or were Greek speakers, while the Hebrews (or Judaizers) were Jewish Christians, or were non-Greek speakers (using either Hebrew or Aramaic). But a closer look at the dynamics of the situation has given modern scholars a more complex understanding of the factors in play. There were Jewish Christians (e.g., Paul himself, and sometimes Peter) among the Hellenists, and gentile Christians (including some at

Antioch) among the Hebrews, and the former could use Aramaic as much as the latter could use Greek.

Then what was the principle of division between these two camps? Scholars now agree that the "Hebrew" Christians thought that Christ's mission was to fulfill Jewish law, not to supersede it—hence the observances of temple worship, circumcision, and kosher food rites were to be continued by Christians. The "Hellenist" Christians were more at home in the culture of the Hellenized Roman Empire, and felt that Christianity could and should exist in that world, separating itself from some (perhaps many) of the Jewish observances. The best translation of the two sets of terms would therefore be "cosmopolitans" for those moving out into the culturally variegated world of the Empire, and "separatists" for those who wanted to restrict the spread of Christianity within the circle of Jewish legal rituals. Not only were both sides Christians, both sides had early founders, apostles, and saints in their company.[2]

The first reported clash between these two parties in the church occurred shortly after the death of Jesus, when the Jewish Sanhedrin executed the cosmopolitan Christian Stephen for blasphemy. This forced the other cosmopolitans to flee Jerusalem, carrying the gospel elsewhere (Acts 6:8–7:3). The Christian separatists stayed behind, since their position was not yet offensive to their fellow Jews. The author of Acts makes the issue at stake in this first split of the church Stephen's attack on Temple worship—in a radical speech probably composed after the destruction of the Temple in 70 CE; but the views put in his mouth are no doubt an extrapolation of the attitude he stood for in the clash with separatists as well as with the Sanhedrin.

The second major conflict between cosmopolitans and separatists took place around 50 CE, over the issue of circumcising gentile converts. The Jerusalem church, under the leadership of James the brother of Jesus, had been demanding circumcision, but Paul and Barnabas won from them the concession that in churches founded by them, away from Jerusalem, they could admit the uncircumcised (Acts 15:6–21). This essentially established a two-track Christian world, one that could not be maintained when—as at Antioch—members from the two tracks flowed together. Peter, when he came to Antioch, at first joined the cosmopolitans in nonkosher meals, but "cut himself off" when admonished by James from Jerusalem. Paul took this as in effect "forcing" the cosmopolitans to toe the separatist line dictated from Jerusalem, breaking the earlier agreement (Gal 2:14). As J. Louis Martyn observes, "Paul observes anything but gentleness" in his attack on Peter—a fact Jerome tried to deny and Augustine would affirm.[3]

But before giving Augustine's interpretation of the Antioch conflict, we should glance ahead to see what course the split between cosmopolitans and separatists took before the rift was healed. Peter was a missionary like Paul—he left the Jerusalem church in charge of James, the Lord's brother. The two missionary apostles, Peter and Paul, were in Rome by the time of Nero's persecution of the Christians, in which they were both martyred—though that is never expressly stated in the New Testament. There is an abundance of indirect and later evidence that, in fact, they did meet their deaths this way. But that raises the interesting question of the omission of this vital information from the text of the New Testament itself.

Scholars have put together the story of their death, at least sketchily, from extra-biblical literature about Nero's reign, and the result shows why Christians did not, for a while, want to dwell on the details of their apostles' deaths. In the nineties a Christian leader in Rome (Clement) wrote a letter that said the apostles were killed out of a "rivalrous grudge"—which does not seem to describe Nero's motive: he killed the Christians as scapegoats, blaming them for the fire in Rome. He was hardly their rival.[4] But according to the Roman historian Tacitus, Nero was not the only agent in the execution of the Christians. He says that Nero first took some Christians prisoner, who explained that they were not responsible for the fire *but informed on others who were*.[5] Another Roman author, Pliny, says that Christians regularly turned each other in during the early decades of their existence.[6] Paul himself speaks of "false brothers" he encountered in the (cosmopolitan) churches he founded, presumably some form of separatists (Gal 2:4, II Cor 11:26—cf. II Cor 11:13).

Oscar Cullmann, Raymond Brown, and others convincingly argue that it was the separatists who collaborated with Nero.[7] Ironically, despite their opposition to the Hellenization of their *religion*, the separatists were *politically* protected by the Hellenized Empire, since Judaism (which these Christians observed) was a recognized cult (*religio licita*), part of the Romans' ruling arrangement with the Sanhedrin in Jerusalem. The cosmopolitans were the vulnerable ones, at the time of Peter's and Paul's deaths, just as in that of Stephen's execution several decades earlier.

What we find, in the first five decades or so of Christianity, is an unremitting opposition between two camps, and the separatist camp seems to win every reported encounter—when the cosmopolitans are driven out after Stephen's death, when Paul can get only partial dispensation from circumcision, when Peter backslides away from Paul in Antioch, and when the separatists turn in Peter and Paul at Rome. No wonder the scriptural writers did not want to give us the full story of the apostles' martyrdom, and no wonder the author of Acts smooths over most of this struggle, entirely omitting the angry outburst of Paul that we began with.

We might ask, if the separatists won over and over in the early days, why the cosmopolitans prevailed in the long run. The turning point was the destruction of the Temple by Roman soldiers in 70 CE. This seemed to vindicate the Christians who had moved out and away from the Temple—so much so that the gospels, which took their final form after this event, speak of Jesus supplanting the Temple. Now Peter and Paul are posthumously triumphant, and a new era begins in Christian history.

It is this tense tale of struggle that Jerome and Augustine blunder into the middle of when they are handling Paul's hot words at Antioch. His is an unmediated report from the front lines of conflict—in fact, the letter containing his words is the second-oldest part of the New Testament that we possess (the first being Paul's letter to the Thessalonians). Jerome's instinct is to do what the author of Acts will do—cover up the signs of conflict in an idealized early church. But Acts simply keeps quiet on Paul's outburst, as on the martyrdoms of Peter and Paul. Jerome goes further—he condones an act of benign deceit on the apostles' part—and that is what disturbed Augustine profoundly, enough to make him challenge a scholar older and better recognized than he was at the time of his first letter on the matter.

Admittedly, neither Jerome nor Augustine knew the whole story that has been put together patiently by modern scholarship, and each came to the interpretation of this passage with his own prior conceptions. Jerome was especially disposed to protect Peter, since Peter was thought (anachronistically) to have been the bishop of Rome (i.e., the first Pope) when he was killed there. Jerome had served a successor to that office when he was secretary to Pope Damasus (a role that made later ages suppose, erroneously, that Jerome was a cardinal). Augustine, on the other hand, though he recognized a special office in the Pope, was not surprised by the notion that Popes could err, just as Peter had in Antioch. In fact, in 418, Augustine would stymie an attempt by Pope Zosimus to intervene in African church affairs by citing a conciliar canon against him, and in 419 he helped mobilize pressures that made the same Pope reverse himself—from exonerating the heretic Pelagius to condemning him.[8]

So, even though Augustine accepted the anachronistic idea that Peter became a Pope, he was able to perceive the plain sense of Paul's letter—that Peter was wrong, and Paul had to correct him. Augustine's own commentary on Galatians—which he was probably preparing when he consulted Jerome's commentary—says:

> Peter accepted the obstacles these men [from Jerusalem] raised, and acted in bad faith, as if he agreed that the gospel could not save gentiles unless they met the heavy requirements of the Law—so Paul made him act in good faith again. And when he did this "in everyone's presence," it was because he had to, so that all would stand corrected by his reprimand. A private remedy for a public wrong is useless (PL 35.2107, 2114).

Augustine goes on to suppose that Peter received the reprimand on the spot, reformed his conduct, and let Paul prevail—which no modern scholar thinks. Paul says nothing of Peter's response, and he leaves Antioch without his old ally Barnabas, who had joined Peter on this point, indicating that Paul was defeated at Antioch by the combined forces of James, Peter, and Barnabas. But Augustine no doubt sincerely thought that Peter would have responded to Paul's justified complaint with an honest admission that he had been wrong:

> And, then, the steadiness and love of Peter—to whom the Lord three times said, "If you love me, feed my sheep"—made him read-

ily accept reprimand even from an apostle called later than he was. For the reprimanded person is more to be admired than the reprimander, since the reprimanded has the harder role. It is easier to see something for correction in another than to see what needs correction in oneself and to correct it readily, either on one's own or at another's prompting—especially when the reprimander was called later, and especially "in everyone's presence." (2114.)

So Augustine, too, bailed Peter out—but not by denying that he could err while admitting that he *could* lie.

Augustine wrote to Jerome with a willingness to be reprimanded, in the spirit he praised in Peter. He wants to know whether there is an argument Jerome can make for his interpretation that would get around the problem of making the apostles act deceitfully. He asks Jerome to correct anything in his own writings:

I find it hard to judge my own work accurately, since I am either too diffident about it, or too defensive. I see, at times, how I err, but I prefer the judgment of better minds, lest, having caught myself out, I go on to acquit myself, treating my own condemnation as a quibble. (Ep 40.4.)

When, at first, he got no answer from Jerome, and then when he got evasive answers, Augustine pressed on—keeping up his requests over the space of a decade—trying to make Jerome explain himself. This was not a casual matter to Augustine, as we see from the fact that he wrote his book *Deception (De mendacio)* while waiting for Jerome's response—he was ready to amend his book if Jerome gave him reasons for further reflection.

I have dwelt so long on the New Testament occasion of this quarrel, since there are five propositions we must grasp in order to understand Augustine's doctrine on lying. The first of these is:

1. *The center of Augustine's concern with truth-telling was the truth of scripture.*

Not only does the Bible forbid lying; it exalts a Christ who says he *is* the truth (Jn 14:6). The ninth item in the decalogue (Ex 20.16) forbids false testimony, yet Jerome claims that Paul gave false testimony against Peter, saying he acted against his conscience out of fear when he knew that was not true. If Paul was lying here, why can people not decide that he is lying elsewhere when he transmits the message of Jesus? Augustine puts aside for the moment whether lying is ever justifiable—but only to say that it is *clearly* not justifiable in a scriptural author, if scripture itself is to be considered true (ep. 28:3–4). Nor is it enough to praise the apostles, as Jerome had, for their regard to their audience's sensibilities. Still relying on scripture, Augustine shows how you can be ingratiating without resorting to deception. Paul himself had said that he preached by entering into the attitudes of the most different kinds of people: "I have become all things to all men" (I Cor 9:22). In this same passage he even says something that could be confused with what Peter did—pretending to think that Jewish observances were necessary: "I have been as a Jew with Jews, to have them to my credit" (9:20). But Augustine continues:

> This was said from kind fellow-feeling, not false pretending. One becomes sick, oneself, to minister to the sick, not with any false claim to having the same fever, but by considering, with an attitude of sympathy, how one would want to be treated if he were the sick one. (ep. 40:4.)

This concern to reconcile different scriptural passages is at the heart of the treatise on lying that Augustine began even before he heard back from Jerome. It also inspired his later work, *The Gospel Writers' Complementarity (De consensu evangelistarum),* where he maintained that different accounts of the same event are not false accounts. To understand how he can make that argument, we must consider the second proposition controlling Augustine's whole discussion of falsehood:

2. *Lying is not a lack of fidelity to the meaning of words but of the proper intention to another person.*

This, the most important aspect of his discussion, sets Augustine apart from any school of thought that allows equivocation, prevarication, or evasion (if only *some* meaning of the words used can be defended as true). In the most basic sense, what one says is irrelevant in itself, apart from the intent to deceive. As Augustine points out, you can lie by speaking the truth, or with a grimace or body language, or even with silence. Being silent can itself be a form of communication. Suppose the police are after a friend of yours, and they ask if he is in the cellar. If you refuse to answer, they will assume from your reluctance to speak that he is there. You will have "told" them that (*Deception* 13). But if silence itself can speak, then it can speak falsely. Suppose you are asked whether you performed some heroic service, and you know that silence will be taken as a modest reluctance to claim what is true (though it is not). Your silence will deceive the questioner. That was your intent; and the intent to deceive is Augustine's definition of a lie.

Equivocators would not consider silence a lie, since silence is indeterminate. It is, of itself, equivocal. You can take from it what you want. The person keeping silent is not responsible, some would claim, for another's interpretation of his silence, any more than a speaker of equivocal words is responsible for the meaning a hearer may take from the several possible ones the words might bear. For Augustine, all such arguments are beside the point. If you believe that silence—or equivocal words—will deceive, you are lying. Even if you fail to deceive, you lie, since you were trying to deceive. If you make a true statement, knowing it will not be believed, and wanting it not to be believed, the statement is true but you are false.

Thus lying is an interpersonal relationship. The instrument you use for lying—true words, false words, equivocation, gesture, grimace, or silence—is unimportant in itself. What matters is that your mind tries to baffle another mind in its quest for truth. Which brings us to Augustine's third controlling proposition:

> 3. *Truth telling is not legalistic or minimalist, but maximalist, an effort to live in the truth.*

Much of moral reasoning on lying, especially in the Catholic tradition, is based on medieval penitentiaries, trying to establish minimal norms of culpability—what is a venial sin, what a mortal? What is allowable evasion or noncooperation? As in any legal context, the offense must be defined, with minimal conditions set for its recognition. For Augustine, the search for truth is a positive requirement for dealing with the God who is truth. Deception is too close to self-deception for a person to muddy his soul with deceit—which is always a veil raised between oneself and the truth. We saw above his confession that it is hard for him to judge his own words, since pride distorts his judgment. Book 10 of the *Confessiones* is one long self-inquest, to clear away from his conscience as much as he can of the fog that falsehood spreads there. Which brings us to the next major supposition that underlies Augustine's discussion:

4. *Lying is a particularly spiritual form of sin.*

Augustine counted the secondarily canonical book Wisdom as part of the Bible, and meditated with special emphasis on the verse, "A lying mouth murders the soul" (Wis 1:11). He used this verse to help him understand the decalogue's ban on false testimony: "This commandment includes all forms of deception, since every meaning a man conveys bears testimony to his own soul" (*Men*. 5.6). It should be remembered that Augustine believed that God entered creatively into every mental act of man, as "the light that enlightens every man coming into the world" (Jn 1:9). That is the profound sense he gave to the Psalm verse (35:9), "By your light we shall see light." To lie was to oppose the light at its very entry point into the soul. This did not quench the light, of course, since God is not so easily defeated. But by trying, so far as that is possible, to shut out the light, the liar darkens his own soul. So the first meaning he gave to a lie's power to "murder the soul" was a kind of suicidal act of the mind on itself. Only secondarily did the lie try to kill the life of the mind—which is knowledge—in another. So lies are not only an interpersonal but an intrapersonal form of violence done to the structure of reality.

It is Augustine's belief that deception is a form of spiritual suicide/ murder that leads him to the hardest thing for a modern audience to accept. When presented with the classic case for justifiable lying—misleading an evil person who is trying to capture an innocent victim—he says that preventing a physical murder by means of a spiritual murder cannot be a good act. Faced with that choice, he says, one must refuse to answer at all rather than tell a lie about the victim being sought—even if the price of that refusal is your own life. He also adds that you must have made it clear that you will answer no questions at all on the matter, lest your refusal to answer just one question "speak" and reveal the truth (*Men*. 13.22). This position seems unrealistically pure—but Christians, after all, were asked to give their lives rather than offer sacrifice to false gods in a pagan temple, and honoring falsehood is an idolatry within the sacred precincts of the soul. Augustine's model here is a bishop from his own home town, Firmus ("firm by name, firmer by his resolution"), who was tortured but kept silent on the whereabouts of a man who had sought asylum with him (*Men.* 13.23).

Can one lie to avoid rape, another's or one's own? "Since the soul is superior to the body, its corruption is the more culpable" (*Men.* 7.10). Augustine has been accused of being obsessive about bodily purity. In fact, he attacks the pagans for setting too much store by that. They praised Lucretia for choosing death rather than dishonor after Tarquin raped her. In *The City of God* (1.19), Augustine says that Lucretia's crime was greater than Tarquin's: "He took her body, she took her life. He raped, she murdered." When Christian women were tempted to suicide after being raped in the fall of Rome (410 CE), he said that the violation of their bodies could not violate their souls if they did not intend what happened. He is consistent here. As the material truthfulness of a statement is not what matters in a lie, but the intent of the speaker, so the material event of rape cannot defile the soul that resists. The superiority of the soul to the body results in merciful advice for the violated women, but harsh demands on those who would prevent such violation by lying. Augustine knows how harsh his teaching is—he says a man should not lie to prevent his own rape, even by sodomization at the mouth or anus (*Men.* 9.13). To violate his own soul is worse than having others violate the body. But truthfulness itself means that one must not obscure the near impossibility of living up to such requirements—so Augustine has one more proposition he must keep in mind.

5. *Truthfulness is a heroic standard.*

Augustine admits that he cannot trust himself to observe his own counsels: "Since we are human, and live with other humans, I admit that I cannot as yet count myself proof against sins that alleviate suffering" (*Contra Men.* 18.36). By "sins that alleviate" he means things like telling a gravely ill man, who is worried about his son, that the son still lives—though he does not. Truth in this case might kill the father, and silence might indicate the truth. "These situations unsettle me—profoundly; but can I say, in the same degree, wisely?" If we are all to comfort each other

with lies that buffer us from reality, whenever reality looks too threaten-
ing, what happens to the possibility of a luminous openness to the God
of truth?

> For when I summon up, before what might be called my heart's
> eyes, the intelligible beauty of Christ, whose mouth never framed
> the slightest thing false—then, though truth glows with intensity
> beyond intensity, unstringing my trembling nerves, yet love of that
> splendor flames through me, making me wish to renounce all
> human ties that pull me away from such truth. But it is hard to
> maintain that feeling, to stick with it when put to the test. (*Contra
> Men.* 18.36.)

So those who tell Augustine he asks too much in the name of truth are
not telling him something he does not experience constantly, while trying to stay as true as possible to the vision of God's "intelligible beauty."
After all, Peter fell into three lies when he denied knowing Christ. He
repented them. He did not deny that they were lies. He did not try to
excuse them.

The worth of Augustine's effort at an entire truthfulness can be registered by looking at the price of deception in the case of Jerome. Augustine did not know, when he first addressed Jerome in his distant
Bethlehem monastery, that he was seeking the truth from one of history's
great liars. Jerome's biographer, J. N. D. Kelly, has shown how his subject
lied whenever it served his purpose to do so.[9] Jerome's responses to Augustine, when asked to explain his commentary on the apostles' conflict
at Antioch, are a string of evasions, counteraccusations, distortions, and
plain denials of fact. At first, since Augustine's opening letter went astray
and never reached him, Jerome—responding to a follow-up letter—im-
plies that Augustine deliberately arranged for the first missive not to reach
him, that Augustine wanted to score points off Jerome without giving
him a chance to answer—though he assures his questioner that he would
not answer in any case, since he is not to be bedeviled by every pert
know-it-all who comes along. (For Augustine, the thing that would be
morally unthinkable is Jerome's assertion that he will not answer Augus-

tine even though he finds signs of heresy in him. Recalling people from error is the first duty of charity for Augustine.) Jerome responded:

> Some of my friends, themselves carriers of Christ (there are many such here in Jerusalem and the Holy Land), have hinted to me that you had as your secret aim to win a vulgar esteem, from the praise of sycophants, by your manipulation of me—to let everyone know that you issued a challenge and I shrank from it; that you, the scholar, wrote letters, while I, the dunce, sat silent; that someone had at last been found to shut up my babbling. Well, I admit I was wary of answering Your Eminence since I was not sure your [second] letter was authentic and that the sword might not (as the saying of one of our lowly folk has it) be smeared with honey. Also, I did not want to be dismissive of a bishop of our faith [Jerome was just a priest] and to answer a correcting letter with correction—all the more because I discerned heretical things in it . . . So if you want to bully with your learning, or show it off, find some youngsters, bright and well-born (Rome boasts many such, I hear), who have the means and will to submit to the labor of debating a bishop on the Scriptures. I am retired from my soldiering, and I should just applaud your prowess not wrestle it with my withered limbs. (ep. 72.2–3.)

When Augustine politely persisted, trying to return the discussion to the passage in Galatians that troubled him, Jerome spewed a variety of contradictory things back at him. He tried to defend his accusation of heresy by saying that Augustine was too nice to the Jews when he said that Peter was observing their practices, not just pretending to do so (as if pretense would be a form of attack on the practices). Then, after accusing Augustine of heresy, he claims that they are not so very different in their views after all—and, besides, Jerome was just repeating what Origen and others have said. After this self-pitying tirade, he returns to his pretense that he is not answering in the first place:

> You—placed, young as you are, on a bishop's pinnacle—may teach the nations, decorating Roman homes with your exotic African

produce, while I am content with whispers to a lowly hearer or reader in my monastery corner. (ep. 75.22.)

Contrast that attitude with Augustine's constant request that others correct him if anything he says is wrong—not just other bishops or clerics, but the hearers of his sermons. It is fascinating to see what lesson he drew from the conduct of Peter at Antioch when—during the very months when he was corresponding with Jerome and writing *Deception*—he chose the Galatians text (outside the normal liturgical sequence of readings) to preach from in a guest appearance at the cathedral of Carthage. Augustine says that he and his host—Bishop Aurelius of Carthage, seated with Augustine in the cathedral—are bishops, and some might think that puts them beyond others' reprimand. But how can that be when their great predecessor, Peter, needed to be recalled from error? "Where Peter was corrigible, dare I claim to be beyond correction? Shall I, a feeble sheep, not be wary of falling into a flood when I see the ram himself still drying out his wool?"[10]

Augustine says that some people (he does not name Jerome) think Peter was just fooling an audience at Antioch, not doing something that really deserved correction. "We are bishops, we follow in the apostles' footsteps—but I do not want to be able to fool you. If something is secretly meant, against what is publicly professed, what sacred responsibility can be trusted? We do not want any license to fool you, or for you to fool us. If you think we may be fooling you, and we think you may be fooling us, where will we find that charity that can believe all things? For Paul says that 'charity believes all things' (I Cor 13:7)."[11]

The idea that Peter might err seems to have been a surprise to his audience, since one of its members shouted out, "What did Paul reprimand in Peter?" Augustine replied, "What Paul himself just said, what he wrote" (in the reading of Galatians that preceded the sermon). But a moment later the same question was asked, and Augustine had the lector read again the passage in which Paul reprimands Peter before all the people.[12] Augustine, so far from holding church leaders beyond all question and correction, draws a sharp distinction between the scriptures, which are always truthful, and those who teach from them, who can err and need constant instruction themselves.

We who study and write about what is written in the sacred books of the bible do not write with the bible's authority—we write as we are advancing, we teach day by day, we pronounce while still inquiring, we talk as we knock for entry. I shall not cease speaking or writing so long as I can be useful to you my brothers, but I beg your charity, by myself for myself, not to treat anything I have written or spoken about scripture as if it were itself scripture . . . Let us revere scripture as scripture, as the word of God, and not treat in the same way any fallible human . . . I would resent it far more if a person accepted my words as scripture than if he should correct me, even where I did not err. Pardon me, now—I see you are concentrating on this point as if you had just heard it for the first time, and I do not want to say more, so you can keep this lesson strongly imprinted in your mind.[13]

Truthfulness for Augustine is a constant joint quest, in which we need to strengthen each other. Error is an obstacle to the quest that must be fought by all. A lie, an error deliberately created and spread to others, is a betrayal of the quest—and the greatest betrayal is to lie about the sacred truths of religion.

---

[1]Oscar Cullmann argues that Aramaic Cephas, the name Jesus gave to Peter, should be rendered as Stone, since that was the point in saying that Peter was the stone on which the church would be founded (Mt 16:17). Actually, Cullmann's translator from the German uses the word Rock—but we do not in English say that a foundation *rock* was laid. We speak of a foundation *stone* for a fortress, or of its being dismantled stone by stone. Cf. Cullmann, *Peter: Disciple, Apostle, Martyr*, translated by Floyd V. Filson, second and expanded edition (Westminster Press, 1962). For the contrast between "tribes" (*ethnē*) and "Judaizers" as "cosmopolitans" and "separatists," see the next note.

[2]For the clash of cosmopolitans with separatists, see Johannes Munck, *The Acts of the Apostles* (AB, 1967), pp. 56–57; J. Louis Martyn, *Galatians* (AB, 1998), pp. 236–40; Thomas W. Martin, "Hellenists" (ABD 3.135–36); A. Dean Forbes, "Stephen" (ABD 6.207–08); Raymond E. Brown and John P. Meier, *Antioch and Rome* (Paulist Press, 1982), pp. 1–8. Brown further divides the cosmopolitans into a liberal wing (typified by Paul) and a radical (Stephen), while dividing the separatists into a conservative group (Peter) and an ultraconservative (James). Cullmann, by contrast, thinks that Peter was moving, ever since the execution of Stephen, toward the cosmopolitan camp, which explains Paul's attack on him for backsliding at Antioch (Cullmann, op. cit., pp. 52–53).

[3]Martyn, op. cit., p. 235.

[4]I Clement 5. He uses a "hendiadys" (two words for one concept), "rivalry-and-grudge," *zelos* and *phthonos*, interchangeable terms for betraying someone out of jealous resentment—

as when the Jews turn Jesus over to Pilate out of *phthonos* (Mt 27:18, Mk 15:10), or turn Christians over to others out of *zelos* (Acts 5:17, 13:45, 17:5). This is exactly the situation of the informants dealing with Nero. For the separatists in Rome, it should be noted that Putative Ambrose ("Ambrosiaster"), though writing in the fourth century, may well be preserving an early tradition when he says that the Christians in that city received their faith "according to the Jewish observance" (*ritu Judaico*)—see Brown, op. cit., pp. 110–11.

[5]Tacitus, *Annals of Rome* 15.44.

[6]Pliny, *Letters* 10.96.

[7]Cullmann, op. cit., pp. 91–100; Brown, op. cit., pp. 122–27. The same forces may have been involved in an earlier clash at Rome (49 CE), when, according to Suetonius (writing about 120 CE), the Emperor Claudius expelled some Jews "because of endless trouble-making stirred up by Chrestus" (*Life of Claudius* 25.4). Most scholars think Suetonius has misunderstood Christus as the common freedman's name Chrestus, and that it was the Christian Jews who were at odds either with Roman Jews in general or with the separatist ("Hebrew") Christians. This would fit with the presumed expulsion at that time of Paul's allies (therefore cosmopolitans), Aquila and Priscilla (Acts 18:2). See Brown, op. cit., pp. 100–2; William F. Orr and James Arthur Walther, *I Corinthians* (AB 1976), pp. 81–82; Peter Lampe, "Aquila" (ABD 1.319). It should be noticed that the author of Acts does not specify why the expulsion took place—which would fit with the unwillingness to look at inter-Christian divisions around the death of Peter and Paul.

[8]For Augustine's dealing with Pope Zosimus, see J. E. Merdinger, *Rome and the African Church in the Time of Augustine* (Yale, 1997), pp. 11–34, 126–30.

[9]J. N. D. Kelly, *Jerome* (Harper & Row, 1975), pp. 64, 65, 78, 107, 149, 150, 178, 201, 239, 252.

[10]Mainz I.9 (one of the sermons recently discovered), François Dolbeau, *Augustin d'Hippone, vingt-six sermons au peuple d'Afrique* (Institut d'études augustiniennes, 1996), p. 46.

[11]Ibid., p. 47.

[12]Ibid., pp. 47–48. For the shout from the audience, see Dolbeau's introduction to the sermon, p. 42.

[13]Ibid., pp. 62–63.

20.

Augustine vs. Consentius

$\mathcal{M}$ ore than two decades after Augustine wrote *Deception*, another attempt to use lying as a religious strategy made him write a second treatise, *Forswearing Deception (Contra Mendacium)*. We now know more about the occasion for this effort, since two letters from the Consentius to whom it is addressed were discovered, in the 1970s, among old manuscripts in Marseilles and Paris libraries. The Consentius letters, along with twenty-six previously unknown letters by Augustine and one by Jerome, were published by their discoverer, Johannes Divjak, in the 1980s. Consentius, it turns out, was a busybody, vain and meddlesome, who wrote to say that he had trouble reading Augustine because of the "forbidding brilliance" (*molesta splendor*) of the *Confessiones*, but that Augustine might want to read some of his own books written to refute various heresies.[1] Consentius, who lived on the island of Minorca off the coast of Spain, was obviously rich enough to indulge his literary hobby of policing other people's orthodoxy, and he tells Augustine that he writes to other famous people, who respond with requests that he keep up the good work. He is a type familiar to any author whose name gets in the news. Though he admits he should read more—he has barely made it through the whole Bible—he comforts himself with the thought that intellectuals can get too wrapped up in their ideas, like Origen—and he even has the nerve to suggest that this could happen to Augustine.[2] For his own part, he can churn out his own treatises without any fear of being too intellectual or "forbidding."

We learn more than we want to know about Consentius himself in the new letter numbered 12* (where the asterisk sets the letter off from number 12 in the old catalogue of recognized letters). More valuable new information comes in his Letter 11⋆, which prompted Augustine's *Forswearing Deception*. Consentius boasts of his ingenuity in ferreting out heretics in Spain, where he claims to have turned up secret followers of the executed Priscillian. A cat's-paw of his, named Fronto, even pretended to be a heretic himself in order to infiltrate the enemy's ranks. Consentius encloses a report from Fronto purporting to tell how he exposed official protection of the subversives by certain Spanish bishops.[3] Fronto sounds like Senator Joseph McCarthy turning up Communists in the State Department. If his story is true, it tells us striking new things about Christian Spain in the fifth century. And even if it is exaggerated, it tells us what overheated imaginations were capable of at that time and place.

Augustine does not show much trust (or interest) in Fronto's charges, in "whether things happened as he says or not" (*Contra Men.* 3.4). What perturbs him are the tactics Fronto claims to be using and Consentius seems to agree with. The two claim that the heretics must be exposed by infiltration since they lie about their real allegiance. For Augustine, pretending to abandon true doctrine and to profess falsehood is a worse sin than the one the schemers are out to punish. We must not, he says, "lure others to the truth by leaving it ourselves, so that, capturing liars with lies, we teach them a deeper kind of lying" (3.4). Christ, he reminds Consentius, warned against wolves in sheeps' clothing (Mt 10:16)—which does not mean that we should, in response to the warning, become sheep in wolves' clothing (6:12).

Augustine takes this occasion to repeat *Deception*'s attack on the attempt to use lies for a religious purpose. He had become dissatisfied with his first treatise. As he recalled in the late catalogue of his own works (*Reconsiderations*):

> I wrote a book, *Deception*, that can be read only with some effort, though it puts the reader through some not entirely futile exercises in mental agility and, more important, imparts the duty to love truth. Still, I decided to delete this from the body of my works, as being too unclear and roundabout—it was thoroughly heavy going. I did not circulate it. Then, when I wrote a later book called *Forswearing Deception*, I was all the more determined to quash the first

one, and bade that be done. But it was not. Thus I came across the undestroyed manuscript while engaged in these reconsiderations of all my writings, and directed that the canceled book should be retained after all, mainly because there are some important things (*necessaria*) in it that are not in the later one.[4]

The important and the "roundabout" passages in *Deception* are probably intertwined—the description of complex hypothetical situations and the classification of lies in subtle categories. Though he did not repeat these techniques in the second book, he must have decided that, on balance, they had their uses. They can mislead the modern reader, though, into thinking in the quibbling manner of those who defend equivocation. In the second book he stresses even more thoroughly and consistently that the intent to deceive is the basic issue in lying.

One reason for this development is that Augustine means to go more deeply into the matter of scripture's truthfulness. Between the composition of his two treatises on lying he had written his book *The Gospel Writers' Complementarity* explaining that inconsistencies in the Bible are not put there to deceive, so they are not lies. This is not an evasion on his part, since he had always taught that one can indicate truth by saying what is literally false, just as one can deceive with true statements. In his commentaries on Genesis, he points out that the creation of the cosmos in seven days cannot be literally true (how can there be a day or a night for the earth, since it is round, which makes it *both* day *and* night at any one moment).[5] That which is *obviously* false cannot be meant to deceive. It must indicate a deeper symbolic meaning. In the same way, "unedifying" tales in the Jewish scripture cannot be recommending immorality— they are told as prophetic types of what would be fulfilled in the New Testament (*Contra Men.* 14.29).

When it comes to the New Testament, Augustine does not deny the inconsistencies, just the intent to deceive. He takes for instance the two genealogies given to connect Jesus with the Davidic line. That in Matthew differs from that in Luke. But one can trace one's ancestry through different ramifications of the family tree. Matthew does not offer his as if it were more accurate than Luke's (which would therefore be false). According to the scripture scholarship of his day, Augustine finds more kings in Matthew's line, more priests in Mark's—so, together, they bring out the complementary characteristics of Jesus, as both kingly and priestly (PL 34.1043–44). A more difficult point about the genealogies is this: each traces the line to Joseph, not Mary, and the gospels claim that Jesus was born of a virgin. Here Augustine makes a surprising argument, proving that Joseph was a real father, though not a father in the flesh (an argument that can resonate warmly with adoptive parents today):

> Why does the evangelist himself call Joseph the father of Jesus (Lk 2:40) but that we are to accept him as Mary's husband, not by carnal intercourse (*commixtio*) but by the coupling (*copulatio*) of the marriage bond? Surely he was Christ's father in an even closer sense than if he had adopted a child born of anyone else but his own wife. (PL 34.1072.)

When it comes to the truthfulness of Jesus' own statements in the gospels, Augustine faces a problem that modern scholars, in general, do not. He thought that Jesus, by virtue of his divinity, was always omniscient.[6] Then how can he say, for instance, that he did not know who touched him when he felt power flow out from him (Lk 8:45)? Augustine believes that the woman healed by touching Jesus was a gentile, and Jesus was saying that he, as God, had not yet recognized her under the old dispensation, meant only for the Jews (*Contra Men.* 13.27).

Augustine works conscientiously through every objection he can think of to the truthfulness of scripture. Since he is not a fundamentalist in the modern sense, he does not try to make the words literally consistent. Scripture is a teaching instrument, meant to reveal the ineffable through symbol and parable (what Newman called "economy"). The allegorical approach to texts was an established part of the literary criticism Augustine was heir to, and things like number symbolism were widely accepted.[7] Of course, a modern critic can say that allowing a literally false statement in order to signal a higher meaning opens the way to all kinds of equivocation. But this neglects the key concept. An equivocator uses the slippery meaning *with an intent to deceive.* Augustine's point, throughout, is that scripture is not trying to deceive (to make people believe, for instance, in a literal sense in the seven days of creation). This is not a latitudinarian teaching but a strict one. It controls not verbal formulas but the inner orientation of the soul, which may never side with deception. The resulting treatise is, according to one modern scholar, "the most sophisticated and comprehensive explanation of the writing of the Gospels in all of early Christianity."[8] It anticipates, in places, the use of modern critical tools.[9]

Augustine set the scriptures as a standard of truth, to be observed in all preaching from them, as well as in all actions taken to promote them. His treatment of falsehood in the ministry can be seen from his response to a fraudulent action in the monastery he maintained within his cathedral precinct. A member of the monastic community, a man named Januarius, died in 425. Before he joined the community, he had been a priest whose wife died, leaving him with two children, a son who entered a monastery and a daughter who entered a convent. Required to give up all his property in order to join Augustine's monastic community, he said that he had surrendered his property to a trust for his daughter, in case she should leave the convent. But when he died, his will showed that he had maintained ownership of the property himself, and that now he willed it to Augustine's church instead of to his daughter. Januarius's daughter protested the will. Her brother, out of spite toward her, defended his father's action in depriving her of the property. Januarius's will, his son claimed, was valid and legal.

What was Augustine to do? He announced to his congregation that he had something important to report that concerned them, and asked them to attend in the greatest numbers his next sermon. In that homily (Sermon 355) he revealed the scandal, and said that the bequest to the church he would never accept. It was the product of fraud, of the monk's broken vow. To accept it would make Augustine a partner in deceit, taking profit from it—he wants the community to know why he has to refuse what they might feel they had a right to accept.

Then what was to be done with the property? Augustine set up a panel to adjudicate the division of the property between the two children, himself presiding with the help, "under God's guidance, of a few loyal and respected brothers from your number, you, the congregation" (PL 39.1573). At the same time he set up another process, asking every member of the monastic community to report on his observance of the vow of poverty. If any undisclosed belongings came to light, the monk must divest himself of them immediately or leave the monastery. Augustine had received all of the monks on the express condition they were entering the monastery under its existing rules. He had the right to strip them of clerical status if they had not observed their vows. He had announced that policy at the outset, but now he renounces it—for a characteristic reason. He does not want to tempt the brothers to lie or pretend that they have no property in order to protect their status. "I would not have false monks here. It is bad enough—who does not see it?—to break one's vow. It is even worse to make a false pretense of observing it" (PL39.1753).

Augustine set the monks a date to make their reports, and to make their decisions. After that date, he promised the congregation, he would report the results, since the laity had the right to know about the monastery they were supporting with their donations. When the day came, he went through the reports in public, man by man (Sermon 256). In the first place, he was happy to say that he had not been required to adjudicate between the children of Januarius after all—they had settled the matter on their own, splitting the property equally. Second, he was able to report that none of his priests any longer owned property, and the deacons, who had not made final settlement of goods held for them by their families, were divesting themselves of it—emancipating slaves in some cases, making division of jointly owned goods in other cases so they could sell their share. An interesting instance under this last head is that of Augustine's own nephew, Patrick, named for his grandfather (Augustine's father). Patrick owned some property jointly with his sisters, Augustine's nieces. Augustine insisted that he extricate from that proprietorship what was his share, and sell it, giving away what it sold for. After this complete audit of every man's condition, Augustine said that he was now satisfied all his monks were in compliance. But should he find that any were not, his original policy would be reinstated, and they would lose their clerical status:

> I had said, and I realize I said it, that if they did not want to undertake the duties of our community life, I would not remove their clerical rights. They would have to leave and live by themselves, in

whatever way they could find to live a godly life, and I made it clear to them how grievous a thing is breaking a vow—yet I preferred to have brothers live thus maimed rather than mourn their death: *the man who lives a lie is dead* [according to Wisdom 1:11, "A lying mouth murders the soul"] . . . But now that they have chosen to live, with God's help, in this community, if any of them should live with a lie, if he should be found to possess any property, I will not let him divest himself of it and stay, but I will delete his name from the clerics' register. Though he should appeal from me to a thousand councils, or sail to any other arbiter wherever—anywhere he can—yet, so help me God, he shall not be a cleric so long as I am a bishop. You hear me. They hear me. But I hope in God, in His graciousness, that since they have now gladly accepted this rule of life, they will observe it simply and exactly. (PL 39.1580.)

Augustine's conduct could not be more distant from the handling of church scandal in our time. He acted with entire openness, inviting scrutiny, including lay participants in the tribunal to handle disputed property, reporting results of his investigation as soon as they became available. Contrast that with the Vatican's conduct when it was involved in the financial scandals centered around the Ambrosian Bank in Milan (the city where Ambrose himself had baptized Augustine). Archbishop Marcinkus and his deputies changed their residences to the Vatican, in order to be beyond the reach of Italian law. The Pope's newspaper denied debts that the Vatican nonetheless paid ($250 million), giving no account to the church faithful of where this money came from. The Pope himself met privately with the Italian President at the very time when the banking scandal was the main topic of relations between the Vatican and the President's government, but denied (implausibly) that the subject came up.[10]

Or contrast Augustine's treatment of Januarius, who tried to give his money to Augustine's church, but in an irregular way, with Pope John Paul II's protection of his fellow Polish priest, Michael Zembrzuski, whose fund-raising for a New Jersey shrine to the Virgin was exposed by the Pope's own investigators. The Pope ignored their report, covered up the scandal, and kept Zembrzuski safe from public condemnation.[11] It may be said that the public has no right to know things that are settled according to the conscience of their superiors. Augustine would have none of that. He said conscious rectitude is not enough. Church authorities owe church members a reputation for honesty.

> Conscience and reputation are different things. Conscience is for oneself, reputation for one's neighbors. Whoever tends to his conscience but neglects his reputation is being cruel to others—especially in a [church] position such as ours, about which the Apostle [Paul] wrote to his followers: "Present to everyone a pattern for doing good works" [Ti 2.7]. Sermon 355. (PL 39.1569.)

Augustine said that the church's reputation for truthfulness must be scrupulously preserved: "It is our duty, with the Lord God's help, to have care for our conduct and for our reputation, that those who admire us should not be confounded by those who accuse us" (PL 39.1574). Some modern churchmen think that having a care for reputation entails covering up flaws and failure. For Augustine, it meant just the opposite—it meant not having the reputation of liars who protect vice in the name of virtue.

The denial and lying around sexual scandals in the church is another kind of deception that Augustine did not countenance as a bishop. When it became known that one of his deacons had accused one of his priests of a homosexual overture, Augustine wrote a long letter to his congregation (he was away at a council in Carthage, so he could not follow his normal practice of discussing such matters in a sermon), asking that the congregation pray for the suspended clerics until more could be established about the charge's truth. Once again, he would make a full report, and there was no denial that such things could occur.

> Before God who bears witness to my inner self from the time I first took up his service, I make open avowal to you, my charitable ones, that—just as I can hardly find men better than those who live observantly in monasteries—I cannot find worse men than monks who fall into sin. I even think that the passage in Apocalypse [22:11]

is expressly descriptive of them: "The virtuous man is called to greater virtue, the vile to greater vileness." (ep. 78.9.)

And just as Augustine would not cover up for priests who claim to serve the God of truth, he would not shirk responsibility for his own failings. Once, in order to install a new bishop where he was badly needed, he hastily put in a man whom he had not tested sufficiently, and who proved to be a disgrace to the community. Augustine publicly repented, and offered to resign his own office. In a public letter to the Pope he wrote:

As for me, Your Beatitude, I am debating whether to resign the exercise of my bishop's office and devote myself to merited penance, tortured as I am by fear and anguish over two possible outcomes— either that I shall have to see a church of God losing its members because of a man I imprudently made bishop, or that (may God prevent this) a whole church may be lost, along with the man himself. (ep. 209.10.)

Augustine's standard of truth has been called too high and demanding. He certainly knew how strict were its demands on him. But how could he settle for conduct less honest in a church that proclaims itself a servant of the God who *is* the truth?

---

[1]Johannes Divjak (editor), *Lettres de saint Augustin* (Etudes augustinienness, 1986), pp. 230–32.

[2]Ibid., p. 246: "Though we now grant that bishop Augustine writes things beyond our caviling, what judgment will the future make of his works?" Though people have tended to suppose that the Consentius of the new letters is the same Consentius with whom Augustine discussed the Trinity and Christ's risen body in the known correspondence (ep. 119–20, 205), Raymond Van Dam points out that the Consentius of those letters is not as cheeky and flighty as the new man. Van Dam, " 'Sheep in Wolves' Clothing': the Letters of Consentius to Augustine," *Journal of Ecclesiastical History* 37 (1986), pp. 515–35.

[3]Ibid., pp. 186–222.

[4]*Reconsiderations (Retractiones)*, 1.27.

[5]*First Meanings in Genesis (De Genesi ad Litteram)*, 1.12.

[6]For modern scholars' conclusions that Jesus was not always omniscient, see Raymond E. Brown, *An Introduction to New Testament Christology* (Paulist Press, 1994), pp. 31–59.

[7]On this, see the essays in Duane W. H. Arnold and Pamela Bright (editors), *De Doctrina Christiana: A Classic of Western Culture* (University of Notre Dame Press, 1995).

[8]David Laird Duncan, *A History of the Synoptic Problem* (Anchor Bible Reference Library, 1999), p. 112.

[9]Genre criticism, for instance, when Augustine says that only one animal is referred to, not two, at Mt 21:5, since Matthew is using the parallelisms of Hebrew poetry (PL 34.1138–39).

[10]Jonathan Kwitny, *Man of the Century: The Life and Times of Pope John Paul II* (Henry Holt and Company, 1997), pp. 460–62, 492–93.

[11]Ibid., pp. 248–49, 267–69, 335, 339.

21.

The Truth That Frees

What does it mean to say that Christ *is* truth (Jn 14:6)? Not that he speaks truthfully, or defends the truth, or represents it, but that he, simply, is truth? One effort at an answer to this question has a chance of being adequate, because it is as radical as anything must be to match the revolutionary gospels. René Girard, the cultural critic, argues (in a substantial body of work) that human societies are established by an initial violence that both controls later expressions of it and validates them.[1] This is reflected in the "founding murder" discoverable in so many cultures—the murder of Abel by Cain, or of Remus by Romulus—as well as in the scapegoats sacrificed to avert threats to the community (Jonah, Oedipus, Prometheus). The community builds itself around a shared enmity and seals its bond by a sacrifice of the object of its fear. Girard notes the way Aeschylus's Furies express this in his tragedy, *The Eumenides* (996–97):

> For many ills one attitude is the cure,
> When it agrees on what to hate.[2]

The salvific outcome of such creative destruction is the sacred—which is revived in all forms of religious sacrifice. This universal trait of sacrifice is meant to placate—to flatter and, at the same time, bribe—appropriately violent sets of gods. Envious rivalry (which Girard somewhat misleadingly calls mimesis) leads to and is assuaged by concentration on a foe (or its surrogate), on whatever must be destroyed that the people might live. After that, the state is made the guardian of the violence that articulated its structure in the first place. Since the surcease achieved by hatred is based on unreasoning contagions of panic, the whole fabric of social life is essentially a structure of deception, beginning with self-deception. That is why Jesus calls Satan the prince of this world, "the father of lies" (Jn 8:44), the embodiment of the whole system of violence.

Girard is a believing Christian—a Roman Catholic, in fact, with whom I used to go to Mass when we both taught at Johns Hopkins. It will be clear that his radical anthropology is consonant with the doctrine of original sin. In fact, Girard's thought is very close to Augustine's, though he rarely quotes him. Augustine, too, maintains that the City of Man was founded on the murder of Abel, and that it lives by violence, in opposition to the City of God, which is founded on, and operates on, love.[3] This recognition of love as a *structural* principle is far from wishy-washy do-goodism. Jesus indicts the whole world of creative hatreds and architectonic violence:

I say, to all you who can hear me: Love your foes, help those who hate you, praise those who curse you, pray for those who abuse you. To one who punches your cheek, offer the other cheek. To one seizing your cloak, do not refuse your tunic under it. Whoever asks, give to him. Whoever seizes, do not resist. Exactly how you wish to be treated, in that way treat others. For if you love those who love back, what mark of virtue have you? Sinners themselves love those who love back. If you treat well those treating you well, what mark of virtue have you? That is how sinners act. If you lend only where you calculate a return, what mark of virtue have you? Sinners, too, lend to sinners, calculating an exact return. No, rather love your foes, and treat them well, and lend without any calculation of return. Your great reward will be that you are children of the Highest One, who also favors ingrates and scoundrels. Be just as lenient as that lenient Father. Be not a judge, then, and you will not be judged. Be no executioner, and you will not be executed. Pardon, and you will be pardoned. Give, and what will be given you is recompense of crammed-in, sifted-down, over-toppling good showered into your lap. The excess will reflect the measure of your excess. (Lk 6:27–40.)

Jesus speaks for a God of topsy-turvydom, the Highest who sides with the lowest. Giving to ingrates is the way to imitate this God. Scoundrels are his pets. As Jesus says in Matthew (21:31), "Quislings and whores are entering the Kingdom before you [chief priests]." This is a particularly provocative thing for Jesus to say, since part of the enmity that would try to make him a polluted scapegoat came from his mixing with the "unclean," with quislings and sinners (Mt 9:11; Mk 2:18). The whole category of the unclean arises from the sacred realm of sacrifice, and he is defying that at its root.

This challenge to the founding principle of the world's very existence unites Christ's foes around him—all the enmity of the powers that be, Jewish and Roman, soldiers and the mob. Girard even notes the unifying effect of scapegoatism in the New Testament itself (Lk 23:12): "On precisely that day [of Jesus' trial] Herod and Pilate were reconciled, after their previous enmity." The followers of Jesus disperse, unable to resist the harmony of hate that blossoms from sacred violence. They have still to learn that when Jesus says one can only follow him by taking up the cross (Mt 10:38), this means meeting the violence of the world with unresisting love. Only this willingness frees one from the dominance of the power system called Satan.

Girard claims that Christ reveals the emptiness of worldly power's claims, but how can this be? When the world unites to oppose him, and his followers either desert or are silenced, isn't this just another instance of successful scapegoating? Girard distinguishes Christ's situation from that of scapegoats, who either agree with their accusers, or oppose them by arguing from the same principles of power that are invoked against them. Only Jesus acts on a principle of total nonresistance to violence, which removes the rationale for sacrifice. He presents a vindicated innocence to refute the conviction of guilt. Girard finds a prophetic forerunner of Jesus in the Job who protests his own innocence, who refuses to accept the logic of his accusing "comforters."

Girard's most radical assertion is that Jesus is not a sacrifice. His Father is not one whose aggressions need to be bought off. Jesus is not an item of barter in the exchange system set up by sacrifice; God does not accept victims. He sides with the victim against its slayers, reversing the whole logic of placation. The prophets of Israel had moved toward the insight that God does not want sacrifice, but Jesus turns their hesitant questioning of the system into confident assertion of its irrelevance. This is clearest in his opposition to the Temple activities that all revolved around sacrifice. His "cleansing" of the Temple was not an attack on peripheral abuses like money exchanges in the forecourt. He is rejecting the validity of sacrifice as an avenue to God—a view of the episode that Raymond Brown finds John's text capable of bearing.[4] "Do not make my Father's house a house barter" (Jn 2:16). The commerce in victims is ended.

Jesus promises to destroy the Temple and raise it up again—not the former Temple, where sacrifice was conducted. His risen body is the new Temple, the presence of the Father in Christ, and Christ's presence in the body of believers. This Father is not a distant figure whose wrath is to be pushed away, who can be approached, ritually, only in fear and trembling. He approaches us, in the Christ who incorporates us as living stones into his living Temple. Augustine notes the paradox involved in Christ's calling himself the path to the Father: "I am path and truth and life—no one arrives at the Father except through me" (Jn 14:16). The Father is already here when the path is here, speaking to us: "Where should we go but to him? And how should we go but by way of him? So he goes to himself [as truth] through himself [as path], and we go to him by way of him, and both of us—he and we—arrive at the Father."[5] The approach to God is not by ritual or violence, but by *receiving* the approach of Christ.

Passage after passage in the gospel takes on new intensity when looked at through the lens Girard has provided. Take the famously knotty words at John 16:8–11:

> When the Defender [Paraclete] comes, he will expose the world's lie about sin, about conformity with God, and about criminal execution—about sin, because they do not recognize me [as sinless]; about conformity with God, because I am the one who arrives at the Father (when you lose sight of me); and about criminal execution, because the Prince of This World is the one convicted.[6]

The world, that is, takes Jesus as the polluted one, heaping sin on him, hoping for reconciliation with God through offering him up as a sacrifice. Yet it is this very act of scapegoating—the Satan system of condoned violence—that is being condemned. The lying pattern collapses when triumph over the victim becomes a triumph of the victim.

Girard makes it clear why the triumph of Christ is a struggle with Satan. Jesus lets the violence of the world system defeat itself on his dying body—instead of this being a sacrifice to a vengeful God, it is a paradoxical defeat of the torturer. The fallen world of satanic resistance to God causes the final violence, not any placatory act demanded by the Father. The only sacrifice by Jesus is his offering of his innocent body to the fury of the sacrificial system that is being canceled. This was exactly the position of Augustine. In an early work, he opposed the ransom theory of Christ's death, the theory that Jesus was a substitute who accepted the suffering that the Father wanted to inflict on others—as if the Father could find satisfaction in causing pain: "The Lord's was obviously not a death of ransom but of restoration (*dignitatis non debiti*)."[7]

In a late work, *The Trinity*, Book Four, Augustine spells out his meaning at greater length. God reconciles us to Himself through the Incarnation—Augustine always made Christ's birth as man the hinge of the drama, not the "atoning" death. In *The Trinity*, he speaks of reconciliation as a harmonic feat of God. Satan's force is one of terrible simplicity, the erring spirit that has no bodily component, and asks for immolation of flesh to his higher spirit. The sacrificial system, just as in Girard's work, is the devil's discipline—"oppressing life with a claim to purification by rites and sacrifices that insult God" (4.3.17). But just as the Trinity has a higher unity than Satan's single and isolated spirit, so Jesus as the one Person with two natures, human and divine, brings man's divided soul-body into harmonic union with God. Thus Christ could "become our friend in the fellowship of death when our enemy boasted he was above us by not condescending to join us in that" (4.3.18).

So the system of God's truth is an escape from the whole regime of false claims that trap humanity in the violence of sin. Truth is a moral discipline as well as an intellectual one. If we are incorporated into the Christ who is truth, it becomes clear why Augustine is so troubled by the mere idea of a Christian lie, a churchly deception. Paul had said that those incorporated into Christ should not make the body of Christ complicitous in sexual sin:

Don't you realize that your bodies are Christ's limbs? Then can I make Christ's limbs a whore's limbs? Unthinkable—unless you do not realize that whoever fuses himself with a whore is one in body with her, according to the text, "The two shall become one flesh" [Gen 2:2]. Whoever, by contrast, fuses himself with Christ is one in spirit with him. (I Cor 6:15–17.)

We saw earlier that Augustine counts spiritual sins worse than physical ones—lying is worse than fornication, since it is a cooler choice to corrupt the soul rather than the body. So Paul's condemnation of prostituting Christ's limbs makes, a fortiori, for even harsher judgment on one who would prostitute Christ's mind. For a Christian, for one who is incorporated into Christ, to engage in deception is to make truth itself, so far as that is possible, tell lies. It returns one to the lying system of the Prince of This World, where one prevails by darkness, by the obscuring of reality, by erasing it (so far as one is able). This fails to honor the truth that Christ brings, that Christ *is*—the truth that he says will set us free (Jn 8:32).

The preceding chapters deal with the connection between a Christian's truthfulness and Christ's truth. The New Testament link between the two is brought about by the Spirit when he fills Christians so they speak without restraint. This open speech is *parrhēsia*, which literally means "speak-all" (*pan-rhēsia*), holding nothing back. In the Christian texts, it means the speech of one totally transparent to the message being conveyed, the truth of God's word. No filter of falsehood stands between the Spirit and the proclamation that issues from the speaker's mouth. Over and over in the Acts of the Apostles, the disciples are said to have openness in their speaking.[8] This is both free speech and freeing speech: "As they were in prayer, the place where they were meeting vibrated and they spoke, as liberated (*meta parrhēsias*), the word of God" (Acts 4:31). In the gospel of John, Jesus sometimes does not speak with *parrhēsia*, but in signs and parables, because he has not completed his mission (10:24, 11:54, 16:25). But when he incorporates believers into his body by the power of the Spirit, "the Defender will come, to expose the world's lie" (16:8).

The early fathers of the church often pondered the meaning of Christian *parrhēsia*. They made it a mark of the free communication with God that Adam had enjoyed and then lost. Origen says that the candor disappeared when Adam tried to hide from God after his sin, having a darkness now that clouded his free address to his maker.[9] Methodius of Olympia said that as Adam covered his naked body with animal skins, so he covered his mind's *parrhēsia* with falsehood.[10] Athanasius said that Adam lost the contemplation of God that was paradise when he lost his "unashamed *parrhēsia*."[11] But at Pentecost, the Spirit restored the *parrhēsia* that Adam had, the free access to God which makes one no longer hide from truth, to the members of Christ's body: "Let us, as liberated (*meta parrhēsias*), approach the throne of grace, to receive mercy and find grace for our every need" (Heb 4:16). So we know one way to test the Spirit's presence. Where she is, there is *parrhēsia*. What does that say about the church today?

What would a church that had, like Jesus, broken out of the violence of the world's lying system look like? It would be a victim, not a victimizer with Satan. Newman, marking the "scandal" of Pius IX's relying on French troops to oppress his own Roman subjects, said, "When he is persecuted, he is in his proper place—not when he persecutes."[12] The whole church, in other words, would be that eschatalogical sign that Paul VI restricts to the celibacy of the priest—a proleptic life in the reign of God (*basileia*) that Jesus said is "here for you" (Lk 17:21).[13]

It would be a church filled with the Spirit, speaking openly of glad access to God. It would not build flimsy barricades against the truth about past Catholic attitudes toward the Jews. It would not stand on pride to reassert, against all evidence, past attitudes on contraception. It would not involve the whole subject of sex in a darkness created when women were considered inferior and sex bestial. It would return to the baptismal cluster of freedoms, the multiple declarations of independence, at Galatians 3:26–28:

> Baptized into Christ.
> you are clothed in Christ,
> so that there is no more
> Jew or Greek,
> slave or free,

man and woman,
but all are one, are the same
in Christ Jesus.

This church would not restrict the priesthood to men. In fact, it would not restrict the priesthood to priests—to magicians of the eucharistic transformation. It would not deprive whole communities of their own priests rather than relax a code of celibacy never imposed on the apostles.

It would not bring in substitutes for the Holy Spirit, making the Pope the monarch of the church. It would not make Mary an empress—drawing on the imagery of the world's violent system. It would not silence the free voice of the Spirit in believers' hearts.

If one wants to know what such a church would *not* be, all one has to do is look at the first Vatican Council, where schemes were hatched to foist a doctrine on the faithful by surprise, where the Pope pursued a stealth strategy, deceiving his own followers by pretending that the Council was not called to do his will. It would not suppress freedom of speech, hiding its proceedings behind a veil of silence, quashing the voice of conscience in the attending bishops, changing its decrees in secret before the final vote. It was not only the faithful, the critical, the questioning, who were excluded from that Council. The Spirit was excluded. None of the Council's distinguishing characteristics—secrecy, coercion, deception—is a characteristic of the Spirit. The old system of sacrifice was brought back, the one canceled by Christ on the cross—only here the believers were sacrificed to an idol, to the papacy. Pius IX stood not for all-speak (*parrhesia*) but for no-speak (*ou-rhesia*), for blind subjection, not liberation in the Light, the Light who enlightens everyone who comes into the world (Jn 1:9).

Christ, Augustine said, is the way to the truth and *is* the truth. Every truth leads to him. Only falsehood blocks the path which he is. "Through him we travel to him." That is why the church lie was the worst lie in his eyes—the use of falsehood to proclaim the truth. He would have said that the new papal sin, of deception, is worse than the vivider old sins of material greed, proud ambition, or sexual license. It is spiritual sin, an interior baffling of the Spirit's access to the soul. It is a cold act, achieved by careful maneuvering and manipulating, a calculated blindness, a shuttering of the mind against the Light.

But where can this church of the Spirit be found? Not in some imagined purity of the past. There were no good old days of the faith apart from what faces us today. There was betrayal and bitterness in the clash of Paul with Peter, Peter with Paul, as in the betrayal of both men to Nero. Then where is the church of Pentecost, that original feast of multilingual multi-culturalism? It is anywhere the Spirit breathes freedom into a Christian community—where peacemakers are at work, where Sister Prejean is telling people that capital punishment is revenge and not a Christian action, where Daniel Berrigan is caring for those stricken with AIDS, where people unite to help the helpless, where Philip Berrigan is telling us that no one has the right to build weapons that can destroy the world.

When John the Baptist asked whether the reign of God had arrived, the answer of Jesus was simple: "The poor have the good news brought to them" (Mt 11:5). At a time when we hear that Catholics are less true to their belief than in the past, the campus churches I know have young people readier than I and my friends were at their age to work on soup lines, to minister to the inner cities. The Spirit is in them. She needs no license from the Vatican to repeat, in barrio, in ghetto, and in slum, the sign given John the Baptist.

I do not think that my church has a monopoly on the Spirit, which breathes where She will, in every Christian sect and denomination. In fact, She breathes through all religious life, wherever the divine call is heeded, among Jews and Buddhists and Muslims and others. But we Christians believe She has a special role to complete Christ's mission in us. Unworthy as we are, She calls us. She even calls the Vatican. All Christians need to respond to that soliciting. Including Popes.

---

[1]The basic text is René Girard, *Violence and the Sacred*, translated by Patrick Gregory (Johns Hopkins University Press, 1977). Girard's application of his insight to the gospels is most extended in *Things Hidden Since the Foundation of the World*, translated by Stephen Bann and Michael Metteer (Stanford University Press, 1987).

[2]René Girard, *Job, the Victim of His People* (Stanford University Press, 1987), p. 148. The French translation Girard works from does not bring out enough the typically Greek word play on *one* and *many*, registered in my version. The text is thus even closer to Girard's thought, which stresses the need of *unanimity* in the social act of violence.

[3]Augustine, *City of God* 14.28, 15.5, 8.

⁴Raymond Brown, *The Gospel According to John, I–XII* (AB 1966), p. 122. Girard admits that opposition to sacrifice is not reflected in the Epistle to the Hebrews, but this letter seems to have been written before the temple was destroyed and to reflect the Separatist Christian attitude of the 60s CE—see Raymond Brown, *An Introduction to the New Testament* (AB 1996), pp. 691–703. For a negotiation of the differences between Girard's antisacrificial approach and older sacrificial views, see Raymond Schwager, "Christ's Death and the Prophetic Critique of Sacrifice," *Semeia* 33 (1985), pp. 109–23. Christ's priesthood in Hebrews is the *end* of sacrificial priesthood.

⁵Augustine, *Interpreting John's Gospel* 69.2.

⁶Brown, op. cit., p. 711, on the commentators' problems with this passage, beginning with the sense of *elenchein* (expose the lie).

⁷Augustine, *Analysis of Some Theses in the Letter to the Romans* 48, text in Paula Fredriksen Landes, *Augustine on Romans* (Scholars Press, 1982), p. 19.

⁸Acts of the Apostles 2:29, 4:13, 4:29, 4:31, 9:27, 9:29, 13:46, 14:3, 18:26, 19:8, 26:16, 28:31.

⁹Origen, *On the Oration* 23.4, cited in G. J. M. Bartelink, "Quelques observations sur *parrhesia* dans la littérature paléo-chrétienne," in *Graecitas et Latinitas Christianorum Primaeva, Supplementa III* (Dekker & Van de Vegt, 1970), p. 20.

¹⁰Methodius of Olympia, *On the Resurrection* 225.3.

¹¹Athanasius *Against the Pagans* 2 (PG 25.8).

¹²Stephen Dessain et al., *The Letters and Diaries of John Henry Newman* (Oxford University Press, 1978–), 25.217.

¹³For this translation of *entos hymōn*, see Joseph A. Fitzmyer, *The Gospel According to Luke X–XXIV* (AB 1983), pp. 1161–62.

Key to Brief Citations

AB	Anchor Bible (Doubleday), Volumes 1– (1964–)
ABD	Anchor Bible Dictionary (Doubleday), Volumes I–VII (1992)
Acton	Lord Acton, *Essays*, edited by Rufus J. Fears (Liberty Classics), Volumes II and III (1985)
Contra Men.	*Contra Mendacium* of Saint Augustine
ep. (epp.)	Letter (Letters)
Men.	*De Mendacio* of Saint Augustine
N	*What Will Doctor Newman Do?* by John Page (Liturgical Press, 1994). Newman's complete correspondence on papal infallibility, with excellent analysis by Page
PG	*Patrologia Graeca,* edited by Jacques-Paul Migne
PL	*Patrologia Latina,* edited by Jacques-Paul Migne
ST	*Summa Theologiae* of Thomas Aquinas

Acknowledgments

I am grateful to James Carroll and Eugene Kennedy for reading the whole manuscript and offering valued suggestions. Specialists helped me with particular subjects—Peter Hayes on the Holocaust, Peter Brown and James O'Donnell on sections devoted to Saint Augustine, Sylvia Demarest on pedophile priests. My agent Andrew Wylie and editor Trace Murphy expertly performed their essential services. The members of the Sheil Center at Northwestern University provide me continuing information and inspiration on the Christ that they are. The book is dedicated to the conscientious priest who had the profoundest effect on my life.

Index

A

Abortion, 2–3, 17, 221–29
  and baptism of fetuses, 222
  in cases of rape or incest, 222–23
  and development of the soul, 225–28
  historical attitudes toward, 222
  and humanity of fetus, 222–23, 225–26
  to save mother's life, 223
  and science, 228–29
  women's right to, 221
Abstinence, and the rhythm method, 100–1
Abuse, sexual, 175–86
Acton, Lord, 1–2, 11
  on church's historical record, 258–59
  devotion of, to Catholic religion, 237–39
  and infallibity decree, 249–50, 252–54
  as modern historian, 233–39
  opposition of, to infallibility decree,
    255–59
  and the *Rambler,* 238
Adultery, 101, 167
AIDS, 189, 193
Albert the Great, 109–10
Ambrose, 154
Ambrosian Bank scandal, 299
American churches, shortage of priests in,
  151–52
Ammonius, 135
Anglicans, and women priests, 104
Anti-Defamation League (ADL), 18–19
Antioch conflict, 277–83
  correspondence between Augustine and
    Jerome about, 288–90
  and division in early church, 278–81
  Saint Augustine's interpretation of, 282–83
  Saint Jerome's interpretation of, 277–78
Anti-Semitism. *See also* Holocaust; Jews
  and Bolshevism, 35–36
  Humani Generis Unitas, 30–40

  and orthodox beliefs, 18–19
  and Pius XI, 29–33
  since the Holocaust, 20–21
  vs. anti-Judaism, 13–14, 18–19
Antony, Saint, 135–36
Annulments, 170–72
Apologia Pro Vita Sua (Newman), 264–66
Apostles. *See also* individual apostles
  marriage of the, 125, 128–30
  and ordination of priests, 156–58
  and power of consecration, 139
  as priestly examples, 104–5
  symbolism of the Twelve, 156–57
  women as, 115–16
Apostolic succession, 155–62
Aquinas, Thomas
  on baptism of fetuses, 227
  on cultivated ignorance, 9
  on development of the soul, 225–26
  on falseness of immaculate conception
    theory, 210
  on Jews as deicides, 20
  on sex, 76, 81
  on women as priests, 107
Archives, Vatican, 233–34
Aristotle
  on development of the soul, 225
  on inferiority of women, 108
Artificial insemination, 188–89
Asceticism, of priests, 145–47
Ascetics
  moral authority of, 134–35
  power of early, 134–37
  role of, in priestly celibacy, 135
Athanasius, 134, 135–37
Aubert, Roger, 246–47
Augustine, Saint, 6
  on the ability of church leaders to err,
    290–91
  on Antioch conflict, 282–83

Garry Wills is an adjunct professor of history at Northwestern University. Wills received a Ph.D. in classics from Yale and has had a distinguished career as an author, with books such as *Lincoln at Gettysburg*. He has received numerous accolades, including the 1978 National Book Critics Circle Award for Criticism (for *Inventing America*) and the 1993 Pulitzer Prize for General Nonfiction (for *Lincoln in Gettysburg*). Wills is a member of the American Academy of Arts and Sciences, and his articles appear frequently in the *New York Review of Books*.